Righteous Indignation

Righteous Indignation

Religion and the Populist Revolution

JOE CREECH

University of Illinois Press

URBANA AND CHICAGO

⊗ This book is printed on acid-free paper.

Library of Congress Cataloging-in-Publication Data
Creech, Joe W., 1964-
    Righteous indignation : religion and the populist revolution / Joe W. Creech, Jr.
        p. cm.
    Includes bibliographical references and index.
    ISBN-13: 978-0-252-03074-1 (cloth : alk. paper)
    ISBN-10: 0-252-03074-5 (cloth : alk. paper)
    ISBN-13: 978-0-0-252-07315-1 (pbk. : alk. paper)
    ISBN-10: 0-252-07315-0 (pbk. : alk. paper)
    1. United States—Church History—19th century. 2. Christianity and politics—United
States—History—19th century. 3. Populism—United States—History—19th century.
I. Title.
BR525.C74   2006
277.3'081—dc22   2005034417

Contents

Preface

Populism was a political reform movement with political aims, yet it captured loyalty, evoked opposition, and in the process created drama as few other political movements have in American history. It could do this because Populists believed they were part of a larger, sacred narrative unfolding in the 1890s, a sacred narrative in which political reform was only one member of a coterie of religious, economic, and social reforms being carried out by God and God's own servants. Populists' reform agenda rested on a cluster of evangelical patterns of thought foundational to what most southerners thought it meant to be Christian, southern, and American, and it was the forsaking of these ideals by certain corporate business interests, the two main political parties, and the major Christian denominations that were for Populists at the root of the economic, social, and political turmoil of the 1890s. While Populism in some parts of the country attracted followers from a variety of causes and backgrounds—socialists, women's suffragists, utopian idealists, labor activists, old Greenbackers and union labor thirdites—Populists in North Carolina had been white Democrat or black Republican stalwarts who converted to Populism in order to restore the principles of Jeffersonian democracy and Lincoln republicanism to a state and country besieged by the forces of tyranny and centralization: corporate capitalism, denominationalism, and party plutocracy. Their white detractors recognized the very real threat Populists posed to certain ideals they also held to be sacred—party fealty and white supremacy—and succeeded in destroying the movement with a ferocity rarely seen in American politics. In doing so, they also forced a reconfiguration in the way many North Carolina evangelicals situated themselves in the nation and cosmos, for at stake in the political battles of the 1890s was the nature of North Carolina's soul—the future viability not only of American liberty but of the Kingdom of God itself.

Acknowledgments

I would like to thank the many people and organizations that contributed to this book, starting with those archivists and historians who led me to sources, listened to ideas, and evaluated my work along the way. These include Catherine Gaylord and Walter Johnson with the North Carolina Discipliana Collection at Barton College; Donald Lennon at the East Carolina Manuscript Collection; Michael Pelt and Gary Barefoot at Mt. Olive College; Connie Keller at Elon College; Tenee Graham and Lloyd Johnson at Campbell University; Mable Berry at the Primitive Baptist Archives in Elon College, North Carolina; Jackie Sims at the Reformed Church of America archives at Catawba College; William R. Erwin and the staff at the Manuscript Division at Duke; John Woodard and Julia Bradford at the North Carolina Baptist Collection at Wake Forest; the gracious and knowledgeable staffs at the Southern Historical Collection and North Carolina Archives; William Sutton; Carolyn DeSwarte Gifford; Robert McMath; Paul Harvey; George Marsden; Jim Turner; Gail Bederman; Scott Flipse; John McGreevy; Jay Case; Julia Walsh; Beth Schweiger; Dan Stowell; John Wigger; James Beeby; Francis R. Hodges; Mark Schwehn; Martha Marble; Donald Mathews; David Hall; Grant Wacker; Russ Richey; and especially Joseph Steelman and the late Lala Carr Steelman. I also want to thank the faculty members of Christ College at Valparaiso University who have read and listened to many of my ideas and given me invaluable help in moving from a dissertation to a book manuscript. Too, I want to thank the referees who read this manuscript for their insight and admonitions, and I especially want to thank Joan Catapano and her staff at the University of Illinois Press for their guidance and expertise and for making my first book publishing experience so enjoyable. The responsibility, of course, for how I have used and interpreted their criticism, advice, and help is mine alone.

Second, I wish to thank those who supported my writing financially at the dissertation stage. Grants and fellowships include an Archie K. Davis Fellowship from the North Caroliniana Society; a Zahm Travel Grant from the University of Notre Dame; and a fellowship from the Pew Program in American Religion at Yale.

I must especially thank Walter Nugent, my graduate and dissertation advisor, whose guidance and support have not only shaped this work of history but the life and thought of this historian. It was Walter who first introduced me to Populism, though of the western variety, and pushed me to integrate my interests in religious history with the main questions and issues addressed by political historians. He also has been a model of precision and clarity in thought and writing. His handiwork can be seen throughout this book.

Finally, I want to thank my wife, Cyndie, and my children, Steven, Lane, Greg, Oksana, and Madison, for their patience and longsuffering as I was sequestered in my office and in front of many a microfilm reader for the past several years. They are my inspiration.

Dedicated to Joe Creech, Sr., and to
Linda Laughter Creech—Dad and Mom

List of Abbreviations

BR	*Biblical Recorder*
CA	*The Caucasian*
CTP	Cyrus Thompson Papers
DU	Durham, NC: Manuscript Division, Duke University Library
ECP	Elias Carr Papers
ECU	Greenville, NC: East Carolina Manuscript Collection, J. Y. Joyner Library, East Carolina University
FA	*The Farmers' Advocate*
FWB	Mount Olive, NC: Free Will Baptist Historical Collection, Moye Library, Mt. Olive College
HM	*Hickory Mercury/Times Mercury*
LPP	Leonidas L. Polk Papers
MBP	Marion Butler Papers
NCB	*The North Carolina Baptist*
NCBHC	Winston-Salem, NC: Smith Reynolds Library at Wake Forest University, The North Carolina Baptist Historical Collection
NCDAH	Raleigh, NC: North Carolina Division of Archives and History
NCDOC	Wilson, NC: North Carolina Discipliana Collection, Barton College
OCALA	*Proceedings,* National Farmers' Alliance and Industrial Union, 1890
PF	*The Progressive Farmer*
PNCFA	*Proceedings,* North Carolina State Alliance
RCA	Salisbury, NC: Reformed Church of America Archives, Catawba College
SHC	Chapel Hill, NC: Southern Historical Collection, UNC-Chapel Hill
TS	*Tarboro Southerner*
WT	*Watch Tower*

Introduction

In the spring of 1894, some thirty or so miles east of Raleigh, North Carolina, a renegade group of Populists acting without sanction from the local and state leadership canvassed Nash and neighboring Edgecombe counties with fliers urging voters to "Look to Jesus" in the coming off-year elections, and without doubt they fully expected Jesus to instruct voters to elect their slate of local candidates. Hoping to avoid confusion in the upcoming People's Party county convention, these Populists circulated their list of nominees among local Farmers' Alliances and elsewhere, pointing out to their "friends in the Democrat and Republican Parties" that they had selected "good men" and that they needed "a county paper to teach our people." Hoping that they were "men that fear God and love his commands," they ended with a salutation "in love to all parties."[1]

To those familiar with Populism, several items in this story have a familiar ring: grassroots involvement, the link between local Farmers' Alliances and People's Party clubs, and the centrality of education and reform papers to the cause. What is surprising, however, is the blatant elision of religion and politics. Most students of southern religion assume separation of church and state to have been the rule in this period, and even though historians have noticed connections between the organizational structures and rhetoric of Populism and evangelicalism, so intimate a combination is striking. This close connection makes more sense, though, when we consider the origins of Populism in Nash and Edgecombe counties.

Populism came early to these counties located along the line where the Piedmont hills of North Carolina level out into sandy pine forests. In late March 1892, well before the larger explosion of Populism later that summer, a group of white and black Alliancefolk gathered at two "mass meetings" in Whitakers on the Edgecombe-Nash line to organize a county People's Party. Believing that the Democratic and Republican parties had forsaken American ideals of self-government by allowing committees, combines, and town hall rings to set those parties' agendas, local Alliance leader J. M. Cutchin justified their radical third-party action by explaining that this state of political tyranny was the primary cause behind the dire economic conditions they faced as farmers. He concluded that "there are only two parties to-day, and they are the oppressed and the oppressor," adding, "there is no hope save in revolution." Methodist lay leader and Alliance paper editor J. B. Lloyd responded to the local Democrats' accusation that these Alliancefolk were "cranks" by likewise appealing to the ideals of popular sovereignty:

> America is a country whose citizens . . . rejoice in the freedom of thought, action and speech. . . . They are taught to believe that they are endowed by their Creator with certain inalienable rights. There are no political or religious restrictions. . . . But when they [Populists] assemble to give expressions to their opinions regarding political issues they are denounced and denominated "cranks." Why? Simply because *they think for themselves* and *will no longer be led,* or *forced* to obey the *dictates* of the *political bosses.* . . . Do the farming and laboring people of Edgecombe County feel compelled to subordinate their views on political matters and obey the dictates of a few? We believe not.[2]

The farming and laboring people attending these meetings belonged primarily to two local Alliances, Maple Swamp and Whitakers, that met at Whitakers Temple Methodist Protestant Church and Bethany Christian Church (Disciples of Christ) respectively. These two local churches, as well as their parent denominations, had ecclesiastical legacies that emphasized the kind of self-government Populists like Lloyd and Cutchin celebrated. Both the Disciples of Christ and the Methodist Protestant Church (not to be confused with the larger, more prominent Methodist Episcopal Church, South) were small, predominantly rural denominations that broke away from the Baptist and Methodist Episcopal denominations around 1830 in order to maintain lay leadership and local autonomy in matters of church government; that is, they rejected the "tyranny" of their denominational leaders who attempted to impose their "dictates" upon local congregations. As Cutchin and Lloyd attest, these ecclesiastical emphases on individual religious freedom, once politicized, undergirded the Populist contention that the Democrats and Republicans threatened to destroy Americans' God-given right to self-government.

Look to Jesus!

TO THE BRETHREN OF THE PEOPLE PARTY:

We a part of the People Party suggest the names below for our officers for the year 1894:

MEDER WILLOFORD, or JOHN GREEN, for Sheriff.

MACK BRANTLEY, for Surveyor.

F. F. EURE, for Register of Deeds.

One legged GUSS BRYANT, or EDDIE STRICKLANE, for Clerk of the Court.

NICK BODDIE, or D. H. FINCH, for County Representative.

Our friends in the Democrat and Republican parties are invited to vote with us if they think we have made a good selection, we have tried to select good men. It is requested that a copy of these names be sent to each Alliance in the County and that the Secretary of each Alliance circulate them among their people, so that we may not have any trouble in our Convention. We as a party need a County Paper to teach our people. We send this in love to all parties, and truly hope we are men that fear God and love his commands.

People Party.

"Look to Jesus" Flyer

Probing more deeply, these two particular churches in Whitakers had even broader connections to statewide and national Populism. As for Whitakers Temple, Cutchin was an elder at the church as well as a leader in the state Alliance and eventually the Populist Party, while the former pastor at Whitakers Temple, Rev. G. E. Hunt, was a Populist organizer and office holder in Davidson County farther to the west. Moreover, another leader at the mass meetings, Populist state legislator and Whitaker's Alliance officer J. C. Bellamy, was the son of John Fletcher, one of the founders of the Methodist Protestant denomination. Turning to Bethany Christian, Dr. W. T. Mayo, who donated the land on which Bethany church was built, was a leader at one of the Populist mass meetings, a member of Maple Swamp

Alliance, and a Populist candidate for several county offices. J. L. Burns, who organized Bethany church in 1874, was an Alliance lecturer and then a Populist organizer who faced rotten eggs for fighting white supremacy in 1898. A former minister at Bethany was M. T. Moye, whose brothers, E. A. and A. J. Moye of nearby Pitt County, where Populism was also centered in several Disciples of Christ congregations, were prominent Disciples of Christ lay leaders as well as two of the most important Populist leaders in the state, E. A. running for Congress and several state offices as a Populist and A. J. serving as Populist doorkeeper to the state assembly. Moreover, Burns and the Moyes were close friends with J. M. Mewborne (or "Brother Jimmy," as he was known at church), a Disciples of Christ elder, organizer, and church planter in nearby Lenoir County who became president of the state Alliance and ran as an Alliance Democrat and then a Populist for several state and national offices. In their private correspondence with other Populist Disciples of Christ leaders, Mewborne, Burns, and the brothers Moye made it clear that their denominational relationships served them well as a Populist organizational network. In this light, and given the additional involvement of local Methodists, Baptists, and Free Will Baptists in the Populist cause along the Edgecombe-Nash line, the elision of religion and politics in this flier should not surprise us if it were not for the conventional notion that southerners did not mix religion and politics.[3]

* * *

In order to understand the organizational, intellectual, and emotional factors behind this flier, it is necessary to examine exactly how Protestant evangelicalism influenced the rise, fall, and characteristics of Populism between 1886 and 1900. Although not every Populist was an evangelical (and vice versa), the situation in Nash and Edgecombe counties was not unique; throughout the South evangelical ministers, lay leaders, and congregations, in conjunction with local Farmers' Alliances, were at the fore in local Populist Party organization. As a result, evangelical ideas about politics, democracy, economics, and relationships of class, race, and gender not only shaped Populists' blueprint for reform but, more important, motivated Populists to set duty to God above allegiances to party and at times even to race in order to restore what they understood to be America's God-given system of economic liberalism and political freedom. As their religious ideals shaped the way Populists understood themselves and their movement, they wove their political and economic reforms into a grand cosmic narrative pitting the forces of God and democracy against those of Satan and tyranny. As they did so, these patterns of thought energized the movement with a sacred, even apocalyptic sense of urgency. Evangelical Populists confronted reprobate Democrats and Republicans with the same vehemence with which they assailed Satan; they recruited new Populist converts with revivalistic intensity, and they sought political reform with a fervor usually reserved for seeking salvation from sin.

Especially important to Populists like the congregants at Bethany Christian and Whitakers Temple was what they called "Jeffersonian democracy," "Christian liberty," or simply "freedom," by which they meant economic independence on a personal level, laissez-faire capitalism in the political sphere, freedom of conscience in politics and religion, and the inherent "tyranny" of centralized or "concentrated" people (urbanization), wealth, political power, or denominational leadership. Working from this ideal, Populists believed the economic hard times, political corruption in the two old parties, and the drift toward centralization among a number of Protestant denominations signaled in the 1890s a crisis in American democracy. In their minds, losing these ideals of freedom in any one sphere—economic, political, or religious—would eventually poison the whole of Christian civilization in America. Such a catastrophe would lead to warfare between the classes or races, the loss of American manhood and liberty, political tyranny in the form of plutocracy or anarchy, and religious "Romanism."

Healing the situation required unified reform on all fronts. On the religious front, many evangelicals attempted to decentralize denominational machinery and reemphasize local autonomy and individual spiritual experience. On the economic front, financial reformers attacked trusts and embraced free silver in an effort to head off corporate and financial centralization and thus preserve personal economic liberty. On the political front, white and black Populists sought to restore Jeffersonian democracy and Lincoln republicanism through a new and separate political party that stood firm for popular sovereignty.

And yet, there is more to the story. Because of its central place in southern culture, evangelicalism shaped not only Populism but opposition to it as well, since nineteenth-century evangelicalism, multifaceted as it was, displayed both countercultural and conservative tendencies. On the countercultural side, evangelicals' egalitarian, antielitist, and liberal strains fastened to certain social fissures to help engender Populism's assault on the southern economic and political "powers that be." On the conservative side, however, because evangelicalism was also entrenched in the centers of political, economic, and cultural power in most of the South, it sacralized the status quo and thus influenced evangelical Democrats to reject and ultimately quash the People's Party. In fact, the volatility of southern politics in the 1890s and, in particular, the vehemence with which Populists and non-Populists did battle, reflected both sides' alignment along this central fissure within an evangelicalism that informed basic southern understandings of politics, economics, and especially race. In other words, because evangelicalism so deeply molded southern ideals and ways, it was able to propel such a powerful movement of social change and such an equally forceful backlash against that change. Thus, in short, understanding Populism in North Carolina and the South means viewing it as the political component of a far broader southern cultural-religious phenomenon.

Evangelicalism, then, fundamentally shaped the way Populists perceived the world and formulated solutions to its problems. Evangelicalism provided leadership and organizational models for the movement, and evangelical beliefs infused the movement with meaning and motive force. Emphasizing the religious components of the Populist revolt therefore broadens our understanding of both Populism and southern religion, for only by seeing the religious component in their thinking can we come to terms with Populists' sense of mission and meaning, and only when we see how evangelicals fought as they did over politics in the 1890s can we fully comprehend their place in nineteenth-century southern society.[4]

* * *

So who were the Populists? The germ of Populism was the Southern Farmers' Alliance, the most dynamic, widespread farmers' movement in American history. The Southern Alliance (as distinct from its northern counterpart) commenced in 1877 in Lampasas County, Texas, as a secret society of farmers and ranchers pushing a variety of political, economic, and social reforms.[5] After a slow start, by the mid-1880s the Alliance had expanded across Texas, and in 1886, under the leadership of Dr. Charles W. Macune, the order spread throughout the South, achieving particular success in North Carolina, Georgia, Alabama, and Mississippi. Although the Alliance excluded blacks from membership, in 1886, Confederate veteran and Baptist minister Richard Manning Humphrey established the Colored Farmers' National Alliance and Co-operative Union that worked in concert with its white counterpart. In 1889 the Alliance absorbed the Arkansas-based Agricultural Wheel, and in 1890 the Kansas and Dakota branches of the Northern Alliance joined the Southern Alliance, giving it a membership exceeding 2.5 million. Even with such a powerful national presence the pride of the Alliance, however, was a vast network of suballiances in which farmers educated themselves in subjects ranging from planting techniques to producerism and eventually to third-party politics.

The immediate impetus behind the Alliance was economic—farmers were suffering under crop lien in the South, mortgages in Kansas, and lack of control over pricing structures everywhere. To ease these "hard times," the Alliance offered programs ranging from self-help to "progressive farming" to cooperative stores and marketing ventures. As indicated by these endeavors, while Populists idealized the agrarian life they thought was slipping away, they also promoted market-oriented farming and enjoyed the benefits of industrialized society; it was not industrialization in general but *unfair* economic practices that they opposed.

While the Alliance stressed cooperative economic action, it was also active in politics, and by 1890 the Alliance had become a powerful political force. In an effort to remain nonpartisan, southern Alliancefolk avoided "Alliance tickets" and instead lobbied certain candidates to support an Alliance agenda aimed at economic reform. By 1890, this agenda included typical nineteenth-century economic and political reforms: antideflationary monetary reform (greenbacks and silver), antimonopolism, various labor planks, government regulation of transportation and communication, banking reform, a graduated income tax, direct election of senators, federal assistance to farmers, and in some places women's suffrage and prohibition.

Though many of its leaders in the Southwest and West had belonged to third parties such as the Greenback and Union Labor parties, in the Southeast the Southern Alliance usually worked through the Democratic Party. Given the number of former third-party folk in the leadership of the Alliance in the Midwest and Southwest, cries for a third party were, however, not long in coming. In Topeka, Kansas, on 12 June 1890, the People's Party was born with the backing of the Alliance, the Knights of Labor, and an assortment of former Greenbackers, Union Laborites, and other reform activists. The new party won spotty state-level victories in the Kansas elections of 1890, though almost all Alliancefolk in the southern states continued to work with the Democratic Party. In 1892, however, Populists established a national party and achieved marked state-level success in the Southwest and Southeast even as the Alliance entered a period of steady decline, since many Alliance Democrats abhorred the close connection between their order and the third party.

The People's Party had solid state-level success in the off-year elections of 1894, often through "fusion" with one or the other national parties, and it was poised to alter the national political landscape in 1896. Needing a national issue to galvanize support outside just the South and West, in 1896 many Populists concluded that supporting the issue of free silver—the reintroduction of silver in addition to gold as specie—would unite Populists with reformers in the two old parties and pave the way for national power. That summer, however, the Democrats surprised the Populists by endorsing most Populist reforms and by nominating for president William Jennings Bryan who, though not a Populist himself, strongly identified with the People's Party. The move fostered a joint nomination with the Populists (with different running mates), but after Bryan's defeat, Populist enthusiasm waned due to an up-turning economy, divisions within the party over fusion, antifusion laws in the Midwest and West, and, in the South, a virulent white supremacy counterattack by the Democrats. In 1908, the last year of the party's existence, Populist presidential candidate Tom Watson garnered only 28,000 votes.

The upper-south state of North Carolina ultimately produced perhaps the most powerful Populist movement in the country. Populism got its start there in 1886, when a number of indigenous "farmers clubs" coalesced under the leadership of Col. Leonidas Lafayette (L. L.) Polk and his weekly paper, *The Progressive Farmer*. In 1887, the Southern Alliance subsumed Polk's Association, and Alliance leaders, who in North Carolina were predominantly Democratic stalwarts, controlled the state Democratic Party by 1890. Between 1890 and 1892, however, the Alliance grew dissatisfied with the state Democracy, and by the summer of 1892 thousands of Alliancefolk formed Populist Party clubs that also attracted black voters discouraged by the Republican Party.

In 1892, though, excitement exceeded actual organizational mobilization as together, black and white Populists polled a respectable but ineffectual 17 percent of the state vote. The Democrats, however, polled only 49 percent of the vote, and so in the off-year election of 1894, Populists fused with Republicans to sweep into office and revolutionize the state's political structures. This coalition nevertheless crumbled in 1896 as the state People's Party pursued contradictory and confusing fusion arrangements that divided the party and alienated thousands of black voters who refused to support a Democrat like Bryan. In the white supremacy campaign of 1898, the Democrats exploited these divisions with intimidation, violence, and murder, winning back the legislature and in 1900 implementing a "literacy test" that effectively disfranchised blacks and discouraged many white farmers from voting—a move that J. Morgan Kousser has so effectively argued not only killed the Populist movement and black vote but introduced the classic elements of twentieth-century southern politics: widespread voter apathy and a one-party system.[6]

Even though the story of Populism appears straightforward, pinpointing the movement's basic ethos has been tricky for historians. For while Populists seemed at times progressive and countercultural—advocating government regulation of the economy, supporting labor concerns, and in places promoting black franchise—they also denounced socialism and labor strikes as anarchical, hoped to limit government spending, and declared city life and many aspects of modernity deleterious. These opposing tendencies seem less contradictory, however, once they are understood as part of a religious ethos, for like the evangelicals that filled Populism's ranks, Populists can best be understood as part of a restorationist movement.

Having been largely unaware of Populism's religious roots, most historians interpreting the movement have, however, presented two other models for understanding these contradictions in the Populist outlook. One school of thought, usually associated with John D. Hicks (*The Populist Revolt,* 1931) and C. Vann Woodward, casts Populists as vanguards of progressivism standing against corporate capitalism and promoting reform and government regulation. Woodward, along with Walter Nugent (*The Tolerant Populists,* 1963), also believes that economic grievances provided the primary impetus behind the movement in the South and Midwest.[7] Since the 1970s, the most influential work from this perspective has been Lawrence Goodwyn's *Democratic Promise* (1976), which interprets Populism as a "movement culture" in which the cooperative economic ventures of the Alliance prompted the rudimentary formation of a working-class consciousness that, had it found political success, might have challenged the rise and political influence of industrial capitalism.

In contrast to this first school of thought, in the 1950s, under the specter of McCarthyism, academic sentiments turned against the Populists, and Richard Hofstadter summarized these sentiments in his Pulitzer Prize–winning *The Age of Reform* (1955). Hofstadter's Populists were hardly Jeffersonian anticapitalists; rather, fed by irrational conspiratorial theories and neurosis over their declining social status in the new industrial America, they were backward-looking localist reactionaries or, in other words, paranoid, nativist, anti-intellectual rural McCarthyites. In criticizing the older tradition of Hicks and Woodward, Hofstadter correctly observed that Populists' economic status actually differed little from that of their non-Populist neighbors. In the long run, however, many of his other assessments faltered because they lacked sufficient evidence.[8]

The religious interpretation of Populism offered here harmonizes parts of both of these schools, presenting a more satisfying picture of Populism as a restorationist movement. What does this mean? North Carolina Populists were restorationists in the same sense as were the restorationist-minded religious reformers like those at Bethany Christian and Whitakers

Temple who were at the movement's center. While such religious reformers attempted to restore the ideals of the apostolic church within the modern church, in like manner, North Carolina Populists hoped to restore the ideals of Jefferson, Jackson, and Lincoln within an ailing political structure. Thus, they were on the one hand backward looking, yet on the other radically independent of immediate tradition as they looked to a more distant past in order to move into the future.[9]

Seeing North Carolina Populists as restorationist, then, strikes a via media between casting Populists as liberal-minded progressives or paranoid reactionaries. On the one hand, like other religious reformers, Populists saw themselves as "reformers," "kickers," "progressives," and "agitators"—as enemies of the status quo. Their heroes were Gladstone, Jefferson, and Jesus the agrarian radical, and they placed themselves in solidarity with the Irish, the regulators, the patriots of 1776, and labor organizations so long as they avoided strikes or violence. On the other hand, reform came through return—return to the social equilibrium of a bygone day through the restoration of proper political, economic, and religious relations. Hence, unlike Progressives a decade later who considered the "modern" all the rage, Populists took their cues from the past.[10]

Religion, however, does not explain all of the features of southern Populism, and three issues are particularly important in understanding the movement. First, Populism was primarily a *political* rather than an *economic* movement. For while the economic hardships of crop lien, tenancy, and the lack of money and credit made farmers anxious, they also made Democrat and Republican farmers anxious. If we take it for granted that economic hardship caused general angst in the 1890s, we are still left wondering why some people sought relief through the Populist Party and others did not. Populists saw their party as the best avenue for economic relief because they believed in finding political solutions to economic problems and that the corruption and loss of democratic principles in the two old political parties was the direct cause of their economic turmoil, not the other way around. Democratic and Republican farmers might also have been less than satisfied with their parties, but for whatever reason—white supremacy, geography, or party loyalty—they did not want to break with their traditional party affiliation. For Populists, the surest remedy for restoring democracy, and in the process restoring economic opportunity, was to create a pure, untainted vehicle for electing pure, untainted reformers to office—the People's Party. Understood in this context, decisions to fuse, to adopt free silver, and the like, derived from strategies to elect Populists who could legislate financial reform.[11]

Second, the rural/urban schism so prominent in the South after the 1880s was the most important social determinant of Populist voting. Rooted in the concerns of farmers, the Populists' political agenda had little relevance for urban professionals, mill owners, and millworkers, evangelical or not. The power of this rural/urban cleavage to shape Populism is an especially important point, for while stressing Populism's link to religion, it would be wrong to assume that such intellectual or cultural factors were all that mattered to Populism. Though they shared, for the most part, a common theological outlook with their rural counterparts, evangelicals in urban areas (or in the Northeast, Midwest, etc.) simply did not become Populists. Thus, in determining the components that created the Populist mind, not only must evangelical and other intellectual elements be considered, but so also must rural identity. The rural-based Alliance was therefore a critical crucible in which certain preexisting evangelical ideals bonded with a cluster of rural social and political problems to create a uniquely religious rural reform agenda. That said, of course, it is necessary to note that not all rural folk became Populists either. Geography, ties of kinship, or commitments to white supremacy, among other things, also contributed to the decision to become a Populist.

Finally, blacks in North Carolina voted the Populist ticket to a far greater degree than many historians have imagined. North Carolina Populism, in fact, owed its victories in 1892 and 1894 almost entirely to the powerful bloc of black Populist voters in the eastern part of the state, and blacks' flight from the party in 1896 forever crippled its future goals. The white supremacy campaign of 1898 and the disfranchisement of blacks in 1900 must therefore be understood as an attack on both Populism and blacks, for in North Carolina, Populist voters in the eastern part of the state were, in fact, predominantly black. In North Carolina, then, Populism was a biracial movement, and North Carolina Populists' ability to forge such a biracial movement gave it the success that eluded Populists in such southern states as South Carolina.[12]

* * *

While teasing out these religious connections helps us better understand the nature of Populism and southern politics at the turn of the twentieth century, it also expands our perception of late nineteenth-century southern evangelicalism.[13]

Evangelicalism is a religious movement with roots going back to the Puritans, to seventeenth- and eighteenth-century continental pietism, and to the British Quakers and Methodists. More than any other factor, evangelicalism's stress on an individual and experientially assured conversion or spiritual "rebirth" has distinguished it from other forms of Protestantism. This stress on individual rebirth, coupled with evangelicalism's voluntary and often congregational "low church" structure, has also produced at times a kind of egalitarianism based on the assumption that all stand equally sinful before God regardless of social status and that all have equal access to God's salvation. Likewise, such evangelical-style individualism has often produced a stress on the freedom of conscience—that is, the idea that each individual should experience rebirth and select belief systems without the coercion of church or state hierarchy. These emphases have maintained within the movement a strong antielitist rhetoric often aimed at affluent clerics, elites, government officials, and those bearing the general marks of erudition. Additionally, in colonial America, the movement's attendant millennialism coupled with emerging democratic and republican ideals to produce a sort of "civil religion." Evangelicals imagined that their stress on freedom of conscience was integral to America's political and ideological destiny, and most evangelicals were convinced that America was God's chosen nation—Winthrop's "City on a Hill."

Along with these more liberal tendencies, evangelicalism has, contrariwise, been a conservative social force capable of maintaining cultural stability because of its pervasiveness and because of its stress on personal and community discipline. And by the 1870s and 1880s (and perhaps earlier), evangelicalism was indeed the established religion and sacred pillar of the "powers that be," bourgeois or otherwise, in the South.[14]

In the end, the situation in the late nineteenth-century South was thus akin to Puritan New England or Mormon Utah; evangelicalism was an inescapable presence. For southern blacks and whites whose religion was a central integrating force, evangelical patterns of thought provided the gestalt for interpreting economic, social, and cultural phenomena.[15] Biblical ideas and language that evoked two millennia of ecclesiastical and theological meanings were so pervasive that even those thousands who were only nominally religious found it necessary to be immersed in evangelical ideas and interpersonal networks to maintain business and community relationships, to educate children, and to engage in political, theological, and philosophical debates.

As historians such as Charles Regan Wilson and Donald Mathews have ably demonstrated, by having achieved such a central place in the southern psyche, evangelicalism stabilized or legitimated many elements of postbellum southern society. It helped mythologize the Old South and undergirded conservative gender relations. Moreover, its ambivalence on vindictive justice and penchant for sacralizing hierarchies of race created an environment hospitable for lynching, Jim Crow, and black disfranchisement. Yet, on the other hand, its egalitarianism, values of justice and equability, restorationist reform impulse, and stress on individual conscience complicated evangelicals' relationship to their prevailing culture. Even the most socially conservative evangelicals, if only in their prayer closets, often felt uneasy about an outlook that so legitimated the status quo or that seemed elitist.

Critical to understanding nineteenth-century evangelicalism and its connection to Populism is recognizing the pervasiveness of this tension between evangelicals' inherent conservative and countercultural tendencies. Most interpretations of nineteenth-century southern evangelicalism have, with good reason, emphasized its conservative aspects. The predominant model for understanding evangelicalism in the period has, in fact, been that of "cultural captivity," which assumes that white southern evangelicals were captive to the pervasive southern culture and were thus conservative guardians of the status quo. Indeed, there is no question that the South had its share of socially conservative Protestants, and certainly in only the rarest of instances did southern evangelicals challenge cultural constructions of race and gender. Nevertheless, the existence of evangelical Populists highlights the presence of rural, theologically conservative southern evangelicals who, by tapping into their countercultural, libertarian tendencies, supported labor activism, critiqued the emerging ideals of corporate capitalism, deplored social injustice, and equated political with spiritual salvation. In short, connecting evangelicalism to Populism helps mark the period from Reconstruction to disfranchisement as one full of diverse options for the political and social involvement of southern evangelicals.

Finally, the disillusionment following the defeat of Populism, along with the disfranchisement of three hundred thousand black and white voters, had profound ramifications for the political and social outlook of twentieth-century southern Protestantism. While southern evangelicals in the 1880s and 1890s were politically active in a variety of ways, after 1900 many of those same folks became largely apolitical by adopting premillennial dispensationalism or by fully embracing the separation of church and state. Thus, southern evangelicalism fits into the same basic chronology other historians have used to understand the late nineteenth-century South: diverse options for race relations and politics prior to 1900 transformed into a one-party political system marked by voter apathy, Jim Crow, disfranchisement, and white supremacy. Likewise, an evangelicalism teeming

North Carolina Map, 1900. Courtesy of the North Carolina Office of Archives and History of the North Carolina Department of Cultural Resources, Raleigh, North Carolina.

with options for engaging society prior to 1900 was replaced by one that buttressed social, cultural, and political norms.[16]

* * *

Woven into these political and religious questions are certain assumptions about the nature of history, human behavior, and religion. Identifying these assumptions is more than a mere intellectual exercise, for behind them lurks the question, "So what; did religion really matter?" In other words, if southern evangelicalism was perhaps the predominant discourse of meaning in the South, what does it tell us about Populism to connect the two, besides simply identifying one of its intellectual sources?

In the most general sense, we must reckon here with the ability of religion to stimulate movements that challenge their pervasive cultures. Especially where it is central to or legitimates a predominant culture, religion can, as with Populism, shape the social and political agenda of movements offering a radical, though often complex, critique of that very culture. For Populists, their religious convictions had an inner cultural logic that drew on ideological, social, and religious traditions foundational to their understanding of what it meant to be Christian and American. It was indeed because of their central place in southern culture that these convictions could so powerfully interpret, symbolize, and sacralize the social, cultural, and political phenomena of the 1880s and 1890s and in the process help embolden a movement urging fundamental social, cultural, and political reform.[17]

More specifically, these religious convictions motivated Populists for at least two reasons.[18] First, because of their centrality in the southern psyche, and because of the way they defined the sacred in southerners' lives, Populists' evangelical ideals stood above southern society and thus had the power to judge and even condemn elements in it. In the case of Populism, this meant the power to condemn economic, political, and religious practices that ran contrary to God's established rules or his "moral governance." Adherence to God's rules—a fixed set of ideals having to do with proper religious, economic, and political conduct—endowed the movement with a sense of sacred duty, a sacred sense of prophetic "rightness," as it framed the questions and answers to the turmoil of the 1890s. Culturally speaking, religion acted simultaneously as legitimator and judge of the status quo.

Second, Populism was fixed in religious ideas that infused its tangible political and economic goals with transcendent or sacred meaning. Populists' observers and detractors were correct when they labeled Populism a "religious" movement, for, indeed, its religious language was more than a mere discourse, ideology, or moral orientation. Behind Populists' rhetoric was a devotion not only to ideals but to the God they perceived to be the author of those ideals. In the Alliance and People's Party, political and economic goals fused with evangelical goals of salvation and the establishment of the millennium. The result was a movement imbued with a religious fervor that matched the ultimate, prophetic certainty and seriousness of the ideals and hopes that propelled it. Populists saw economic and political problems and solutions not in temporal terms but in moral and spiritual ones. Certainly many Populists who lacked such beliefs often utilized evangelical language to galvanize support, making it function as cultural discourse or as a rhetorical tool. That they did so, however, with such effectiveness, demonstrates the degree to which their audiences believed in the ideals and were motivated to act accordingly.

For what distinguished a Populist in 1892 from her Democratic neighbor down the road was gnawing deep down in her liver—a gnawing intuition that the state and nation suffered a disease far more virulent than mere "hard times"—that it suffered an ailment whose sores needed more than the mere topical salves of crop diversification, tariff reduction, railroad commissions, or other ointments the Democratic and Republican parties offered. The infection ran deeper, much deeper, to the heart of what it meant to be a free Christian American. The divine democratic experiment begun in 1776 was failing and the fault lay with the trusted servants of government and religion whose job it was to ensure just such a catastrophe from happening. With a furor that matched the ultimate, apocalyptic scale of the problem, Populists perceived their old parties as sick unto death and left them to die. In their stead they sought to reestablish God's moral governance in America through the restoration of evangelical, democratic ideals.

* * *

What follows are three sections concluded by a brief Epilogue that covers the religious ramifications of Populism's defeat. Section 1 outlines the basic intellectual contours and history of southern evangelicalism pertinent to this study. Section 2, which details the emergence of the Farmers' Alliance, analyzes the social conditions that precipitated the agrarian revolt of the 1880s and examines the connections between the Alliance and southern evangelicalism. While Sections 1 and 2 are descriptive, Section 3 narrates the rise, success, and demise of the People's Party in North Carolina and further analyzes the religious connections that prompted the Populist revolt.

Since both the Alliance and the People's Party focused on state and local politics, concentrating on a single state is often necessary to navigate the complicated details of fusion arrangements, local political and economic issues, and demographic or geographical complexities. Hence, this book focuses on North Carolina—a state with a powerful and influential Populist movement and one that has substantial archival sources. Although North Carolina provides the historical setting for this story, many of the observations and conclusions, especially concerning the relationship of religion to the movement, are applicable elsewhere, though different players, groups, and attitudes might have changed the specific ways this relationship played itself out.

Evangelical Establishment

"We Are Not the Free Men Our Fathers Were"

Hebron Christian Church, founded in Lenoir County in the eastern part of North Carolina in 1878, was typical of most Disciples of Christ congregations. Although the restorationist Disciples of Christ exaggerated many of the liberal and egalitarian tendencies of evangelicalism—rejecting all creeds; discarding, to varying degrees, denominational apparati; and relying almost solely on lay leadership for churches' week-to-week activities—they conducted those activities in ways similar to those practiced by many rural southern congregations. Hebron had no paid pastor; this congregation of thirty-three men and thirty-one women was led by two brothers, J. M. and Levi Mewborne. While both Levi and J. M. farmed all of their lives, J. M., or "Brother Jimmy," as they liked to call him at Hebron, gained fame in the 1880s and 1890s as the premier Farmers' Alliance lecturer in the eastern part of the state. In 1890 J. M. ran for Congress as an Alliance Democrat and in 1893 and again in 1894 was elected president of the state Alliance. He also became a Populist, serving as a state senator in 1895, as elected commissioner of agriculture in 1896 and 1897, and as superintendent of the state penitentiary in 1898. All the while he, along with Levi, led Sunday morning worship and Sunday evening prayer services at Hebron.[1]

The Sunday services consisted primarily of hymn singing and scriptural exhortation. Insisting on "exhortations" or "lessons" rather than on prepared sermons, the members at Hebron expected leaders to read a portion of Scripture and then comment on that passage extemporaneously while other members, both women and men, chimed in with their interpretations. This

J. M. Mewborne. Private
Collection, Courtesy of
Martha Marble.

way, they believed, Scripture did not merely provide "pegs" on which to hang "doctrines of men"; rather, such a participatory, egalitarian approach enabled "the life-giving thoughts of God" found in the "Holy Book" to penetrate "every man's intellect, conscience and heart."[2] Topics covered in these lessons included calls for holy living, moral courage, winning the lost, trusting in God, the need for Christian education, and, on the eve of the 1888 election, Brother Levi covered "the duty which we owe our country."[3]

Even though there was little variation in the week-to-week activities of the church unless there was inclement weather or a member passed away, on 4 October 1891, after Brother Levi had finished his exhortation on "the resurrection of Lazarus from the dead," the church secretary recorded that "after regular services the assessment plan adopted by the [North Carolina Christian Missionary Convention] was discussed for some time but final action was put off until next Sunday." Obviously causing some ill feelings at Hebron, this assessment plan demanded a six-year congregational pledge to give money to the Disciples' overarching convention on pain of forfeiting membership.[4]

Debate over such ecclesiastical matters was not new to Hebron or to most other southern evangelical congregations; in fact, evangelicals during the period spent far more time wrangling over ecclesiology than just about anything else. At Hebron, for example, just a year earlier both Brother Levi and "Brother Jimmy" exhorted the church on "the right way of raising funds for the Missionary Convention," and the congregation now opposed this particular proposal because it was an affront to its ideals of ecclesiastical autonomy. Even though such assessment plans were common in the more centralized denominations like the Methodists or Presbyterians, to these Disciples, who fifty years earlier had left the Baptist denomination because they believed it had become too centralized, such a measure reeked of "denominationalism." Thus, the following week, the secretary recorded: "The assessment plan was voted on and rejected, and our delegates [to the Convention the following week] were directed to introduce resolutions . . . providing for its discontinuance, and should the Convention decide against us, to ask that our name be stricken from the roll."[5]

Despite its stand, Hebron apparently acquiesced, or, at least, the Convention accepted its protest, since a year later the church pledged to give half of its annual treasury to foreign missions; nevertheless, the members' opposition to such denominational centralization, especially where money was concerned, reflected a critical point of conflict not only among Disciples but among other evangelicals in the late nineteenth-century South.[6]

In fact, the discussion at Hebron that October was one instance in a conflict that had been growing among North Carolina Disciples for some time. For although the Disciples treasured congregational and individual autonomy, in the 1870s denominational leaders successfully urged Disciples in the state to establish a standing "Missionary Society" based on financial membership that would enable the church to spread the gospel more efficiently.[7]

Its establishment was not without opposition, and it was none other than "Brother Jimmy" who led the losing battle in the 1870s against the society, arguing that such denominational centralization constituted a radical "New Departure" not only from the founding principles of the Disciples of Christ but from the New Testament or "apostolic" pattern of church governance. Mewborne was not against financial support for missions per se but rather opposed a centralized and mechanical procedure that required a predetermined amount of money as a prerequisite for membership and that then funneled the money through a committee. He believed instead that the apostolic pattern for distributing missionary funds dictated that individual churches collect money, "as the Lord has prospered them," and then send that money to support the missionaries or programs of their choosing. Such local control was sensitive to the financial needs of its congregates; it would not overburden them; neither would it let wealthier members get away without paying their fair share. Drawing on the idea that centralized "machinery" such as the proposed missionary society was an inherent threat to individual liberty, he warned fellow disciples that, just like the "Romish church, Methodist church, [and] Baptist church," such "'Christian Missionary Societies,' so called" would inevitably "see fit to place a collar about [their] neck" if they did not "submit to the powers that be."[8]

While Hebron was a small church in a relatively small denomination, its concern about the proper relationship of individuals and local churches to denominational "machinery" was also shared by the largest group of evangelicals in the state: the North Carolina Baptist State Convention, a part of the overarching Southern Baptist Convention. These tensions were always just below the surface for Baptists, who, like the Disciples, treasured individual and congregational autonomy even though they channeled missionary and outreach funds through a standing state missions board. While the distribution of funds was the primary point of contention between localist and centralizing Baptists in the late nineteenth century, in 1891 a most unlikely event set off a storm of anticentralization rancor: the founding of a second statewide Baptist newspaper, the Fayetteville *North Carolina Baptist.*

The trouble started when the editors of the *North Carolina Baptist* (all good Alliancemen) decided to charge $1 for annual subscriptions rather than the $2 charged by the official state paper, the *Biblical Recorder.* Although it was not the editors' intention, many Baptists perceived the *North Carolina Baptist* as the paper of the "common man" in contrast to the "aristocratic" *Recorder.* A paper war ensued that spilled over into the state convention as rumors flew that the older *Biblical Recorder* and the convention would censure the upstart *North Carolina Baptist* for daring to challenge the *Recorder*'s place as the state organ. These rumors prompted a Baptist who called himself "Watchman" to insist that Baptists would never submit to such coercion, since they were "especially fond of liberty."

"Watchman" also believed that the threat to the *North Carolina Baptist* epitomized a more general tendency among the officers, editors, or board members of the state Convention to consolidate and centralize power with which they might coerce local churches, associations, and individuals to do their bidding. Just as was the case in political parties, so did Christian denominations need democratic checks and balances against concentrations of power. One editor of the *North Carolina Baptist* captured well the fears not only of "Watchman" and other Baptists, but of "Brother Jimmy" and a host of other evangelicals who were "especially fond of liberty":

> Everywhere now-a-days we find machines . . . Times were when the church in conference could discuss the various questions affecting Zion. Slowly but surely plans were developed. . . . And the whole church had a part in whatever

was done. The results were the outgrowth of free and full discussion. . . . But now—ha! All that has changed. Committees and Boards and Societies report, and the church is expected to accept whatever the machine grinds out. Time is saved. Perhaps greater growth is secured. But Baptist usage is violated, and general interest is killed. . . . We are rapidly exchanging a democracy for an oligarchy. We are taking the first steps toward the absolute monarchy, Popery. . . . If machine methods are the best we submit; but we still know that we are not the free men our fathers were.[9]

* * *

This assertion that Baptists were no longer the free men their fathers were dovetailed with Populists' assessment that, in America, economic, political, and religious liberty was eroding in the late nineteenth century. While this represents one way in which Populist and evangelical thought mingled, there were many others as well, for when North Carolina Populists talked about what it meant to sing "Goodbye, Old Party, Goodbye," they did so with the language of Zion. This was not surprising, for even though not all southerners were evangelicals, North Carolina was unique in that more than 95 percent of its churchgoing population belonged to evangelical denominations, and if we include Episcopalians and Lutherans in that number, it jumps to over 99 percent. As so many historians have pointed out, from the Civil War forward evangelicalism was the most important intellectual and institutional presence in the South (and much of the nation), and North Carolina was certainly no exception.

In order to appreciate the intricate ways in which Populism and this religious juggernaut intertwined, we need to understand the history and thought patterns of southern evangelical Protestantism. More to the point, in its thought and history, evangelicalism was marked by a central irony critical to the story of Populism. In their hearts, most late nineteenth-century evangelicals imagined themselves antiestablishmentarian and countercultural, yet they found themselves established at the center of southern society. Southern evangelicals viewed their heritage as one of dissent and confrontation; early evangelicals had rejected established churches and proclaimed a mission to convert the world to bold new ways of thinking about the Christian life, theology, ecclesiology, and relations between church and state. For a few, these bold new ways of thinking had even meant overturning cultural conventions on race, family, and gender. In America, evangelicals furthermore fastened these theological emphases to democratic or republican political ideas and classic economic liberalism to sacralize the American experiment in freedom. Evangelicals thus embodied a deeply politicized liberal, democratic impulse that eventually gave Populism a sense of sacred duty.

Concurrent with this liberal impulse, however, were evangelicalism's emphases on conformity to church discipline and to the economic, cultural, and political "powers that be." Evangelicals believed that advancement in Christian maturity required individual and congregational discipline. Discipline involved adherence to fixed codes of belief and action. Such obedience was necessary because evangelicals believed that, by embodying these codes, such people became the means by which God governed the economic, moral, and political affairs of the world. In North Carolina, conformity to such divine ordinances ultimately meant adherence to cultural, racial, and political norms; such conformity was summarized by the command to submit to the "powers that be."

As they wed, therefore, these multivalent theological emphases to the idea that God had special designs for the United States and the South, southern evangelicals created their own religious-political establishment. Indeed, by the late nineteenth century, Methodists, Baptists, Presbyterians, and even groups like the Quakers and the Disciples of Christ found themselves at the heart of economic, intellectual, and political life in North Carolina. Yet many of these same evangelicals were also beholden to myths of origin, historical narratives, and beliefs emphasizing individual autonomy and antielitism that had the potential to overturn it all. Thus, as highlighted by the tensions at Hebron and the controversy over the *North Carolina Baptist,* by the late nineteenth century, southern evangelicalism was reaching a point of crisis. Evangelicals like "Brother Jimmy" saw denominational centralization as a tyrannical threat to American liberalism or freedom; denominational centralizers saw local control as a threat to efficiency and progress, and especially to social, political, and economic stability. To understand evangelicalism's relation to Populism is to understand the political ramifications of this tension.

1. An Established Antiestablishmentarianism: Nineteenth-Century North Carolina Evangelicalism

Trying to make sense of the different evangelical denominations in late nineteenth-century North Carolina can be a daunting task. Finding consistent patterns even in the ways they related to one another is often fraught with contradictions. For example, while most of these denominations regularly consigned one another to hell over matters as seemingly insignificant as baptismal formulas or ritual foot-washing, even groups as antithetical as broad-minded Arminian Disciples of Christ and radically Calvinist, isolationist Primitive Baptists shared ministers, meeting houses, and a common religious language and set of knee-jerk reactions. Even within particular denominations themselves, decisions over what relationship Christians ought to have with the larger culture or what it meant to be faithful to particular ecclesiastical nuances sometimes erupted into fratricidal schism laced with irony. Methodists, for example, ostracized the break-away holiness movement using the same regulations with which the Church of England had ostracized Methodists a century or so earlier. President John Kilgo of Methodist Trinity College (later Duke University) demeaned these passionate holiness folk as uneducated simpletons but was himself praised for the way his preaching captured the old-time, emotional appeal of the Methodist camp meetings derided fifty years earlier by the northeastern intellectual establishment Trinity now sought to emulate.

Nevertheless, as daunting as the task appears, tracking a path through these denominational labels, intellectual peculiarities, and ecclesiastical preferences provides the necessary roadmap for understanding the complex ways these religious institutions related to Populism. Again, the critical component of this relationship was that evangelicalism, a movement that claimed an iconoclastic mantle, found itself, especially after the Civil War, at the center of southern intellectual, social, and political life. It was therefore in a position to shape, legitimize, and sacralize both sides of the Populist revolt. The political battle between Populists and Democrats, in fact, paralleled in many ways the denominational conflict over centralization we saw with "Brother Jimmy" and the *North Carolina Baptist*. What follows, then, is a brief description of the denominations, an account of how they developed before and after the war, and, finally, a more detailed description of the late nineteenth-century tensions between local autonomy and centralized denominational efficiency that left many rural evangelicals with the sense that their sacred ideals of democracy were on shaky ground.

* * *

So what were these denominations and their basic dynamics? We turn to the smaller restorationist denominations in a moment, but first, on to the largest white denominations in the state and South: the Methodist Episcopal Church, South, and those Baptists associated with the North Carolina State Baptist Convention, an affiliate of the Southern Baptist Convention (sometimes called "Missionary Baptists"). White evangelicals in these denominations, along with blacks affiliated with their sister denominations, constituted about 75 percent of North Carolina's church membership. While both of these denominations were so large and geographically diverse that they defy easy generalization, both exhibited characteristics common to many if not most evangelicals.

To begin with, Methodists and Baptists maintained a social outlook that was simultaneously antielitist and elitist. On the antielitist side, Baptists, for example, had a reputation for being provincial, backward, uneducated, and unrefined well into the twentieth century because of their exclusivistic membership requirements (including postconversion baptism), rigorous discipline, and the practice of closed communion (only Baptists could participate). This reputation was only aggrandized by their emotional revivalism and predominantly rural demography. Moreover, Baptists believed that they needed to be separated from the worldliness of southern society, which meant abstaining from drinking, dueling, horseracing, fighting, dancing, card-playing, and theater. Rural Baptists and Methodists also insisted on simple, straightforward or "plain speech" sermons by plain-folk preachers, and they stood ready to denounce the fashionable trappings of gentility and the sins of avarice associated with urban money-getting. These emphases, born in the colonial and antebellum periods and extending, especially in rural churches, into the twentieth century, put Methodists and Baptists at odds with many aspects of the larger southern culture.[1]

All told, however, Baptists and Methodists were never quite able to draw a clean line of separation between themselves and larger society, or, as they would call it, "the world"; neither did all of them resist the pull of urban or plantation wealth. For example, many Baptists, like other evangelicals, crossed the lines of sacred and profane in the eighteenth century when they participated in the regulator movement, the Revolutionary War, and when they linked arms with infidels and deists to help disestablish the Anglican Church. Crossing lines of class, throughout the antebellum period Methodists and Baptists clambered up the ladder of social mobility as their churches attracted "up-and-comers" as well as those city and rural gentry who had already arrived. Moreover, as they drew in southern slaveholding planters, most southern evangelicals relaxed their earlier antislavery leanings. Finally, like other evangelicals, Baptists and Methodists balanced the sense of pathos, excitement, and emotional intensity in their camp-meeting revivalism with an earnest stress on education. As they established themselves in hamlets, towns, and cities, urban Methodist clerics in particular developed a sophistication that rivaled that of the Presbyterians and Episcopalians. Thus, by the eve of the Civil War, even though rural folk populated innumerable meeting houses, Methodists and Baptists counted among their members many of the social, educational, and political elites in both the rural and urban sectors of southern society.[2]

Superior to Baptists and Methodists in prestige but not in number (a sore point for many of them) were the Presbyterians and Episcopalians. Southern Presbyterians and Episcopalians nevertheless exerted a cultural, economic, and social influence in the state beyond their numbers; Presbyterians and Episcopalians were overrepresented, for example, among politicians, manufacturers, and college presidents. Specifically, Episcopalians remained a fixture of elitism in the east among wealthier planters in rural areas and merchants in River and Coastal towns like Wilmington and Fayetteville. Presbyterianism similarly coupled social gentility with a tradition of Calvinist theological erudition that gave the denomination and its ministers a well-deserved reputation for intellectual prowess. That said, however, in the eighteenth and early nineteenth centuries, congregations in both denominations—and especially rural Presbyterians—adopted an intense revivalistic piety that Presbyterians coupled with their rational Calvinism and Episcopalians joined to their sense of gentility.

Frequently sharing the same ground as Presbyterians were Lutherans and German Reformed (German Calvinists), who often held religious sway in areas of the Piedmont settled in the eighteenth century by the Pennsylvania Dutch. Except for pockets of ecclesiastical conservatism in the western part of the state, most Lutherans and German Reformed churches adopted the theological emphases of evangelical revivalism, making them in many ways difficult to distinguish from the Baptists and Methodists with whom they often shared revival meetings, buildings, picnics, and preachers.[3]

In the end, then, despite ecclesiastical and theological lines of distinction, and despite a growing distinction between rural and urban congregations, these Protestant groups shared, for the most part, a common evangelical outlook, which, when joined to their general aversion toward doctrinal hair-splitting, established a southern-style ecumenism by the late nineteenth century. Among these larger groups, denominational titles, though a source of competition or theological debate, rarely marked significant lines of social or cultural schism. Neither was anticlericalism an important line of social cleavage. As in Puritan New England, the distinction in social position and theological education between the laity and clergy was minor. Since most church boards held the deed to the church building and could almost always dismiss pastors at will, and since churches inevitably had scads of "local preachers," organizers, and armchair theologians, it behooved local pastors not to separate themselves too far educationally, culturally, or socially from their congregants. Moreover, for many rural southerners the local preacher was an important community leader and one of the best local sources of literary, philosophical, legal, historical, and political insight.

Turning our attention now to the smaller groups, most could be characterized as restorationist denominations, meaning that they adhered to a reform impulse that at some point had led them to break away from a larger ecclesiastical body. Some of these smaller denominations, though, had roots going back to the seventeenth century; these included the Free Will Baptists in the east (related to the old Arminian sect associated with Rhode Island's Roger Williams) and the Quakers, who populated the far northeastern corner of the state and a swath of Piedmont counties anchored by Greensboro and Winston(-Salem) known as the "Quaker Belt." This Quaker Belt had a long tradition of oppositional politics: abolitionism before the Civil War and Republicanism afterward.

Other restorationists, however, broke away during the antebellum period; these included the Primitive Baptists (1827) and Disciples of Christ (1841), who broke from the Missionary Baptists, and James O'Kelly's Republican Methodists (1792), later known as the "Christian Connection," and the Methodist Protestant Church (1828), both of which broke from the Methodist

Episcopal Church. Added to the mix were two important schismatic movements of the 1880s and 1890s: the Gospel Mission movement among the Baptists and the holiness movement among Methodists, Free Will Baptists, and a few other denominations. Noteworthy is that most of these smaller denominations were decidedly rural—some, like the Methodist Protestants, exclusively so.

Because the restorationism of these groups influenced the Populist outlook, this religious ideal deserves closer inspection. Religious restorationism in the Western Christian tradition has generally included three elements. First, historically speaking, restorationists believe that their sect (and often their sect alone) represents a holy remnant that has kept alive the true, unadulterated message and ecclesiastical structure of the early church or the Bible. As they lay out their histories, Protestant restorationists take pains to show how a scarlet thread of their sectarian faithful kept alive various traditions throughout the "dark ages of Constantinianism." Baptists, for example, highlight various sectarians who practiced adult baptism or voluntaristic ecclesiology. Pentecostals, on the other hand, uncover those who spoke in tongues. Each group usually has a peculiar set of emphases. For instance, two Free Will Baptist historians identified themselves as part of a persecuted minority of "reformers" that traced its lineage back to the Apostles: "[Christ's] followers . . . *were first called Christians in Antioch*, A.D. 41; then Montanists in A.D. 171; then Novationists in A.D. 251; then the Donatists in the fourth century; then the Paulicians and the Waldenses; then General Baptists in 1611; finally they were called Free Will Baptists in North Carolina in 1690."[4]

Second, in the intellectual sense, these groups attempt to reproduce the exact theological and ecclesiastical ideals of the Bible, New Testament, or early church. Many restorationists therefore reject instrumental worship, missionary boards, paid clergy, and other practices not mentioned specifically in the New Testament. Others pick up and incorporate apostolic practices: Free Will Baptists, for example, have adopted foot-washing and anointing with oil since they are mentioned in the New Testament; Pentecostals and some holiness folk have similarly practiced supernatural healings, miracles, and speaking in tongues. Still other restorationists call their organizations "Christians" or "Disciples," since denominations were not a part of the early church (for this reason, restorationists are often, though in contradictory ways, ecumenical or, as they put it, "tolerant," seeing denominational disagreements as extrabiblical). Along this same line, some restorationists reject creeds (not just particular creeds, but the idea of a rule of faith itself) as foreign to New Testament practices. James O'Kelly's Republican

Methodists, for example, ceremoniously burned their minutes at the conclusion of their annual conferences to ensure that no "traditions of men" would replace individual instruction through the Bible alone. Finally, some groups such as Quakers, O'Kelly's Republican Methodists, and certain holiness and Pentecostal groups practice a more far-reaching critique of cultural norms, challenging things such as hierarchies of gender and race that they believe run counter to the social patterns outlined in the Bible.[5]

Two restorationist groups, the Primitive Baptists and Alexander Campbell's Disciples of Christ, deserve a bit more attention because of their prominent roles in the Populist revolt, and, too, because of the way their opposing tendencies shed interesting light on variations within this restorationist outlook. To understand both of these movements, as well as the Methodist restorationist groups, we need, however, to understand first just how evangelicals thought about denominational oversight, for even though restorationists touted various theological points of departure, it was ecclesiology that usually drove them to break away from larger denominations.

As they worked out their ecclesiologies, most evangelicals attempted to balance centralized discipline and efficiency in missionary and evangelistic endeavors with their ideals of voluntarism and local autonomy. Local Baptist congregations, for example, ordained ministers and owned their buildings, though, for the sake of efficiency, they established "associations" and eventually "conventions" to oversee discipline and expansion; Methodists, Presbyterians, and the like, worked out different arrangements, but most attempted to strike the same balance.

From the 1790s into the 1830s, however, denominations began to face "antiepiscopacy," "anticonvention," or "antimissionary" protest, and among Baptists, this protest took two forms. A first group of Baptists took the name "landmark Baptists," meaning they upheld or hoped to restore the true "landmarks" of the Baptist faith, one of which was the rejection of overarching associations. For this reason, landmarkers urged individual congregations to break all associational ties. A second group of Baptist restorationists were liberal, Arminian sectarians who called themselves "reformers" and then simply "Christians" or "Disciples." In North Carolina, "Brother Jimmy's" Disciples of Christ—followers of Alexander Campbell—represented the largest of these liberal reform groups.[6]

Though "landmarkism" would not become a noticeable faction in North Carolina until after the war (its strength was in Tennessee, Kentucky, and northern Alabama), in 1827 its shock waves produced the Old North State's radically Calvinist, localist, and vociferously antielitist Primitive Baptists, a truly unique group on the American religious landscape. Primitive Baptists rejected all authority outside the local congregation and refused to commune with any other denominations, since they were tainted with worldliness. In contrast to most other landmarkers, they also opposed all missionary and evangelistic activity on localist, Calvinist, and antirevivalistic grounds. Moreover, they rejected the use of musical instruments in worship, paid clergy, and ministerial education, since these were not mentioned in the New Testament (and largely on antielitist grounds). They also opposed temperance or prohibition on the grounds of individual conscience and of separation of church and state, and because opposition to drink was associated with secret societies.[7]

In contrast to the localist and Calvinist conservatism of the Primitive Baptists, Alexander Campbell's "reform movement" was Arminian and enjoyed open communion with other Protestants; Disciples liked to call themselves "liberal." Disciples of Christ were also anticreedal and intensely millenarian in their unashamed city-on-a-hill patriotism; they were confident that their "reform movement" was pushing America toward the millennial reign of Christ. Reflecting this merger of patriotism and evangelical thought, Disciples used the language of Jeffersonian democracy to oppose the "tyranny" of denominational centralization expressed in Baptist associationism; such associations posed a threat, they believed, to God-given individual and congregational liberty.

Among Methodists, O'Kelly's Christian Connection and the Methodist Protestants expressed a liberal ethos similar to that of the Disciples (though the Methodist Protestants retained a belief in creeds). In 1792, O'Kelly opposed the "monarchy" behind Methodist Bishop Francis Asbury's assertion that a bishop's authority took precedent over local clerics and congregations. The Methodist Protestants similarly broke away because the Methodist hierarchy was unwilling to seat local lay preachers and lay delegates at its annual conferences. In breaking away, Methodist Protestants asserted that they were protecting their "republican world" against "ecclesiastical monarchy."[8]

All three of these liberal-leaning groups—the Disciples, O'Kellyites, and Methodist Protestants—along with the Quakers and Free Will Baptists who were similar in orientation, comprised something of a restorationist coalition in nineteenth-century North Carolina. Each group sent delegates to the others' annual conventions, and there were a number of attempts after the Civil War to unite the groups formally, though ecumenical talks usually broke down over the issue of creeds.[9] Even though each of these restorationist groups taken individually only amounted to several thousand members, by 1890 their combined strength was 658 churches and 49,756 white members, making them a strong cultural presence on the North Carolina religious landscape. For the sake of comparison, Presbyterians had 282 churches with 27,477 members. All of these groups were dwarfed, however, by Baptists, with 1,480 churches and 153,648 white members and Southern Methodists with 1,288 churches and 114,385 white members.[10]

Just as the older denominations had begun to climb the ladder of affluence and expand numerically before the Civil War, as we saw with "Brother Jimmy's" concerns, these restorationist groups (except the Primitive Baptists) moved rapidly toward denominational centralization after 1877 in order to expand within the state and overseas, and by 1900 all had established centers of higher education and boasted a theologically trained clergy (again, except for the Primitive Baptists, who were always unique). These restorationist groups therefore found themselves facing many of the same denominational tensions felt by the Baptists and Methodists in the antebellum period—in particular, tensions between local autonomy and centralized denominational endeavors.

Finally, much of what characterized white evangelicalism also characterized its African American counterpart, but with some important distinctions. Southern black evangelicalism developed in tandem with white evangelicalism in the crucible of slavery, so even though the two shared certain beliefs—conversion, baptism, and in some cases ecstatic worship—the context of slavery meant many of these beliefs took on profoundly different meanings for African Americans. Although introduced to evangelicalism by whites, slaves quickly made it their own. In clandestine meetings held in "brush harbors" beyond the pale of white control, slaves developed their own rituals, selected their own leaders, and found psychological release through religious ecstasy. For these slaves, conversion and baptism not only meant immersion into the family of God but also into personal dignity based on God's acceptance. Hence, evangelicalism helped slaves subvert the slave system as they imagined themselves to be the children of Israel held in Egyptian bondage awaiting a Moses or Jesus to set them free.

After 1865 black evangelicals realized this freedom from white control politically, socially, and religiously, though in a limited way. Institutionally, to the shock of paternalistic whites, blacks wasted little time in establishing churches free from white control. These churches included independent Baptist churches, "sister" Disciples, Episcopal, Presbyterian, and other denominational affiliates, and the African Methodist Episcopal Church (AME) and African Methodist Episcopal Church of Zion (AMEZ), both transplanted from the North. By the late nineteenth century, the black church increasingly functioned as the primary public sphere for black men and women in southern society. For black men, and especially black preachers, the church provided a base for Republican political involvement and mobilization for suffrage and civil rights. In the end, the black church became, even more so than for southern whites, the central social and political institution for the developing African American community and culture; as C. Eric Lincoln has written, the black church was the "womb of black culture."[11]

* * *

Even though white evangelicals occupied positions of power, wealth, and prestige before the Civil War, the process of justifying slavery, fighting a righteous crusade against the Yankee infidels, and then redeeming their society from unscrupulous Reconstruction oppressors situated evangelical institutions and thought at the center of southern economic, political, and social life after 1877.

Regarding slavery, although they continued to believe that Africans were humans, by the 1830s white evangelicals, except for Quakers and some O'Kellyites, offered a spirited defense of slavery and by doing so legitimated not only the slave/master relationship but general paternalistic relationships of power and submission, making hierarchical relationships of race appear "proper."[12] Having sacralized slavery, most southern evangelicals extended their defense of the "peculiar institution" to a defense of Confederate nationalism after 1860. After the war, evangelical thought helped southerners come to grips with defeat and the process of Reconstruction as they interpreted these dire events as God's chastisement for failing to live up to southern or slaveholding Christian ideals. As Reconstruction ended, southerners again turned to evangelical ideas to imagine the return of white Democrats to power as the Lord's "redemption." As historian Daniel Stowell has pointed out, in southerners' minds, the Democrats represented the saving arm of God who "redeemed" the righteous folk of the South from the grasp of godless Republicans and incompetent blacks. Even after Reconstruction, through civil rituals such as memorial dedications, many evangelicals helped create and maintain the myth of the "Old South" and "Lost Cause." In that same spirit, Methodists, Baptists, and Presbyterians vigorously maintained denominations separate from those of their northern counterparts. By the late nineteenth century, then, evangelicalism was at the core of what it meant to be a "southern patriot."[13]

Of course, war, emancipation, Reconstruction, and redemption brought a mix of blessings and curses to black Christians. While they enjoyed newfound freedom, exercised certain civil liberties in voting and office-holding, and established their own churches, Christian freedpeople still chafed under evangelical views of "proper relations" as whites continued their paternalistic care for blacks. For example, white southern churches helped blacks build church buildings and schools, donated lands, buildings, and literature, and helped set up organizational machinery. Blacks acknowledged their indebtedness to white assistance but also resented the paternalist strings attached.[14]

While both black and white evangelicals were busy expanding their cultural influence in the South, they also extended their physical presence. Like other southern institutions, southern churches reeled under the devastation following the war. Missionary efforts lay in ruin, ministers went without pay, colleges lost their endowments, and publication boards, administrational infrastructure, and newspapers were in shambles. Northern Methodist denominational leaders even confiscated Southern Methodist church property under the aegis of martial law.[15]

In response to this devastation, southern evangelicals reconvened their annual meetings (dormant since 1861) and by 1866 began laying the blueprints for an era of unprecedented institutional and numerical growth. Driven by reasons ranging from the proclamation of the gospel to demonstrating to the Yankee infidels that they could match them brick for brick and conversion for conversion, Methodists, Presbyterians, Baptists, along with the restorationist sects worked hard to standardized Sunday school literature and hymn books, to professionalize the ministerial ranks, and to centralize and expand evangelistic and missionary activities. Denominations especially stressed education, developing secondary schools, and strengthening or establishing denominational colleges. By 1900, every primary denomination in the state (except the Primitive Baptists) had an institution of higher learning, and some institutions, like Wake Forest (Baptist), Davidson (Presbyterian), and Trinity (Methodist, later Duke), established national reputations.[16]

These first-rate colleges and the push for education, however, illuminated the old ambivalence between elitism and antielitism that also persisted well into this period. For example, while one Baptist bemoaned the fact that "other denominations love to throw it in our face that we are behind in educational matters," regularly in attendance at Wake Forest's commencements were the governor, both senators, and every other important politician and educator in the state. Further attesting to this ambivalence, Princeton-educated W. A. Graham, Jr., a leading Baptist in Lincoln County and son of W. A. Graham, Sr., North Carolina's antebellum Whig governor, wrote in the early twentieth century that "while . . . God needs not a man's learning . . . if there had been no advance in the education of the ministers, the Baptists could not have done the work they have in the past quarter of a century." Yet, to the contrary, Graham immediately noted, "If all our ministers in the past had been highly educated, they would have been above the people and the Baptists could not have done the work they have."[17]

Interestingly enough, women in both white and black denominations came to the fore in raising the funds necessary to support this denominational expansion. In fact, "the ladies" usually outpaced the men in adopting many of the techniques of efficiency and centralization that would later be associated with "scientific management." Although, as in antebellum times, women's activities were confined largely to the local scene, certain denominations, such as the Free Will Baptists and O'Kellyites (who ordained women), seated women at annual conferences. In most cases, however, women flexed their denomination-wide strength through women's conventions that operated independently from the larger, male-dominated ones.[18]

Meanwhile, as towns and cities in the South and North Carolina experienced tremendous growth after Reconstruction, urban churches in the midst of prosperity innovated while rural churches maintained their old buildings and traditions. Townsfolk often met in newly constructed, even ostentatious buildings and hired well-paid preachers to preach every Sunday rather than the rural custom of once a month. They also became more socially stratified than their rural counterparts, with professionals and first families attending "First Churches" and mill workers attending mill-owned churches—though often alongside mill owners.

These developments intensified a growing urban/rural tension among evangelicals that, though present before the war, became the major social and rhetorical source of schism within southern denominations in the 1880s and 1890s. On the one side, denominational leaders, who increasingly came from urban churches, saw rural congregations as backward or as part of a "country church problem": not enough pastoral guidance, poorly constructed buildings, poor stewardship, and lack of support for denominational programs. In short, country churches were not "progressing."[19] On the other side, rural evangelicals saw urban churches and their hollow "churchianity" as the epitome of all that was bad about towns, though, since many rural evangelicals had never been to a town of over 2,500, their denunciations were often colored by northern evangelicals' characterizations of cities such as New York and Chicago whose evils included centralized and corrupt political rule by bosses and rings and moral degradation typified by prostitution and whisky. While such vices might have been visible in the streets of Chicago, New York, or San Francisco, North Carolina evangelicals

looked at their own cities of Wilson, Fayetteville, and Wilmington and imagined similar scenarios. One righteous farmer, in fact, prophesied that his
sleepy town of Clinton in Sampson County was none other than "Satan's
Seat" (a reference to Revelation 2:13).[20]

Black churches experienced similar conflicts. Urban and rural church
leaders, too, came into conflict over the middle-class black strategy of earning cultural, social, and political equality through "respectability." Many
middle-class blacks saw poor, uneducated, rural blacks, with their ecstatic
worship and uneducated preachers, as a hindrance to Christian and racial
uplift.[21]

This urban/rural line of cleavage was moreover intensified by the
period's denominational expansion—expansion that, as in the Disciples of
Christ, revived antebellum debates over the nature of denominational
authority. On the one side, many denominational leaders, often taken,
again, from urban churches, pressured congregations to set aside local initiatives in order to fund denominational directives in the name of efficiency
and progress. On the other side, rural evangelicals undergirded the anticentralization backlash.[22] These localist sentiments also rekindled landmarkism in the form of the Gospel Mission movement, an attempt by several
Baptist churches and associations to bypass the state Baptist Convention
and finance missions activities directly, and it prompted numerous
Methodists and Baptists of various sorts (especially Free Will Baptists) to
embrace the iconoclastic holiness movement.

The holiness movement centered around the theological position that
Christians, after having been converted through a primary act of God's
grace, in one way or another had to receive a "second blessing" of God's
grace that removed the desire to sin. After 1906, the Pentecostal movement
grew out of the holiness movement and added other features. Southerners
learned this theological motif largely from northern holiness sources and
thus maintained close ties with northern evangelists and with the northern
wings of their denominations. Some holiness advocates also combined this
theological emphasis with a rigid antielitism as they attacked fashion,
wealth, "First Churches," and centralized church bureaucracy; others taught
more exotic doctrines such as divine healing, exorcism, and speaking in
tongues. Among white North Carolinians, the holiness movement took
root especially in Methodist and Free Will Baptist churches in the Cape Fear
region in the middle of the 1890s. In order to censure holiness ministers, the
Methodist Episcopal Church, South, banned all Methodist ministers from
public preaching who were not invited by the ordained minister in charge,
and this prompted holiness advocates to form their own churches and

denominations. Numerous black independent and denominational congregations also embraced the movement as holiness doctrines thoroughly
leavened the southern black church.[23]

The Gospel Mission movement hit the state about the same time. Drawing on landmarker restorationist strains, Gospel Missioners argued that this
"apostolic" or "biblical" plan of direct congregational support for missionaries and new churches would enable missionaries and church planters to
respond directly to God's call, would prove "economical" since it would not
require salaried bureaucrats and would enhance the manly independence
of churchgoers who would not bow to the board's ecclesiastical lash. High-
lighting the urban/rural rhetorical line common to the movement, one
leader wrote that "this new (old) plan . . . accommodates itself to the country churches especially" since "the present work [NC mission board] is projected and run from the standpoint of the wealthy city churches and men of
high salaries." In spite of such charged anticity rhetoric, however, the movement interestingly drew much of its support from large city churches where
wealthy benefactors apparently wanted more control over their benefi-
cence. In response to the movement, the state Mission Board, while censur-
ing many of the movement's leaders, argued that its centralized methods
were the most efficient means for sending "money and men" overseas.
Unlike the holiness movement, however, Baptist polity did not allow for the
expulsion of the Gospel Missioners, and so, even though a few associations
temporarily departed the convention, the movement gradually waned at
the turn of the century without creating lasting institutions, but only after
it had touched off a great deal of debate and denominational strife.[24]

Like the wrangling of "Brother Jimmy" and his Disciples denomination
and the battle between the *Biblical Recorder* and the *North Carolina Baptist*
(a strong advocate of the Gospel Mission movement), both of these movements testified to a growing concern over the relationship between local
autonomy, often couched in arguments advocating freedom ("not the free
men our fathers were") against the swelling bureaucratization or "centralized tyranny" of the denominations brought on by postwar expansion.
Hence, there was a growing sense among North Carolina evangelicals that
centralizing forces threatened their American freedom to run their congregations as they pleased.

* * *

Finally, keeping in mind all these theological and ecclesiastical nuances,
schisms, and contradictions, how did these evangelicals relate to southern
society by the 1880s? Perhaps the best way to answer this question is with a

typology identifying three categories. A first group, comprising the leaders of the largest denominations in the state, maintained a cozy relationship with the status quo. Their denominations were so large, of course, that it would be impossible to generalize about how individual Baptist, Methodist, Episcopalian, Presbyterian, or Lutheran congregants or congregations related to the wider society, since such relations varied widely depending on social and geographical factors. Nevertheless, at the denominational level, officers and the official pronouncements tended to be centrist or conservative. Local congregations, associations, and individuals within these denominations often parted with these official, more conservative pronouncements; in doing so they, in fact, produced much of the intradenominational struggle during the period we just saw. The denominational leaders, however—often educational, political, and economic power brokers—had a vested interest in the political and economic welfare of the state and attempted to steer their denominations in directions amenable to political and economic stability.

Second, there were evangelicals who simply opposed prevailing cultural norms outright, and in North Carolina the most obvious examples were Primitive Baptists on the localist/conservative side and holiness/Pentecostal folk on the radically countercultural side. Both groups, in different ways, withdrew from the southern public sphere. Primitive Baptists, with their highly exclusivistic, decentralized church life and theology, refrained from participating in social clubs like the Knights of Pythias, in political activity outside of voting, and in any reform activity (especially prohibition), all to ensure individual and congregational purity and autonomy. On the other side of the spectrum, holiness folk acted outside the public sphere by rejecting its conventions through emotional ecstasy, exotic and innovative theologies, links to the North, and sometimes subversion of gender and racial categories. Holiness folk also eschewed social clubs, though, unlike Primitive Baptists, they tended to support prohibition. In sum, both groups existed on the fringes of a southern society in which they did not feel entirely at home.

Third, white members of smaller, more uniform denominations, as well as certain constituencies in the larger ones, consistently walked a fine line between evangelicals in these other two categories. These evangelicals included Free Will Baptists, Disciples of Christ, German Reformed, Methodist Protestants, the Christian Connection, and, in some cases, Quakers, as well as members or congregations (especially rural ones) in the larger denominations. Like the officers of the larger denominations, evangelicals in this third category maintained an inclusive ecclesial outlook and were part of the southern public square; they joined secret and social societies, attended the state university, took part in public debates, and participated in electoral politics at all levels. Yet, unlike the first group, these denominations or congregations were predominantly rural, and, most important, considered themselves "reformers," "restorationists," or "reform bodies," meaning they had broken from larger denominations in an attempt to restore the true church or had, from the start, maintained a restorationist or separatist stance. Thus, integral to their denominational myths of origin and historical narratives was a strong, countercultural, egalitarian, voluntaristic, and independent impulse.

As we will see in Chapter 6, although there were always exceptions to the rule, Populism found strong support in this third group of evangelicals and especially those who belonged to restorationist, reforming sects such as the Disciples of Christ that had traditions of political activism, democratic ideals, and American millennialism, and that were predominantly rural.

2. Men and Machines: Freedom, Conformity, and the Complexities of Southern Evangelical Thought

Long before it achieved its place of cultural centrality in the South, evangelicalism, as it emerged during the mid-1700s, distinguished itself from other forms of Protestantism by stressing individual conversion and voluntaristic church government. These ideas were new and challenging—as radical to some religious conservatives as deism or infidelity. In the South, early Baptists and Methodists further challenged the social hierarchy as they claimed equality among men, women, and Africans. In short, evangelical thinking blossomed among cultural outsiders and iconoclasts.

During the period from about 1790 to 1835, or the "Second Great Awakening," these ideals coupled with the methods of revivalism to propel this evangelicalism across the South and the rest of the country. As evangelical emphases crossed denominational and class lines, they forged the predominant religious motif of the nineteenth century, and even though this widespread success brought varying degrees of conflict, something of a Protestant intellectual consensus developed as preexisting denominations, in whole or in part, embraced the theology and practices of evangelicalism. Except for the more rigid Calvinism of the Primitive Baptists and of theologically acute Presbyterians, the confessionalism of certain Lutherans, and the moralism of some Episcopalians, Protestants in North Carolina adhered to most of the same theological and philosophical ideals, and these ideals shaped not only religious presuppositions but social and political ones as well.[1]

In looking at the aspects of evangelical thought pertinent to Populism, we need to pay particular attention to how these sometimes contradictory patterns of thought aligned with the institutional and social developments examined in the previous chapter. More specifically, evangelicals' commonsense approach to human nature, institutions, economics, and political action, along with their belief in "God's moral governance," indelibly marked the contours of the Populist reform strategy. At the same time, their ideals of freedom, millennialism, antielitism, and belief that God especially favored the poor sacralized Populism's mission to restore American democracy. Ironically, evangelicals' conservative tendencies—tendencies often inherently and ironically joined to their more liberal ones—helped mobilize opposition to the Populist cause. If there is a key that unlocks the complexities of the evangelical mind, perhaps it is the movement's basic epistemological and cosmological grounding: commonsense.

* * *

Providing a basic foundation for the way southern evangelicals understood how people, society, and God worked, Scottish-based commonsense thinking stressed the ability of all people to apprehend and conform to certain axioms, ideals, or "principles" by which God ruled heaven and earth. This way of thinking therefore influenced the way evangelicals understood the processes of thought, perception, learning, and government (moral, ecclesiastical, economic, and political), how people and institutions ought to behave, and how "proper" class, race, and gender relations ought to appear.

This pattern of thinking—called "commonsense" by the unsophisticated or "Scottish Moral Philosophy" by the erudite—was rooted in the thought of eighteenth-century philosophers such as Thomas Reid. Formal Scottish Moral Philosophers like Princeton's John Witherspoon (1723–94) and Brown's Francis Wayland (1796–1865) taught that correct economic, political, or moral activity had to conform to eternal axioms that governed the proper relationships between God and humans, humans and humans, men and women, parents and children, governments and the governed, and so on. Yet they also believed that humans were themselves responsible for understanding and acting in accordance with these proper relations; hence, proper action involved both the nonrational passions that were tied to the will along with the higher faculties or reason used to apprehend these axioms.

In order to involve both the rational and nonrational aspects of the human psyche, Scottish Moral Philosophers believed the conscience served as an arbiter between the passions and reason. The conscience, once informed through reason with the knowledge of right and wrong (the awareness of axioms or principles), would then arbitrate between higher and lower passions to connect unction to right behavior. Thus, reason would judge an action to be moral, or right, by an external locus of authority (natural law, the Bible, etc.) and at the same time utilize heartfelt unction involving the will (moral activity was thus based on motive, not outcome, as utilitarians argued).

As evangelical theologians wed this philosophical outlook to their ideas about salvation and to their social/political thought, they argued that, as the conscience was renewed by Christ, and as the rational faculties were educated in the laws of God, the conscience could arbitrate between sinful passions and godly passions to produce sinful or godly acts (strict Calvinists and Arminians argued about the finer points here).

Furthermore, most evangelicals linked this way of thinking to the idea of "God's moral governance." Evangelical theologians argued that, since acting according to godly axioms produced right behavior, if all members of a society acted rightly, that society experienced the "moral governance" of God, or more simply put, was in line with the way things ought to be. Although not every rural Baptist could articulate the philosophy of Thomas Reid, literate clergy in the antebellum period were well versed in these ideas and passed their general contours on to the laity.[2]

By the late nineteenth century, even though fewer southern academicians adhered to formal Scottish Philosophy, its basic premises, in various degrees of sophistication, along with the notion of God's moral governance, remained strong in the southern evangelical mind and engendered a number of often contradictory intellectual/social trajectories, since commonsense thinking had both egalitarian and hegemonic implications. On the egalitarian side, for example, it stressed the innate "common" ability of all people to think and act morally regardless of social classification. In the postwar South, evangelicals therefore had confidence that anyone could understand God's ways through reason or inductive study of the Bible. On the hegemonic side, however, this outlook stressed conformity to absolute rules—an idea that could support relationships of power or social control, including oppressive ones. This was especially evident in matters of race, gender, and sometimes class. For example, even though southern evangelicals granted blacks a degree of equality, most nevertheless understood white supremacy to be divinely ordained. Similarly, with only a few exceptions, evangelicals also opposed anything that upset a strict doctrine of separate spheres among the "sexes."[3]

In sum, then, commonsense thinking often supported the status quo as believers submitted to the "powers that be," which often implied submission to cultural norms. And yet, this conservative tendency was counterbalanced by evangelicals' stress on individual apprehension of truth and the sanctity of conscience. These latter notions of "freedom" infused evangelicals with strong liberal tendencies as they considered themselves champions of religious, economic, and political liberty.

Evangelicals rooted their emphasis on freedom of conscience and their more general egalitarian tendencies in their insistence that an experiential conversion experience—a radically personal, inductive, and passionate sense of knowing one belonged to God—was essential to salvation. Specifically, evangelicals believed that all people were equal before God in a state of sin, and likewise that all people could apprehend the divine without the mediation of priest or church. Drawing on this egalitarian, individualistic impulse, evangelicals averred that an individual believer, armed with a sanctified conscience, could read the Bible, develop ethical and theological positions, and deliberate such matters without political, ecclesiastical, or, in some cases, creedal coercion. One Baptist insisted along this line that his denomination was "democratic" and bred "independence" because "the Baptist reads the Bible for himself and teaches his children to do likewise."[4]

This stress on individual autonomy, especially as it combined with American democratic political thought, caused southern evangelicals to think of themselves as historical champions of freedom of conscience and religious toleration. Drawing on their restorationist leanings, for example, two Free Will Baptist historians writing in 1898 announced that "the [Free Will] Baptists claim the high honor of being the first who, in England, asserted the right of conscience.... [Theirs] were *the first articulations of infant liberty*—the first utterances of the voice of truth and pure Christianity issuing from the pioneers of the soul's freedom." They also compared themselves to Anabaptists, who believed *"that it is not only unmerciful but unnatural and abominable, yea monstrous, for one Christian to vex and destroy another for differences on questions of religion."* Similarly, the editor of the Baptist *Biblical Recorder* stated in 1892 that his brand of Baptists "believe in the entire freedom of the conscience" so long as it was "enlightened by the teachings of God's word" and furthermore that "Baptists have ever ... [been] ... marked as a peculiar people" in "their intense love for both civil and religious *liberty*."[5]

This emphasis on individual freedom, however, combined with other emphases in sometimes contradictory ways. Evangelical discipline, for example, stressed conformity to external rules and regulations ranging from general moral axioms to denominational and congregational strictures, for once having become church members, most evangelicals either willingly or not-so-willingly submitted to the discipline of the church. Even though these emphases on freedom and discipline might seem contradictory, the way evangelicals connected conscience to discipline was nevertheless critical to their understanding of the limits of freedom, for evangelicals believed church discipline was a tutor that molded the conscience into conformity with God's moral governance. It would be wrong, therefore, to assume that evangelicals were libertarian in their advocacy of conscience. One Baptist, for example, warned, lest he be considered an anarchist, antinomian, or libertine, that "the conscience, not properly enlightened by the Bible, is not a safe guide: nor can the mind decide wisely . . . without bowing to the authority of God's book, and making it the only true standard of appeal."[6]

This connection between conscience and conformity to God's governance was also critical in shaping evangelical political thought. Again, evangelicals believed that when Christians acted according to their sanctified consciences, their obedience to religious, economic, or political truth put them in harmony with God's governance which ensured a well-oiled society.[7] Thus, they fought the twin evils of ignorance and political coercion that could bind the conscience and thus thwart God's governance. In doing so, evangelicals emphasized not only the importance of Christian education but also feared the power of civil governments to bind human conscience. This emphasis on conscience was at the heart of Protestants' assaults on papal hierarchy, for example, and once politicized in the seventeenth and eighteenth centuries, this belief undergirded evangelical attacks on religious establishment and furthermore supported liberal ideals of toleration and republicanism or democracy.

When they looked back on the revolutionary period or when they thought about American democracy, in fact, North Carolina evangelicals believed their institutions were essential to American religious and political freedom. When American evangelicals conjured up their sacred narratives and myths of origins—when they summoned up the spirits and deeds of the past—they inevitably pointed out how their early stresses on individual and civil liberty were central to their institutional identities and even to American democracy itself. In doing so, evangelicals used political and theological conceptions of liberty interchangeably. Myth, of course, might not have conformed to reality, but whether James O'Kelly had been a champion of Jeffersonianism or merely a local autocrat was beside the point when one O'Kellyite in 1912 imagined O'Kelly the foremost American "advocate of religious liberty and antagonist of ecclesiastical tyranny . . . the liberty loving patriot . . . [who] could not brook the fastening of an ecclesiastical hierarchy upon the American church" and who "wanted a church without episcopacy, because it comported better with republicanism."[8] So, despite the degree to which antebellum evangelicals were *actually* democratic or egalitarian in their thinking (a point of debate among historians), by the late nineteenth century, southern evangelicals believed that their denominations had worked in a reciprocal manner with American democratic ideals to ensure the uninterrupted success of American individual, civil, and religious liberty.

Evangelicals furthermore imagined their religious emphases on liberty, conscience, and Christian maturity foundations for democratic government more generally, and this helped render porous for them the divide between the sacred and the political. Most southern evangelicals believed, for example, that the vote was the voice of the conscience that in turn reflected the voice of God—*vox populi, vox dei*. They moreover considered religious liberty and their voluntary ecclesiastical institutions tutors for civil liberty, for reliance on one's conscience in religious matters, they believed, led to a general independence about the things of life, meaning one could cast a vote or serve one's government independent of the suasion of party favors, greed, or self-interest. Repeating a favorite Baptist legend "that Thomas Jefferson got his idea of the constitution . . . from noticing . . . the system of government of a small Baptist church near his home," one Baptist wrote: "America will never know how much she is indebted to the Baptists for the establishment of both civil and religious liberty. . . . To become a Baptist gives a man that religious liberty or freedom that accords with the civil liberty he so much admires, and for which our sires spilt their blood."[9]

In finding biblical justification for their emphases on liberty, postbellum evangelicals usually turned to biblical injunctions to love one another. In other words, loving one another was incongruous with hierarchical relationships of power, at least among enfranchised men. With this emphasis on loving one another, along with their general commonsense emphasis on freedom of conscience, most evangelicals saw some form of democracy as the only system of government suitable for a Christian church or nation. Methodist Protestant Edward J. Drinkhouse, in showing that ecclesiastical and civil governments work on the same principles, argued that "hierarchical," paternal, or oligarchical systems, while efficient, were, nevertheless, wrong, since, in any proper government, "authority is from below upward and not from above downward." He added that a democratic system of government "is but another expression for the incarnation of the gospel of Christ in the social relations."

In ecclesiastical matters, he therefore concluded that hierarchical forms of religious government were "forbidden by Christ's ecclesiastical ideal" and that "a hierarchy in the Church cannot peacefully abide and be ultimately perpetuated in a civil republic." Similarly regarding the absolute verity of political democracy, Drinkhouse wrote: "The peerage of democracy is that every man is a sovereign; every head wears a crown. It may be true that nine of the ten shall be clowns instead of kings; but this is better than that nine should be slaves and one a kingly clown." Opposing "the autocratic rule" of a "Pope or a Prelate" that turned men into "machines," Drinkhouse, in the end, averred: "Personal sovereignty . . . was what the Master taught, what the Apostles taught, what the primitive Church taught, and what the struggling peoples are teaching their rulers the world over; a struggle . . . that will not end until this pyramid stands upon its base, and authority shall work from the many to the few, and not from the few to the many."[10]

While advocating the verity of democracy in church and state generally, evangelicals usually stressed the particular importance of American democracy in God's providential designs. Thus, undergirding the remarks of Drinkhouse, Harrison and Barfield, and the editors of the *Biblical Recorder* was what I term "patriotic millennialism"—the notion that God had special designs for America as the beacon of democracy to the world—that America was Winthrop's city on a hill, the culmination of all that was good in Western Christian civilization. This idea permeated southern evangelicals' speech; for example, Disciple Miss Mattie Ham wrote that, because it resisted British tyranny, "the American government more fully embodies the principles of Christianity than any other political system on the globe." A Methodist lay leader similarly wrote: "If there were any children of God favored above all others of earth, it surely was those of the United States. . . . We faithfully affirm that the United States is a Christian nation."[11]

* * *

Just as it affected their preference for democracy, this ideal of independence or freedom, along with commonsense thinking, also shaped evangelicals' economic views and, more generally, how they thought the rich and poor ought to get along. Most southern evangelicals supported Jeffersonian views of limited government, the sanctity of private property, the verity of fair, honest competition, and the notion that increasing one's wealth, in moderation, was a good thing. Beyond these basics, however, evangelicals split between those who considered economic laws synonymous with the "powers that be" and thus wanted to leave them alone ("we shall always have the poor among us") and those who, in the name of social justice or antielitism, were willing to tinker with the economic system through political or social action. Both of these sides agreed that obeying God's laws of economics led to prosperity and economic harmony, but this latter group was willing to apply pressure against those agents who might thwart such harmony through immoral or unjust practices.[12]

Lines of class or rural/urban identity did not, however, generally determine one's views on the subject. One poor Baptist farmer wrote, for example, that there would never be "social equality," since God made rich and poor alike.[13] In stressing self-reliance as a cardinal virtue of American independence, this

Baptist farmer believed that God's moral governance had determined that those who practiced self-discipline and frugality were rewarded with prosperity while those who wasted time or money pursuing earthly pleasures received their just rewards.

Even while rich and poor alike might have adhered to such a way of thinking, as the nineteenth century wore on, affluence shaped certain evangelicals' thoughts on the subject. Of course, there had always been evangelical elites who looked askance at the poor, uneducated masses, just as there had always been antielitists who ridiculed urbane "aristocrats," but as the rural/urban divide grew wider and more prominent in the late nineteenth century, many wealthy southern evangelicals, especially those in towns or who owned factories, increasingly supported the "New South" gospel of wealth. They believed, in other words, that government financial breaks for railroads and businesses would have a positive trickle-down effect on the economic health of the entire South as it helped develop indigenous southern enterprise and as it attracted outside investment. They then linked this commercial prosperity to religious prosperity, reasoning that money earned in the name of capitalism would eventually support church initiatives. Much like our Baptist farmer, such evangelicals appealed to the "powers that be" in order to thwart the meddling of reformers who might oppose their vision of the New South.[14]

That they had to hold meddlers at bay, however, points to the presence of evangelicals who held such conservative thinking in contempt. These evangelicals groused that the "centralization" of capital in factories, cities, or large businesses might frustrate God's economic laws and furthermore that "combinations" of wealth and speculative investing were nothing more than the sins of tyranny and gambling respectively. In short, these evangelicals found the general idea that wealthy elites might have a free and easy way with the common folk nauseating.

Typically, rural meddlers located the roots of such avarice in city "First Churches." For example, one Methodist, in castigating city preachers who, "reclining on soft cushions," offered "incense and adulation to the millionaire bondholders, gorged with the wealth they have illegally wrung from the people," suggested that, had these effeminate ministers lived two thousand years earlier, they themselves would have put Jesus "into prison and denounce[d] Him and His followers [as] anarchists, socialists, and communists." Similarly, a Free Will Baptist, reflecting on a new steeple a local church had erected, decried the wealth that had provided this ostentation, assuming that it was the result of "ill-begotten gain taken unlawfully from the hand of poverty." He then called down God's eternal judgment on those, who, like this church's benefactor, "oppress" their "poor countrymen."[15]

Sophisticated analyses of the economic system such as those found in the northern social gospel were, however, rare. In the South, most southern evangelical critiques were not, in fact, based on the ideas of northern social gospelers such as John R. Commons, Richard T. Ely, or George Herron, who combined theological liberalism and progressive economic theories to assault the assumptions of classical laissez-faire political economics. Such social gospel ideas nested in some southeastern urban churches and universities and in southwestern rural areas but had little influence in the rural Southeast. There, common-folk evangelicals drew instead on older Jeffersonian rural ideals, classic economic producerism, and evangelical traditions of benevolence to articulate what historian Paul Harvey identifies as "social Christianity"—the simple yet powerful idea that economic relationships should be guided by the law of love and that God favors the working poor and especially the farmers over "non-producers." One Baptist simply put it like this: "God is at all times in love and sympathy with the toiling tiller of the soil.... God pity the man or the woman whom religion will permit a frown of disgust or a feeling of contempt for the honest and earnest toiler."[16]

As was evident earlier in the harsh words against preachers "reclining on soft cushions," this brand of social Christianity usually dovetailed with evangelical traditions of antielitism, both of which contributed mightily to the Populist ethos. This antielitist tradition was not so much a cohesive, well-thought-out philosophy as much as it was a gut-level, power-packed attitude that scorned ostentation, soft living, city life, and especially "fashion." Although this antielitist outlook had roots in Puritan rigor and Wesleyan holiness, like social Christianity, in the nineteenth century it also meshed with Jeffersonian ideals of agrarian purity and self-reliance.[17]

This antagonism toward erudition and open displays of wealth took a number of specific forms. For example, men, but more often women, eschewed wasting money and time buying fashionable clothing. Evangelical antielitists also derided highfalutin' ministerial elocution by praising ministers who preached extemporaneously or in the "plain style." Preaching extemporaneously, in fact, came to symbolize the "common" preacher in relief to "dude" preachers who "sermonized" with florid offerings steeped in erudition. One wildly popular North Carolina Presbyterian evangelist, William P. Fife, proudly claimed that he "did not know how to prepare a sermon and he thanked God that he didn't." He added that, nowadays in city churches, "there is too much sermon preaching and not enough of the teaching of the religion of Jesus Christ." Native North Carolinian Thomas Dixon, Jr., the state's most popular preacher in the 1890s, similarly mocked the "dainty hands" of "goody-good" city preachers who dispensed "honeyed words."[18]

As we saw with "Brother Jimmy," this antielitism only exacerbated the urban/rural denominational infighting of the late nineteenth century as rural folk often directed their antielitist critiques at the "goody-good preachers" and "town-bred dudes" they believed increasingly controlled denominational machinery. One Baptist, for example, noted that as "our members, especially in city churches, become wealthy, and hence able if disposed to indulge in even the foibles of fashion, there is a decided tendency on the part of some of our preachers to assume the airs and manners of the *fashionable preacher*. . . . What a contrast could be noticed between the . . . humble Nazarene" and "the fashionable preachers of our day!"[19]

As mentioned in the previous chapter, southern rural folk often stoked these rhetorical fires with northern examinations of the pathological problems of city life. The tyranny of centralized political power in the form of bossism, centralized economic power in the forms of trusts and combines, and centralized church life in the form of hireling pastors made city folk effeminate dependents: dependent on political bosses for instructions on how to vote, dependent on banks and employers for livelihood, and dependent on pastors for their spiritual lives. Such centers of effeminate degradation were a blight on the nation as they stifled the voice of the people and made the political system impotent.

* * *

Attacks on city life as emasculating evince another element of the southern evangelical outlook that also combined ideas of free conscience, moral governance, and commonsense thinking: the idea that people and institutions were sacred only insofar as they embodied God's eternal principles. Regarding individuals, southern evangelicals viewed the Christian life as a progression from spiritual infancy, inaugurated at conversion, to full Christian manhood and womanhood. Of course, "manhood," or manliness, often had other meanings in southern life (honor, blood sport, hunting, and general carousing—activities usually considered incongruent with church life), and likewise Christian womanhood dovetailed with more general conceptions of being female, such as possessing an innate spirituality and an ability to nurture. Nevertheless, for evangelical men, who often looked askance at carousing (though not hunting), manhood also meant being a devoted Christian brave enough to stand for the truth of the gospel in a world of infidelity, brave enough to face the arrows of Satan in the form of vice and temptation, and knowledgeable enough in the things of God to evangelize, to lead prayer meetings, church services, or family devotions, and to love fellow human beings.[20]

This idea of manhood shaped what evangelicals considered to be the foundational criterion for the male in public life: that he have the backbone or courage to stick to his convictions; in other words, that he have an enlightened conscience that properly and consistently directed the passions to adhere freely to God's moral principles.[21] Such a one thus attained the crowning virtue of manhood or womanhood: independence. For an independent, manly man, the coercion of political bosses could not sway his conscience-born vote, ecclesiastical mandates or establishments could not influence his conversion or church membership, and he did not depend on a wage, bank, or capitalist for financial stability. True manhood was thus foundational for American political freedom since only true men had the independence of thought not to be swayed by party rhetoric, boss rule, or emotional whim in casting their vote. For women, such independence was largely confined to its proper, "private" sphere, where, even there, they largely genuflected to their husbands' leadership or "mastery."[22]

The opposites of true men were, on the one hand, "Pharisees" or "straddle bugs" who lacked the anchor of an integrated belief system and who were thus blown about by popular opinion or self-interest, and, on the other, children, weak women, and African Americans. Regarding the "Pharisees," such lukewarm "straddle bugs" were not to be trusted, much less voted into political office. It might be added that one might not be born a spineless, emasculated Pharisee—certain environments tended to create them; cities, towns, universities, and Washington, D.C., were particularly suspect. The rural life, however, where men and women could experience self-sufficiency, provided luxuriant soil for proper gender development, as it enhanced independent thinking and thus a strong backbone. It was the job of such independent evangelical men, of course, to make sure such Pharisees did not achieve political or ecclesiastical power. Like men, children, weak women, and Africans required conversion and Christian education to ensure a civil society and a God-fearing church, but until they realized such states of maturity, they required governance by manly men. Most evangelicals were confident, however, that, with conversion and proper education, children, women, and blacks could become independent agents in God's government.[23]

As with manly men, most evangelicals believed institutions of economic production and civil and ecclesiastical government were sacred only if they embodied God's eternal principles, or, in other words, conformed to the way things should be—a belief that was critical to the way evangelicals approached political and ecclesiastical reform. We address political reform shortly, but by the late nineteenth century denominational reformers such as the Gospel Missioners or "Brother Jimmy" believed that their denominational machinery was in danger of abandoning or had already departed from God's principles. Reform, therefore, meant retooling this institutional machinery according to the apostolic blueprint, which reflected God's principles.

Given these reformers' democratic ideals, this ecclesiastical blueprint, as we have already seen, typically ensured a high degree of local control and volunteerism. Again, for such reformers, denominational apparati existed for utility only: to secure adequate pay for ministers, to organize and fund domestic expansion and foreign missions, and to provide ministerial oversight.[24] Reformers believed, moreover, that ecclesiastical governing bodies posed an inherent threat to the liberty of local churches, since, like all governing structures, these denominational bodies were prone to centralization and therefore to "tyranny." Methodist Protestant historian Edward Drinkhouse hammered this point home when he wrote that ecclesiastical hierarchy always threatened "to exert its repressive force against popular liberty . . . by subordinating the individual activity to the uniformity of the system. . . . The man is nothing; the system is everything." He added that "whatever may be its efficient uses," such a system was "radically opposed to that individuality which is the very genius of the gospel." Of course, almost all American Protestants believed that Roman Catholicism represented the ultimate expression of such ecclesiastical tyranny. As Drinkhouse put it: "The Roman Catholic Church . . . as a hierarchy is the perfect ideal of effectiveness in its methods. From the Pope downward there is absolutely no individual freedom. . . . All the actors . . . are but . . . cogs in the wheels within wheels."[25]

The intense denomination building and stress on efficiency in the late nineteenth century was, for many evangelicals, evidence that the American ecclesiastical machinery was indeed becoming tyrannical and therefore had the potential to coerce individual consciences. Even though much of the rhetoric that framed this anticentralization anxiety was antielitist and anticity, the lines of battle did not follow simple lines of class, race, or gender, or even the line between urban and rural churches. Centralizing tensions occurred equally among both black and white denominations; women were among the chief centralizers and supplied ample anticentralizing voices as well, and although denominational denunciations incorporated antielitist language often colored with attacks on city churches and aggregations of wealth, the holiness and Gospel Mission movements were popular in urban areas or led by urbanites. All of these anticentralizers would nevertheless have agreed with one Baptist who wrote, "We need no centralized power in our denomination . . . but . . . we are drifting into the hands of an ecclesiastical authority. We beg you to call a halt . . . we must be free . . . be free men, not slaves."[26]

Denominational leaders, often in the name of progress, did little to dampen the growing conflict. Apparently unaware that financially strapped farmers were calling their efforts to fund denominational initiatives "taxation without representation," they aggravated the situation with their attempts to get local churches to funnel all of their funds into a central agency in the name of efficiency.[27] These leaders insisted further that, if evangelicals were to have the social, political, and economic impact on society commanded by Jesus, they needed to be efficient and further needed to utilize the resources and rules of the city, which meant adhering to urban codes of professionalization and making friends with the city folk increasingly running the southern political and economic show.[28]

* * *

Just as evangelicals like the Gospel Missioners were eager to expose the threats to individual autonomy and personal liberty posed by centralized denominational and economic tyranny, many evangelicals were also concerned about political centralization, which they often identified with the epithet "bossism." From their basic democratic and ecclesiastical preferences, many evangelicals believed that political parties, like denominations, existed for utilitarian purposes and were to operate by democratic principles. The aim of a political party was to embody, through manly men, principles that would extend God's governance. Furthermore, even as Christianity could succumb to mere "churchianity" (all church and no "true" principles of religion), so could democracy forsake the principles of God's governance in favor of mere "partyism" or "partisan politics," in which parties existed only to perpetuate themselves.[29]

While attacks on partisan politics and bossism, along with general concerns about maintaining God-given civil liberty, represented one aspect of southern evangelical views on politics, evangelical discussion became much more complex when attempting to work out the actual, temporal relationship of the church to the state. Evangelicals' thoughts on political action, in fact, vacillated between two rather nebulous foci. On the one hand, evangelicals viewed the relationship between church and state from a conservative perspective marked by ideals such as the "separation of church and state" and their doctrine of the "spirituality of the church." Evangelicals drawn to this view of church/state relations frowned on attempts by Christians, churches, and especially ministers to "meddle" in politics. On the other hand, ideals of patriotic millennialism and the close association evangelicals made between religious and political freedom produced strong calls for Christians to be involved in the political sphere to prevent civil corruption, to legislate moral norms, or to ensure the continuance of civil and religious freedom or even, ironically, to ensure separation of church and state.[30]

Concerning the conservative focus, postbellum notions of separation of church and state and the "spirituality of the church," especially among Baptists, Methodists, and Presbyterians, were rooted in the antebellum debates over slavery and abolition that had split their denominations. Even though antebellum evangelicals were, in fact, politically active in a number of ways, with the rise of abolition, southern theologians articulated the doctrine often referred to as the "spirituality of the church," which relegated to the state all power in the political sphere and to the church all authority in the moral or "spiritual" sphere. The intent of this doctrine was to cast legislation about slavery as a political rather than a moral issue so that evangelical ministers and churches could remain silent on the issue to avoid church schism. The doctrine also enabled southern evangelicals to condemn abolitionists for wrongfully mingling church/state issues. After Reconstruction, the spirituality of the church similarly fueled more general denunciations of political meddlers such as women's suffragists, African American Republicans, unionists, socialists, anarchists, and other religious reformers who closely elided church and state.[31]

Along with well-thought-out ideas such as the spirituality of the church, postbellum evangelicals also adhered to more vague and even contradictory ruminations about "the separation of church and the state." From a commonsense view of obedience to the "powers that be," many evangelicals simply thought politics, like the economy, was best left alone, and, as was usually the case, "leaving it alone" meant acquiescence to the status quo.[32]

Another concern went back to Roger Williams's denunciations of Puritan New England: where the state and church mix, the state corrupts the church. Hence, evangelicals sometimes ignored or denounced politics in general as a corrupting, sinful, and immoral enterprise with which the church should have little business. Many ministers also worried that political excitement doused enthusiasm for revivals or other works of the Lord, and evangelicals also criticized the way allegiance to party lines compromised individual independence. Perturbed by this threat to independence, one evangelical noted in 1896 that a "politics which robs a man of his principles, deprives him of his individuality, causes him to cater to the whims and notions of popular sentiment and makes him a slave to party is the curse of our national life today."[33]

In their support of redeemer governments, however, conservative evangelicals were by no means consistent in their advocacy of separation of church and state. Especially after white political supremacy "redeemed" the South in the 1870s, white conservatives who supported the "powers that be" often intentionally or unintentionally supported the Democratic version of that power. Moreover, opposition to religious meddling itself prompted many a minister to delve into political debate, and in these instances the spirituality of the church continued to function as a rationalization for suppressing unpopular political views. Sometimes, however, conservative evangelicals cast certain political problems as having clear moral imperatives and were thus compelled to political action. Conservative evangelicals, for example, attacked dueling, child labor, divorce, and Reconstruction governments; they debated capital punishment and labor unions; and in particular they denounced women's suffrage.[34]

On the more activist side, many southern evangelicals, rather than using commonsense patterns of thought to support the "powers that be," instead looked to eternal axioms to judge the status of society in terms of what it should be. In the minds of evangelical reformers, axioms became ideals by which temporal social norms were judged. Moreover, mixing this brand of commonsense idealism with patriotic millennialism, many southern evangelicals concluded it was their job to advance the United States toward the democratic ideals on which it was founded, and advancing the cause meant diving into politics.

And a good number of evangelicals were, in fact, less than satisfied with the southern status quo. We have already met late nineteenth-century evangelicals who were concerned about growing economic inequalities or who condemned the partisan nature of politics. Others were alarmed by the influence of the "whisky ring" on politics, while still others worried about the growing Roman Catholic (and Protestant centralizing) menace in American society that, when coupled with other forms of economic and political centralization (monopolies and partisan politics), indicated a general drift in the land toward tyranny. For many southern evangelicals, these sinister forces threatened to move America away from its millennial course, and these evangelicals believed that they had a responsibility, through political involvement, to keep America on its Christian path.

Hence, by the 1880s and 1890s, calls for evangelicals to be more active in politics came from many quarters. One Baptist wrote, "Good government is the fruit of Christianity, it should co-operate with, and sustain religion, by enacting and enforcing such laws as will protect the moral and the good, and abate all nuisances." He then sadly noted, however, that the "Devil is running the political parties of the present day. He licenses crime and when Christians protest against it his children cry out: 'Don't mix politics and religion. . . .' If a man's religion is not worth carrying to the ballot-box on election day, it is not worth anything."[35]

Such general calls for Christians' involvement in politics often meshed with the concerns of the *North Carolina Baptist* editor who feared that North Carolinians of his generation were not as free as his fathers. One Baptist editor, calling America "the receptacle of the purest form of religious truth, and the great palladium of civil and religious liberty," for example, noted that, in the salad days of American democracy, "the American felt that he was in the true sense of the word a *free* man. He called no man master. He freely discussed matters of State and cast his ballot without regard to the wishes or the gold of political or business bosses." But times had changed; the influence of the "immense whiskey combination," "railroad corporations," and "immense trusts" were "striking ponderous blows at the palladium of our liberties." Thus, he warned: "We should remember that no republic can exist permanently that is not sustained by an enlightened Christian people . . . who would as soon think of selling their birth-right for a mess of pottage as to sell their vote or influence for money."[36]

Two specific ways in which evangelicals "went" into politics in North Carolina in the 1880s and 1890s, other than in Populism, were in the battles over "State Aid" to the University of North Carolina and prohibition. The attack on "State Aid" originated among a group of powerful Baptist and Methodist denominational leaders who attacked appropriations to the state college and in particular the free scholarships these appropriations granted to poorer students.[37] This fight was something of a sideshow, however, when compared to prohibition. Calls for the legal prohibition of the sale, manufacture, and consumption of alcohol (and sometimes tobacco) more than any other issue drove even apolitical holiness folk to run for office and to vote as they prayed (Primitive Baptists consistently, however, rejected prohibition as an affront to civil liberty). While calls for prohibition in other regions and times might have been prompted by bourgeois drives for social control, North Carolina prohibition was a grassroots movement concerned with preserving purity in government and American civil liberty. Prohibitionists blamed whisky, and more usually the whisky rings, for enslaving men and producing political corruption, hard times, racial and class problems, family problems, crime, the "money problem," and just about every other social evil one could conjure up. Whisky emasculated men, tortured or left women and children unprotected, and kept blacks from social uplift, and the whisky ring strangled state legislatures and silenced the voice of God through tyrannical boss rule.[38]

Although some evangelicals especially beholden to the spirituality of the church favored "moral suasion" as the means to correct this evil, others became radically politicized and even threatened third-party action since they believed the Democrats (the dry party in North Carolina) had fallen increasingly under the sway of the "whisky ring." One such evangelical, Gospel Missioner M. P. Matheney of Gastonia, was perhaps the most ardent voice among Baptists advocating this sort of activism. In his columns, "Gastonia Gumption" and "A Dish of Hash" in the *North Carolina Baptist*, Matheney foreshadowed the way evangelical Populists would weave together themes of tyranny, centralization, patriotic millennialism, and anti-Romanism to urge preachers into politics. Even though Matheney was not quite ready to advocate a third party in 1891, he was nevertheless convinced that the "Saloonatics" were "entrenched behind the two great political parties in this country, and . . . dictate every nomination." By 1892, he was steadily losing faith in the white man's party and was thus prompted to write something no self-respecting white Democrat would have considered writing ten years earlier:

> It is hard to tell just how far a minister of the Gospel should go in politics, but it is not difficult to see that a minister should use all the power he has to prevent the whiskey curse from being fastened again upon his people, and he is unfaithful to himself and to his master if he does not speak out in a time like this. Of course, there will be some hypocrite or friend of whiskey who will hold his hands in holy (?) horror and say the preacher has gone into politics. Well, if there is any place under heaven where a preacher's influence is needed it is in politics. If the politics of the country are too rotten for the preachers to go into, then it is high time the Christian people of this land had separated themselves from such rottenness and organized a decent man's party where a preacher can afford to go.[39]

* * *

As evangelicals in North Carolina reached the final decade of the nineteenth century, they held many opinions about the economic, political, and ecclesiastical issues they faced. When it came to politics, North Carolina evangelicals, as individuals, congregations, or even denominations, balanced or galvanized around the dual foci of conservative and more activist ideas about preserving America's civil and democratic freedom and America's place as the great beacon of democracy for the Western advance of civilization. These dual foci, when coupled with other tensions between conservative notions of the way things were and potentially radical evangelical views of egalitarianism, liberty, and social Christianity, could produce multifaceted and even contradictory social movements and stances. Such tensions, however, did not exist in a vacuum; evangelicals might have started out as radical opponents of the status quo, but by 1890 they were cultural insiders, though they might not have always thought so themselves. Culturally, this movement that arose to fight established religion, partly because of its theological imperatives to leaven and to save society, partly because of its historical development, and mostly because of its success, had become the established religion, legitimating multiple and even contradictory elements of southern cultural, economic, and political life. At the same time, in its egalitarian and antielitist outlook, and because of its axiomatic thinking, it bore the most potent critiques that could be leveled at these very same institutions, including the church itself. This radical undercurrent, when linked to the reforms advocated by the Farmers' Alliance, proved more than capable of turning southern society on its head in the late 1880s.

SECTION 2

The Voice of God
in the Alliance Whirlwind

"The Christian Religion in Concentrated Form"

Leonidas L. Polk had a habit of signing his correspondence, "In Haste, L.L.P." Indeed, L. L. Polk was a man incessantly in haste to achieve some measure of success greater than that preceding it; he captured Tocqueville's characterization of the restless entrepreneurial American. Born in 1837 to Federalist, Presbyterian planters in Anson County owning thirty-two slaves, Polk was educated at the Presbyterian enclave of Davidson College, though as a young man he was caught up in the revivalism of the local Baptists and affiliated with the denomination for the rest of his life. Eventually Polk sat on the board of trustees at Wake Forest College, served in 1889 and 1890 as president of the North Carolina State Baptist Convention, and helped establish the Baptist Female Seminary in Raleigh (Meredith College). A Whig and a Unionist, Polk nevertheless hearkened to the strains of Dixie in 1861 and achieved the rank of colonel. After the war, with his small plantation in ruins, like many planters Polk divided up his property, set up a post office in his home, published *The Ansonian,* built a Baptist and then a Methodist church, farmed, and eventually named his town "Polkton."

As the depression of the 1870s gripped farmers in North Carolina and elsewhere, Polk and Mecklenburg County planter S. B. "Syd" Alexander established North Carolina's Grange, a phalanx of mostly well-to-do farmers, numbering about ten thousand in the Old North State, intent on making the state legislature more responsive to farmers' needs and on easing farmers' high overhead and transportation costs. The Grange succeeded in establishing a state Department of Agriculture in 1876 with Polk as its first head. By that time, Polk had also secured a seat at the table among a handful of Democratic leaders around Raleigh who basically ran North Carolina's affairs of state.

As the 1880s brought better times, interest in the Grange wilted, and so Polk resigned as agricultural commissioner and took on senior editorial duties at a new Democratic paper out of Raleigh while also pursuing a number of unsuccessful business ventures, most notably his patented diphtheria cure. Polk eventually moved to Boston and then to New York in order to capitalize and market "Polk's Diphtheria Cure," but he returned to North Carolina after he failed to make his fortune.

Once farmers again experienced "hard times," Polk, who never sat still for long, inaugurated *The Progressive Farmer* in February 1886, one of the most important agricultural papers in the country over the next decades. With loads of agricultural advice, a page of jokes and riddles, serials, and "women's" and "children's" columns, this eight-page paper got farmers to talking and eventually to organizing. Grassroots "farmers' clubs" sprang up across the state in 1886 and early 1887 in order to discuss the issues facing farmers, and in response, Polk, along with his old Granger friend Syd Alexander, organized the North Carolina Farmers' Association to oversee these clubs. In the summer of 1887, the Farmers' Alliance of Texas rolled into the state and, recognizing the value of a national organization, Polk oversaw the two groups' merger and became state secretary while Alexander took the reins as president of the newly minted North Carolina State Farmers' Alliance. Polk would rise further in the national organization, serving from 1889 until his death in 1892 as president of the Southern Alliance. Had he not met such an untimely death, Polk, rather than James B. Weaver, would no doubt have headed the presidential ticket for the Populists in 1892.[1]

But that is jumping ahead. Back in 1886, farmers were delighted that the *Farmer,* among other things, was a "$1.00 paper," and this show of solidarity with smaller farmers who could not afford "$2.00" papers illustrated Polk's insistence that his new organization draw in farmers of the "middling" classes, as opposed to the Grange, which had catered more to large planters and political power brokers. It is furthermore not at all surprising that the upstart Baptist "$1.00 paper," the *North Carolina Baptist,* lent its hearty support to Polk, the *Farmer,* and the Alliance, given that all three of its editors were organizers for the Farmers' Alliance. As "middling" rural parsons, the *Baptist* editors typified the sort of rural folk attracted to the Alliance; moreover, as Baptist pastors belonging to the most powerful denomination in the state, they demonstrated the degree to which the Alliance tapped into the mainstream, not the periphery, of southern society. As farmers, though,

L. L. Polk. Courtesy of the North
Carolina Office of Archives and
History of the North Carolina
Department of Cultural
Resources, Raleigh, North
Carolina.

they also perceived the growing cleavage between the burgeoning wealth of
manufacturers and city folk and the growing poverty of the countryside.[2]

As National Alliance president, L. L. Polk gained renown as he traveled
about the country inviting blue and gray farmers to analyze this growing
divide between urban opportunity and rural stagnation. In an 1890 gathering
of the Southern Alliance at Ocala, Florida—a gathering that marked the
height of Alliance power—Polk asked why, given that "no country or people
in all history have been so favored and blessed with opportunity and favorable
conditions for the successful and profitable prosecution of agricultural industries," was it the case that, "instead of the happy song of peace, contentment
and plenty, which should bless the homes of the farmer and laborer of the
country, should we hear the constant and universal wail of 'hard times'?"

The answer, according to Polk, was that a combination of corrupt politicians, monopolists, and the northeastern financial establishment (the
"plutocrats") had enacted "iniquitous" class legislation that distorted the
economic system, and, as a result, farmers could neither obtain money or
credit nor could they control their costs or the value of their crops. Thus,
farmers were enslaved to creditors, Wall Street, railroads, and monopolists
who controlled both the markets and the political process. Again at Ocala,
President Polk argued that, in the face of such economic disequilibrium, the
"holy mission" of the Alliance was "to restore and maintain the equipoise

between the great industrial interest of the country" through cooperative economic and political action in order to invigorate widespread prosperity. Echoing the apocalyptic concerns of the *North Carolina Baptist* in his assertion that farmers faced a growing state of economic slavery, Polk concluded:

> Centralized capital, allied to irresponsible corporate power, stands to-day as a formidable menace to individual rights and popular government . . . so that reflecting, patriotic men, are confronted with the question, whether this is really a popular government founded "on the consent of the governed." . . . We are rapidly drifting from the moorings of our fathers and stand to-day in the crucial era of our free institutions, of our free form of government, and of our Christian civilization.[3]

The Progressive Farmer and the *North Carolina Baptist* shared more than just their support for the Alliance; like so many North Carolina evangelicals, they were also enamored with the Rev. Thomas Dixon, Jr. In late 1890 and early 1891, *The Progressive Farmer,* along with other local, state, and national Alliance papers, began printing the weekly sermons of Dixon that blended southern individualism and evangelical piety with a passion for reform and an intense patriotic millennialism.[4] In these papers, in his Alliance lectures, and from his New York City pulpit, Dixon responded to the same pressures identified by Polk as he proclaimed that the Alliance was God's tool for correcting these political and economic problems propelling America into an apocalyptic abyss.

And Alliancefolk latched on to every word. J. M. Cutchin, for example, a Methodist Protestant Alliance lecturer in Whitakers, began reading Dixon's sermons during his public Alliance lectures. One Alliance devoted a weekly meeting to a Dixon sermon while Allianceman J. G. Mitchell equated Dixon to the venerable L. L. Polk in naming the pair North Carolina's greatest living champions of the masses. Similarly, after having heard Dixon preach on the Alliance, a reporter from *The Progressive Farmer* proclaimed: "Truly he is another Patrick Henry . . . Long live Dixon!" Marion Butler, president of the state Alliance in 1891, wrote: "If we had more preachers who would preach a practical religion, we would have less corruption in politics and less dishonesty in business. Would that the Christian pulpit had ten thousand Tom Dixons."[5] Perhaps more than anyone else, Dixon was able to articulate, in a language common to both agrarian folk and evangelicals, a millennial and patriotic vision of the Alliance that gave it a sense of moral duty and righteous indignation. Just who was he?

Dixon was born to Amanda and Thomas, Sr.—a small planter, slave owner, and Baptist minister—in 1864 in the town of Shelby in the foothills of the Appalachian Mountains. Rarely does one child gain the notoriety of Thomas, Jr., but in the case of the living Dixon siblings, all five achieved national and even international fame. A. C., Tom's older brother, became the most famous Baptist minister in the country in the early twentieth century, taking over D. L. Moody's pulpit in Chicago and Charles Spurgeon's pulpit in London. A. C. eventually edited the *Fundamentals,* a twelve-book series published from 1910 to 1915 outlining the "fundamentals" of conservative evangelicalism; from this series was coined the term "fundamentalist." Tom's younger brother, Frank, gained national fame as a lecturer and eventually as a leader in the Chautauqua Society. One sister, Addie Dixon Thacker, became a renowned author, while Tom's other sister, Delia Dixon Carroll, became arguably the most famous woman physician in the country.

Although Thomas, Jr., would gain wealth and fame beyond his wildest dreams as a white supremacy novelist with *The Leopard's Spots* (1903) and *The Clansman* (1905), much as was the case with Polk, Dixon's peripatetic existence had led him through Wake Forest College, Johns Hopkins (where he studied with Herbert Baxter Adams and Richard T. Ely and befriended Woodrow Wilson), an unsuccessful theater career in New York, and a promising career as a reforming state legislator all by the time he was twenty (a year before he could vote). Discouraged, however, by the corruption of party politics, Dixon left the legislature and went to law school, becoming a successful prosecutor until again growing restless. In 1886 he was ordained as a Baptist minister, and, after quickly moving through a series of pastorates in North Carolina, he worked his way to Boston and then to Twenty-third Street Baptist Church in New York City, from which he would gain international fame, along with the friendship of John D. Rockefeller.[6]

The content of his lectures, writings, and sermons epitomized the contemporary currents and contradictions of evangelical thought. As the preacher of "the people," Dixon spoke a caustic, plain-style message rooted in traditions of antielitism and social Christianity. A theological Arminian, he firmly believed that everyone, with the proper basic education, could understand and debate the most esoteric theological, economic, and political principles. He was furthermore conservative in his dedication to classical economic liberalism, separate spheres for men and women (though he waffled throughout the period on women's suffrage, women in the workplace, and women's ordination), and the natural division of the races. Thus, even though he was fairly liberal theologically, his conservative stands on these issues made him palatable to most southern evangelicals. Despite his conservatism in these areas, Dixon nevertheless thought of himself as a "radical," a "reformer," and a "progressive." For Dixon, the enemy of the

Thomas Dixon, Jr. Thomas Dixon, Jr. Papers, Rare Book, Manuscript, and Special Collections Library, Duke University, Durham, North Carolina.

South was traditionalism—"the most . . . utterly devilish opposition the Master encountered." He called his readers to imitate Galileo and the revolutionaries in France, believing that "progress has always been made by a life and death struggle with tradition and bigotry." Linking his radicalism to his commitment to freedom of conscience, Dixon eventually founded his independent New York City "People's Temple" in 1895 (bankrolled by Rockefeller), to stand against what he considered to be the tyrannical conservatism of the Southern Baptist Convention.[7]

It was out of his commitment to this "plain-folk" liberalism, along with commitments to patriotic millennialism and Christian political action, that

Dixon emerged as the premier evangelical apologist for the Alliance in the early 1890s. In one speech concerning "The Moral Import of the Farmers' Alliance," Dixon, according to one reporter, "argued that the Alliance was the result of divine inspiration" and that it represented "a great social and moral revolution" that "would elevate mankind" and "purify politics."[8] According to another reporter, Dixon concluded that Alliancefolk "represent the grandest moral issues of the age." Dixon warned the "deadbeats and bummers" who discounted such agrarian radicalism that "the cyclone has only begun. They had better seek shelter."[9]

In a manner perfected by Dixon, Alliancefolk across the South combined evangelical ideals, patriotic millennialism, and agrarian self-sufficiency to forge a powerful, evangelical critique of how wealth and power in the late nineteenth century ought to be distributed. In doing so, Alliancefolk blurred lines of secular and sacred, moral and political, as they developed a sacred narrative of democratic redemption. Within this narrative, in fact, American, agricultural, and Christian identities merged to the point that Thomas Dixon could assert without blinking that Alliance principles were nothing less than the "Christian religion in concentrated form."[10]

* * *

As typified in Dixon's speech, the Southern Farmers' Alliance was often described as a "cyclone" sweeping across the South, destroying every vestige of rural political and economic conservatism. The simile was apropos, for even though the Grange and Greenback Party preceded it and farmers' unions would follow, no rural movement in the South or elsewhere matched the Southern Alliance's rapid mobilization and economic and political impact. Aiming to end farmers' economic and political marginalization in the face of urban and industrial prosperity, the Alliance drew on older political, economic, and religious ideas to teach farmers how, through cooperation, they could flex their economic and political might. Through Alliance education, an emergent cadre of fencepost political economists conversant in Smith, Ricardo, and Gilded Age reformers used cooperative leverage to boycott manufacturers and merchants, start local and statewide cooperative stores and manufacturing ventures, and warehouse cotton and tobacco to maximize profits. These farmers built agricultural colleges and institutes, made state agricultural agencies more respondent to farmers' needs, and tried to block the flood of young boys and girls leaving the farm for vainglorious city life. The Alliance moreover influenced state and local politics, forcing the southern Democratic Party to bend to farmers' demands that included railroad regulation, internal improvements, agricultural education, better rural public schools, and financial laws fairer to farmers and debtors. At the pinnacle of its strength, there were 2,221 suballiances and over a hundred thousand members in North Carolina.[11] At the same time a "sister" organization, the North Carolina Colored Farmers' Alliance headed by black Baptist Rev. Walter A. Patillo and white Baptist lay leader J. J. Rogers, claimed a membership of 15,000.[12]

To understand the motives behind this movement, it is important to remember that Alliancefolk were not just experiencing hard times but rather were indignant that urban professionals and other "nonproducers" prospered while they did not. These farmers were not just poor; they were angry, and as Polk made clear, their anger had a target: economic, political, and religious centralizers who had captured the levers of state and local government through "class legislation" and had thus denigrated God's moral laws of economic, religious, moral, and political governance. For Alliancefolk, this represented a political and economic state of tyranny, and righting the situation involved the restoration of popular democracy, meaning that the enlightened masses needed to elect their own to storm the gates of local, state, and national government and recapture the levers of legislative power, returning control of the political economy back to the place it belonged—the hands of the people.

While the Alliance drew on a number of cultural and intellectual agendas to draw these conclusions, and while it approximated other secret societies in format, it was the Protestant evangelicalism of folks like Thomas Dixon that gave the Alliance its basic intellectual orientation, its moral fervor, and, most important, its sense of urgency—its feeling of righteous indignation that greedy, unscrupulous, hell-bound plutocrats had adulterated God's New Israel. More to the point, churches, local preachers and lay leaders, and denominational networks provided an organizational apparatus for the Alliance, and Alliancefolk drew on evangelicals' commonsense thinking, elevation of individual autonomy and conscience, patriotic millennialism, social Christianity, and antielitism to assess the crisis of the 1890s and to formulate a solution. This solution to restore American democratic principles through political action paralleled the way the Disciples of Christ and other religious restorationists sought to restore the ideals of pristine Christianity to remedy the problems of "churchianity."

Alliancefolk, however, did not just mimeograph these evangelical ideals. Within the crucible of the Alliance, rural identities, evangelical patterns of thought, and Jeffersonian yeoman ideals amalgamated into a uniquely evangelical and rural reform agenda. In the process, the lines between the Alliance and Christianity, between farmers and Christians, and between Jesus and

Thomas Jefferson, blurred. Jesus became a radical agrarian reformer and his circle of disciples a Galilean suballiance, while the Democratic and Republican parties became the Pharisees and Sadducees in league with the money changers (monopolists) in the temple. Alliancefolk regularly used the terms "farmer" and "Christian" and "preacher" interchangeably.[13]

In adopting evangelical organizational patterns and intellectual strands, the Alliance, again, mirrored the place of evangelicalism in relation to southern society. With its evangelical-based commonsense outlook, the Alliance reinforced certain elements of that society near and dear to North Carolinians as it blended into the southern landscape. The Alliance, for example, rarely challenged southern norms of race and gender; neither did it explicitly challenge the basic tenets of economic liberalism. Until it began to agitate politically in 1888, the Alliance therefore faced virtually no opposition, and even then only from outdated conservative Democrats who were becoming out of synchrony with most North Carolinians' economic goals.

Thus, and this is a critical point, the Alliance in North Carolina, like the evangelical institutions to which it was linked, did not consist of cultural outsiders; rather, within its ranks were a myriad of "the best farmers" and local political leaders who hoped to join hands with industrialists to herald a new era of progress and prosperity. Yet, like evangelicalism, the Alliance harbored radical conceptions of popular democracy inherently threatening to certain ideas about what form this prosperity should take. If evangelicalism legitimated the Alliance, making it palatable to the status quo and giving it a broad audience, at the same time it imbued the Alliance with a cluster of ideals and a radical undercurrent capable of turning southern society on its head.

3. The Alliance *Vorzeit*

Even though certain intellectual and religious components shaped the Populist movement, it was also tied to specific social, economic, and political developments of the late nineteenth century. Leaving political developments for the next section, this chapter examines the social and economic factors that helped determine the shape and timing of Populism or, more specifically, the Farmers' Alliance. The most important of these factors were a growing urban/rural divide in the South and nation, the marginalization of agriculture in the national culture, political sphere, and economy, and national debates over the nature of money and the role of the federal and state governments in regulating the nation's economy. Perhaps most important, from the late 1870s into the 1890s, the national economy was marked by high interest rates, scarce currency, and low commodity prices—an economy devastating for farmers, especially those in the war-ravaged and cash-starved South. Farmers in North Carolina responded to this economic nightmare with cooperative action first through the Grange and then through L. L. Polk's North Carolina Farmers' Association and *Progressive Farmer*.

* * *

No one doubted that times were hard for North Carolina farmers after the Civil War, but, then, most farmers in North Carolina had never known the plantation wealth of other states like Virginia and South Carolina. Because North Carolina's seventeenth-century proprietors had doled out land in 640- to 660-acre parcels, the state never really developed a plantation system, though some eastern counties boasted a few large plantations.

Rooted in the ideals of self-sufficiency, most antebellum white yeomen could claim roughly the same independence that just about any farmers in the country could—they usually owned a small farm, planted enough food to eat, made their own clothing, and established a small cash crop of corn, tobacco, or cotton. But that is not to say that antebellum North Carolina was a Jeffersonian paradise. Except for the commerce in a few bustling towns along the Cape Fear River like Fayetteville and Wilmington, North Carolina was probably the most commercially isolated antebellum state. Navigable rivers were few, roads were abysmal, there were few banks or even towns, and wages were about the lowest in the country.

After the Civil War the state lay prostrate, with inadequate transportation, a labor shortage, virtually no banking or currency, and the fewest financial assets in the South. Once the political situation was redeemed by the Democrats in 1876, the state's boosters saw economic salvation in a "New South" where progressive, market-oriented cotton and tobacco farmers could join hands with textile, furniture, and other manufacturers in the Piedmont.[1] Such growth, however, was slow to start because of a general economic depression in the 1870s. Compounding the problems of this general depression were the scarcity of capital, currency, banks, and credit in the state, along with high interest rates and low commodities prices brought on by banking and currency regulations that restricted the volume of currency in circulation. Farmers, who were falling further into debt and making less on their crops, felt the brunt of these economic problems most severely.

Debate surrounding these economic problems and, more specifically, the banking and currency regulations that controlled the volume of U.S. currency, evolved into one of the most contentious political issues of the Gilded Age: "the money question." On one side of the money question were "soft money" advocates who wanted to lower interest rates and raise commodities prices first by expanding the money supply with greenbacks or silver and, second, by terminating the national banking system. These soft money advocates were most often debtors (including farmers) or those who felt discriminated against by eastern financial and banking circles. On the other side of the money question were "hard money" advocates—financial conservatives such as bankers, creditors, and those with overseas trade interests—who advocated a small, tightly controlled money supply that would keep inflation down and interest rates high. Most taking the hard money side also advocated the gold standard, which likewise helped keep the money supply in check and facilitated trade with gold-standard Britain. Those involved in the money question also debated the nation's protective tariff, but this issue acted more as an independent variable (though Republicans generally supported the tariff and Democrats opposed it). Most southern farmers disliked the tariff, however, because they thought it raised the prices of manufactured items they needed to purchase.

In order to grasp the kinds of problems the Farmers' Alliance and People's Party addressed in the 1890s, as well as the solutions they formulated, it is necessary to understand the basic issues, regulations, and vocabulary surrounding this money question. Even though the issue pitted "soft money" against "hard money" advocates, the money question itself actually involved three interdependent questions: (1) whether Congress ("the people") or the national banking system ("the private interests") would make money and control its volume; (2) what the nature of money in the United States would be: bank notes (national or private); "fiat money" or "greenbacks" (legal tender minted by the U.S. Treasury with no backing but the word of the U.S. government); or currency backed by metal specie. Those who advocated currency backed by specie further divided over (3) whether to use gold backing principally (monometallists or "goldbugs") or both gold and silver backing without restriction (bimetallists, "free silver" advocates, or "silverites"). In terms of specific public policy, debates over these three issues focused on the role of the government in regulating specie backing, whether to continue the national banking system, and whether to mint standard silver dollars after the United States abolished them in 1873.

Problems surrounding these issues stemmed from federal monetary measures put in place during the Civil War to fund the Union cause. Before the war, circulating currency consisted primarily of bank notes that were redeemable on demand at the issuing bank in "specie," that is, in metallic backing, which up until the early 1870s was almost always gold. Before the Coinage Act of 1873 in effect legalized the gold standard by dropping use of the silver dollar, the United States recognized both silver and gold specie at a minting ratio of roughly sixteen to one (sixteen grains of silver equaled one grain of gold). Because silver was undervalued in this minting ratio during the antebellum period, however, it rarely served as circulating currency. "Specie payment," or the requirement that banks and the U.S. Treasury redeem notes in specie on demand, served as a test of solvency for banks and as a means of regulating the number of notes they could issue; in other words, specie payments served as a means of controlling the volume of currency in circulation.[2]

To finance the Civil War, the federal government authorized special taxes and the sale of war bonds, but there was neither the currency in circulation nor the specie backing in existence to support these measures. Hence, the government expanded the money supply with four policies. First, it suspended specie payments in 1861, which, in essence, took the United States off the gold standard. Second, the U.S. Treasury produced "fiat money" or "greenbacks"—legal tender notes backed not by specie but only by the U.S. Treasury's word. While greenbacks increased the amount of circulating currency, their value inflated to the degree that, by 1864, nearly three greenbacks traded for one gold dollar. Third, the federal government issued short-term bonds that could be purchased with greenbacks. It was unclear at the time of purchase, however, whether the government would redeem them in greenbacks or gold. The federal government clarified this issue in the Public Credit Act of 1869 and the Funding Act of 1870 that mandated the replacement of short-term bonds with longer-term bonds for which both interest and principal were to be paid in coin. For large investors (often northeastern banks and financiers) who had purchased bonds with greenbacks valued to gold at 3:1, repayment in gold coin was a windfall return many poor folk in poor regions viewed with suspicion.

Finally, the National Banking Act of 1863 reestablished a federal banking system that provided the federal government with funds in two ways. First, in order to become nationally chartered, banks had to deposit gold coin in the federal Treasury in return for Treasury bonds; hence, the national banking system provided an additional market for those bonds. Second, the federal government authorized chartered banks to issue "national bank notes" that, along with greenbacks, inflated the volume of currency. Additionally, the act eliminated a significant number of state banks with a back-breaking 10 percent tax on state and private notes. National banks, then, as a centralized banking structure and *private* arm of the federal government, became, along with the Treasury, the primary vehicle for creating money and regulating the money supply. Furthermore, the vast majority of national banks were chartered in the Northeast. Even though the Currency Act of 1870 and the Free Banking Act of 1874 opened up more federal banks in the Midwest and more evenly distributed federal notes, these measures did not aid the South, which, needless to say, had no access to national bank charters during the Civil War and remained isolated from the national banking system long afterward. By 1895, while there was one bank for every 16,600 people in the United States, in the South, excluding Texas, there was only one bank for every 58,130 people.[3]

As a result of all four measures, by the end of the Civil War the Union was experiencing high inflation and, in the minds of financial conservatives in the Northeast, a tarnished reputation with the primary culprit being the $450 million in greenbacks in circulation. Conservatives thus urged both "resumption" of specie payments and "suspension" of greenback production to ease the United States back to the effective gold standard and to remove the depreciated greenbacks. By reducing the money supply and renewing faith in the stability of U.S. currency, both measures would reduce inflation, raise interest rates, and reduce the trade deficit. These aims culminated in the 1875 Resumption Act. Because of a series of compromises, greenbacks, however, remained in circulation. Although there was no severe reduction of the money supply in the Gilded Age for fear that radical surgery would cause economic panic, as manufacturing and agricultural production increased, the money supply remained the same. The bottom line, therefore, was that greenbacks came more closely to equal gold in value, manufacturing and commodity prices went down, and interest rates rose, making lenders a happy lot and creating a devastating situation for farmers and debtors.

As the Gilded Age wore on and the financial panic and depression of the 1870s peaked, the National Greenback Party (1876–84), many southerners and westerners, and a number of manufacturers in places like Pennsylvania increasingly advocated the soft money position, which aimed to decrease the amount of financial power in the Northeast and expand the money supply in order to raise commodity prices and lower interest rates.

To accomplish this, soft money advocates wanted, first, to end the national banking system and, second, to increase the money supply with greenbacks or silver. Regarding banking reform, soft money advocates believed that the national banking system represented "private" banking interests rather than the will of "the people," as represented by Congress, in controlling both the production and volume of money. For soft money folk, then, the national banking system operated outside the nation's political economy and thus outside even the economic laws of supply and demand as it tilted the nation's economy in favor of northeastern financial interests. Furthermore, soft money folk resented the inequitable distribution of banks and notes, the payment of interest for a basic necessity of life (many contrasted profit-generating money to postage stamps), and the fact that national banks received interest both from the government and from issuing notes. They also rightly perceived that banks were unresponsive to the borrowing needs of farmers, who often faced restrictions on using land as collateral, and they were incensed that banks that had purchased bonds with forty-cent dollars during the war were being repaid in gold dollars. In place of the national banking system, soft money advocates promoted a return to state banks or the development of "free banking," meaning that anyone adequately capitalized could issue notes.

In addition to bank reform, soft money advocates wanted to expand the money supply either with greenbacks or, increasingly in the 1880s, the remonetization of silver at a ratio of sixteen to one after it was demonetized in the Coinage Act of 1873, popularly known as "the Crime of '73." Although connecting the volume of currency to commodity prices and interest rates seems complex, in farmers' minds the connection was fairly simple, as illustrated by historian Lawrence Goodwyn. First, they believed money, like any commodity, was subject to the laws of supply and demand, and so in a period with a compressed money supply (like the 1870s forward), money would cost more to obtain; this meant higher interest rates. Second, farmers thought about the effect of the money supply on commodities prices like this: suppose ten farmers represented the entire population of farmers, ten bushels of wheat their entire output, and $10 the amount of money in circulation in 1865. In such conditions, every farmer would receive $1 per bushel of wheat. If in 1890 the number of farmers had increased to twenty and their combined output to twenty bushels and yet the money supply had remained at $10, they would then only receive fifty cents per bushel, and therein, for many farmers, lay the problem of falling commodities prices throughout the Gilded Age.[4]

While Greenbackers advocated a "fiat money" system in which Congress, not the law of supply and demand, controlled the volume of currency and interest rates, and in which Congress, through the Treasury, would oversee the production of greenbacks as the primary means of exchange, free silver advocates, like their "goldbug" adversaries, usually rejected "fiat money" as unstable and ultimately "dishonest" because it had no intrinsic value. Debate over the gold standard, however, was never quite that simple, since both gold and silver came to symbolize a host of meanings outside simple economics. For "monometallists" who advocated the gold standard alone (a position taken by most of the business community by the 1890s), gold, with its intrinsic value, barred "dishonest" speculation in money markets, provided a "sound footing" and a safe mode of exchange, offered "discipline" to the financial markets, and was the "progressive" foundation of a financial system free from impurity and corruption. Furthermore, because Mexico, France, and certain non-Western nations used silver, monometallists regarded silver a metal unworthy of respect; its use, they believed, would tarnish America's financial image among other "progressive" nations and especially the premier trading partner of the United States, monometallic Great Britain.

Silverites, on the other hand, cast the money problem in democratic and antielitist terms. They associated gold with northeastern trusts and tycoons,

Wall Street corruption, and the national banks, while they touted silver as the pure, simple metal of the people, the democratic coin of the "common man." Furthermore, they argued that increasing the money supply with silver would put more money in the pockets of yeomen, artisans, and small manufacturers, and thus secure the independence that ultimately undergirded democratic politics, economic advance, and true American manhood.[5]

Silverites won modest victories with the 1878 Bland-Allison Act and 1890 Sherman Silver Purchase Act that provided for limited coinage of silver. Grover Cleveland's repeal of silver purchases in 1893, though, made silver the preeminent issue in the 1896 presidential campaign between Democrat William Jennings Bryan and Republican William McKinley, otherwise known as "the Battle of the Standards." Bryan attempted to link the South and the West over the silver issue, but McKinley won and returned America to the gold standard with the Gold Standard Act of 1900. Again, the point here is that all of these questions, attitudes, and rhetorical nuances provided the basic lexicon for Gilded Age financial reformers, including members of the Alliance and the People's Party.

* * *

Faced with the devastation of the state's capital, currency, and transportation structures, however, battling over monetary standards seemed perhaps the least of North Carolina's problems in 1865. Slowly but surely, though, North Carolinians pieced together their meager infrastructure and economic well-being after the depression of the 1870s. This process, however, aggravated a growing division between urban and rural folk by giving industrialists and especially the railroads immense power in shaping the state's political and economic status.

Regarding railroads, in the 1880s Governor Thomas J. Jarvis began to privatize North Carolina's state system by selling or leasing its lines to capitalists in Virginia and parts farther north. By 1904 North Carolina's railroad system was completely privatized and controlled by three companies owned or financed outside the state. Because of tax exemptions, freedom from regulation, and the use of state convicts to work on the roads, these private (or "foreign") railway companies radically expanded the state's transportation network. In doing so, as was the case in the rest of the nation, railroads held a great deal of sway in the economic development of the state, since proximity to the tracks determined where new towns evolved, which land values would rise, where factories and warehouses were built, and ultimately where the centers of economic and political power would be. Railroads, however, secured this control by using free rail passes and other perks to influence state legislators to pass favorable laws. Because of the railroads' economic, social, and political power, and because they could set whatever shipping costs they wished, it is little wonder farmers worried about the control railroads had in their lives.

Nevertheless, on the strength of such railway investment, other industries expanded in North Carolina during the 1880s while the rest of the nation likewise experienced a whirlwind of industrial growth. Although there were a few instances of local folk pooling what capital they had to found a factory here and there, most North Carolina entrepreneurs were middling to upper-class folk who had antebellum roots in textiles or tobacco and who made use of prewar capital invested outside the state or who attracted outside investors. Along with burgeoning textile mills in the Piedmont and tobacco-manufacturing centers and warehouses in the east, North Carolinians also cultivated timber and turpentine in the sandy pinewood areas along Cape Fear while furniture factories blossomed in Piedmont towns like Hickory and High Point.

As growth in manufacturing output and nonagricultural wages increased, perhaps the most noticeable result was the explosion of towns, villages, hamlets, and a few major manufacturing and commercial centers like Charlotte, Durham, Winston, Greensboro, and Goldsboro. In fact, the urban population in North Carolina grew from about 55,000 in 1880 to around 187,000 by 1900. Not only did these towns attract thousands of young men and women from the farms by offering new educational and economic opportunities, but they helped to pull the political power of the state away from the more rural east toward the industrializing Piedmont. Moreover, farmers' political clout in local and state affairs was often giving way to town professionals (and especially lawyers) who formed "town hall" or "courthouse" rings that conducted themselves by new codes of professionalization and who took increasing advantage of technological advances such as typewriters, telephones, and mimeograph machines.

This growing divide between urban and rural clout was only intensified by the receding economic viability of farming in the late 1800s. Although in 1865, in terms of currency and banking, farmers faced many of the same difficulties that entrepreneurs did, they nevertheless suffered from their own unique problems and circumstances. From the end of the Civil War through Reconstruction, yeomen and planters who suffered direct wartime destruction of their farm implements and livestock felt the lack of currency, capital, and credit most acutely, while all North Carolina farmers suffered under high Reconstruction property and cotton taxes and diminishing land values. These circumstances hit small farmers especially hard since they usually owned property but had little cash with which to pay their taxes.

In the east, larger planters often moved to town and parceled out their lands to white tenants and black sharecroppers. As a result, by 1880 approximately one-third of North Carolina's farmers tended fields that were not their own, with white tenants outnumbering blacks. Even though it appears these arrangements increased overall farm productivity from 1870 to 1900, among black sharecroppers this system reinforced paternalistic elements of the slave system. White tenants, faced with falling crop prices and mounting debts, were trapped in an unending cycle of economic dependency that was psychologically devastating for those brought up with the yeoman ideals of independent manhood. It is little wonder the mills and factories of nearby towns appealed to so many young rural men and women.[6]

Yet, as bleak as this outlook seemed, farmers in 1880 had many reasons to anticipate working in tandem with manufacturers to bring progress and prosperity to the state. In the first place, farmers matched innovations in manufacturing and transportation with new technological advances of their own. The growth of agricultural "experiment stations," land grant colleges, and "book farming" led to new understandings of weather, soil depletion, and erosion. Manufacturers developed new implements that would cut deeper into and thus help revive depleted topsoil as well as new phosphate fertilizers that expanded cotton culture and plowed the way for bright leaf tobacco.

Moreover, expanded transportation networks opened new markets for many North Carolina farmers to experiment with new cash crops, even though cotton, because it was easy to store, relatively simple to cultivate, and always brought some kind of monetary return, remained the cash crop of choice for most North Carolina farmers. Many farmers, however, tried to diversify in order to fight both overproduction and soil depletion. Though some toyed with other nonperishables like peanuts and pecans, many in the east touted bright leaf tobacco as their salvation while others saw saving grace in "truck farming" watermelons, cantaloupe, strawberries, cabbage, and other perishables, since they could now more rapidly transport these items to fine hotels and restaurants in the Northeast. Too, farmers could not help but notice that railroads ran in two directions; while they took watermelons to Chicago, they also brought goods from Sears and Roebuck to Kinston. The material isolation faced by most antebellum yeomen therefore eased as farmers realized they could order almost anything available to city folk and could also eat exotic oranges, bananas, and canned sardines, as long as the trains kept unloading their bounties. Thus, looking toward the decade of the 1880s, the promise of the New South seemed within the reach of many a white yeoman.

The promise, however, proved illusory.[7] To begin with, cotton prices fell steadily throughout the 1880s and 1890s reaching $0.05 per pound by 1894—a price well below the cost required to cultivate it. Tobacco prices were a little better, but bright leaf cultivation was woefully labor intensive, and so, working alone, few farmers could cultivate enough to make ends meet. Truck farming, too, proved a bust for many farmers who faced wildly fluctuating prices, unfair transportation costs, and dishonest middlemen. New fertilizers were also unreliable because manufacturers often were incompetent or downright dishonest. Finally, new and exciting markets, while offering the promise of high returns, put farmers in a position where distant commodities exchanges determined the value of their labor rather than face-to-face negotiations and the quality of their produce. In the eyes of most farmers, nonproducers such as "warehouse men," merchants, and railroads were making the profit off their labor while they, the producers, were starving. All the more galling was the way Sears and Roebuck dangled from a stick products that people in nearby towns were enjoying—products that most North Carolina farmers would never be able to afford.

Even Thomas Dixon, after he left the ministry and found himself independently wealthy from his white supremacy novels, found out how difficult it was to farm, even with his capital and scientific know-how. After settling into his new home on the Chesapeake, Dixon "determined to get rich on fancy truck farming," and so he put in ten acres of cabbage and fifty acres of cantaloupes. Using hired laborers to do the work and "the most expensive commercial fertilizer," Dixon nevertheless lost over 20 percent of his cabbages to "worms and bugs and lice in succession." Dixon lost more cabbage because it blossomed too early, and he was unable to hire enough hands to pick it. Still, his hopes were high, for according to the papers cabbage was selling at $2.25 a crate. Filled with pride, Dixon "began to pity [his] neighbors who were still struggling with common farming." His glee was short lived, however, after his first shipment brought only seventy-five cents per crate and his second a mere twenty-five cents. Since the cabbages cost him at least $1 a crate to produce, Dixon lamented, "I sent the ploughs into the field and tenderly turned under for fertilizer my crop of cabbage over which I had toiled and yearned and dreamed," adding, "I quietly determined to let someone else raise cabbage."

His cantaloupes fared no better. Although he thought his melons were "the finest . . . New York ever tasted," Dixon sadly announced: "Instead of $3 a crate I had expected, I got an average of 85 cents a crate. They cost me $1.25." Never a man to take things lying down, after a "nervous prostration" Dixon "went to New York" to confront his "commission man" only to find that this nonproducer was selling the crates to hotels for $3.50 each. When Dixon demanded an explanation, the middleman blamed the railroad for rough handling, saying most of the crates were damaged, and so he had had to sell high. Dixon recalled, "I had a pleasant interview with this commission-retailer who was kindly assisting me to bankruptcy." While in New York, however, Dixon took direct orders for his next year's crop, but drought that year made his melons unfit to eat. Dixon then sadly reported, "I retired from the trucking business," adding, "It requires more brain and moral fibre, muscle and soul patience, to successfully run a large farm to-day than to conduct any other enterprise of modern civilization. And town-bred dudes have been known to sneer at 'hayseeds.'"[8]

Although many "town-bred dudes" blamed the "hayseeds'" woes on over-production (which was no doubt true), urban armchair farmers also cited dependency on manufactured food, fertilizer, and clothing, along with poor efficiency or general laziness as contributing factors.[9] Many farmers, however, saw a more immediate cause. Along with dishonest middlemen and speculators, high transportation rates, and a high protective tariff, they believed a lack of currency and credit, which they tied to the lack of banks, and, thus, to the national banking system, was the primary cause of their hard times. For while prices for their crops continued to fall, because neither banks nor cash were available, farmers had to rely on the especially devastating "crop lien" system to procure supplies for the spring. It worked like this. Having little or no cash on hand in the winter and spring, farmers—be they tenants or land owners—secured seed and other supplies on credit from local merchants by using their unharvested crop as collateral. Some farmers also put down other collateral—often a mule or sometimes land—but most furnishing merchants held a lien on the future crop. Interest was high—usually 25 to 50 percent—and farmers additionally paid higher prices to buy "on time." Along with higher prices and interest, fluctuating commodities prices hindered farmers' ability to "settle up." At "settling-up time," a merchant brokered the sale of the crop, and if the crop did not fetch a high enough price to cover a farmer's tab (and by the late 1880s and 1890s, it rarely did), a new lien for the balance was placed on the next crop, creating a deepening cycle of debt for the farmer. If the debt became insurmountable after years of not settling, the merchant foreclosed on the farmer's property, which by that time would have been held as collateral.

It is tempting to overplay an antagonistic relationship between black-hatted merchants and white-hatted farmers. In fact, many merchants were farmers, and both farmers and merchants realized their dependence on each another. Many if not most southern merchants went bankrupt; they themselves were paying outrageous interest to their suppliers and had often extended credit to local farmers with whom they shared bonds of family, friendship, and church, even when they knew they had no hope of repayment. Nevertheless, the system was ruinous to farmers, who fell not only into a cycle of debt but also of dependency, for because a particular merchant held a lien on their crops, those farmers could do business with no one else. Furthermore, since lien holders often dictated that cotton be planted since it always held the safest prospect for a return, the lien system hindered crop diversification. In the cases of black farmers, for whom the merchant was often the landlord or former master, the system only entrenched older race-based relationships of paternalism. In the end, this system of credit, along with the factors mentioned earlier, drove rural sons and daughters to town, increased tenancy, and, when coupled with a growing perception of rural folks as "hayseeds" and "behind the times," fostered a profound sense of psychological loss on the farms.

Country churches, too, experienced the privation of rural life in the 1880s and 1890s. Country parsons remained for the most part bivocational, receiving little or no compensation for their arduous clerical responsibilities. One Methodist minister and Allianceman in Moore County spent countless nights without sleep begging God for economic relief; he even had to sell his horse at one point, meaning that for a while he covered his widespread circuit on foot, often walking twenty miles a day.[10] Lack of currency not only meant country pastors went unpaid and country-church buildings remained in a state of disrepair, but rural churches contributed little to larger denominational initiatives; in failing to contribute, they inadvertently allowed the pastors and lay leaders of more affluent city churches to gain control over denominational initiatives, a process that mirrored the shift of political and economic control from rural to urban folk. Tellingly, one Baptist remarked at the annual meeting of his association in 1873 that his "people needed someone to show them how to obtain some money."[11]

In the midst of these "hard times," many evangelicals in both town and country cast such financial problems in spiritual terms and were primarily concerned about how poverty was affecting their spiritual health.[12] Other farmers and townsfolk drew on strains of agrarian individualism and self-sufficiency to argue that, in order to outlast the hard times, farmers needed to grow their own food, be self-sufficient, and not waste time on politics, church suppers, and lodge meetings. The remedy, in other words, was to pull up their bootstraps and get to work. One farmer and frequent contributor to the *North Carolina Baptist* urged farmers to stop blaming the government, the tariff, and taxes for their problems and to blame themselves for mounting such large debts in their drive to match the wealth of city folk. Another similarly insisted that "hard work" was the cure for their ills, though he noted that such a concept was "very unpopular," since it "allows less time for talking politics, rabbit hunting and attending protracted [revival] meetings." That farmers were "fond of idling" was, for him, the heart of the problem. While it might be tempting to think that these writers simply did not understand the credit problems facing farmers, we can see in them an absolute conviction that farmers ought to be self-sufficient and independent—especially independent of creditors.[13]

That farmers chastised themselves for their dependency, debt, and laziness, however, reflected the despair into which many of them were sinking. Searching their moral actions, contemplating their sins, and striving to work hard in order to find salvation from these hard times was something akin to the dark night of the soul faced by sinners at the altar seeking salvation from hell.

In the mouths of townsfolk or denominational officials, however, such "boot strap" language became condescension, fueling the "hayseed" stereotype of rural folk and increasing concern over the "Country Church Problem." Primitive Baptist Elder P. D. Gold, editor of the state paper and an oddly urban and urbane Primitive Baptist minister living in the tobacco boomtown of Wilson, for example, gained quite a reputation in Nash, Wilson, and Edgecombe counties for his condemnation of farmers who blamed others for their "hard times." Writing to the local Democratic paper in February 1892, this city pastor must have irked farmers immeasurably when he wrote:

> What good does it do to cry hard times? We notice that people stop labor about two weeks at Christmas. That will not help to relieve hard times. Many farmers buy their flour, meat, corn &c., besides buying everything families wear. That does not help to relieve the hard times. They also buy their horses and mules. This does not help to relieve hard times. Grumbling and murmuring aggravate hard times. What is there of this trouble that we have not brought on ourselves? There is plenty of corn and wheat made by those that plant and sow enough, and pay proper attention to it. Neither famine, pestilence, nor war has afflicted our land. One trouble is that when times are tight as at present many people will aggravate the trouble by not paying their debts as far as they can.

After angering farmers, Gold mildly urged creditors not to "force a debtor's property to sale when it will sell for so little on a tight market." After further angering farmers and debtors, Gold concluded by mixing common-sense thinking with equalitarian strains: "The rich and the poor ought not to be arrayed against each other, for the rich need the poor to labor for them, and the poor need the rich to give them remunerative employment, and God is the maker of them all."[14]

Failing to give Gold an active ear, many rural evangelicals would neither take these insults nor the social and economic realities behind them lying down, for by 1892, the year Elder Gold made his pronouncements, the Alliance had already exploded across the state, driven by evangelical lay leaders and ministers who developed a unique Christian political critique of the problems facing farmers—a critique empowered with righteous anger toward the attitudes expressed by the likes of Elder Gold.

* * *

In its early days, however, the Alliance probably did not seem so radical, for it followed a long line of farmers' unions in North Carolina that stretched back to the 1830s. Moreover, even though the Knights of Labor never made a real impact outside Wake and Durham County factory workers and black day laborers, the ideas of reformers such as Edward Bellamy, Richard Ely, Hamlin Garland, and Henry George were making their way into North Carolina's state university, religious colleges, and civic lectures, affecting such future reformers as Thomas Dixon, Jr., and Populist leader Marion Butler. Too, reforming Democrats like Josephus Daniels, Walter Clark, and Redeemer governor Zebulon Vance, who believed in industrial progress but also in an even economic playing field for farmers and laborers, constantly nettled more conservative Democrats or Republicans who focused solely on making the state attractive to outside investment.

The most important precursors to the Alliance, however, were the Grange and L. L. Polk's *Progressive Farmer* and North Carolina Farmers' Association. Active in the 1870s and 1880s, the Grange introduced many farmers to the potential, on the one hand, of "book farming" and cooperative economic ventures and, on the other, of their need to have a voice in the state legislature. During the 1870s, the Grange attacked speculation on commodities, established several cooperative enterprises and educational exchanges, and, most important, established the North Carolina Department of Agriculture in 1877. Many small farmers, however, were put off by the pretentiousness of the Grange's elite leadership and elaborate rituals. Too, its genteel and academic goals seemed more concerned with the status of farming as a profession than with bringing immediate relief to small farmers' most pressing problems: lack of credit and money as well as control over prices. As one Allianceman put it: "The Grange was a grand organization and ultimately resulted in no material achievement for the sons of toil."[15]

The Grange nevertheless laid the groundwork for L. L. Polk's more successful North Carolina Farmers' Association, initiated in 1886 with the introduction of his *Progressive Farmer.* Polk's Farmers' Association differed from the Grange in a number of ways. Farmers' clubs, for example, organized on their own initiative and then connected themselves with the Association, which gave the movement deeper grassroots. The Association (and the Alliance after it) also offered a lower cost for membership and a less elaborate ritual.[16]

The Association and the *Farmer,* did, however, draw on the Grange's three main emphases of economic cooperation, political action, and education in "progressive" farming techniques. Although it never had the opportunity to establish any cooperative economic ventures (the Alliance would take these up in 1887 and 1888), through a series of traveling "Farmers' Institutes" and the guidance of the *Farmer,* the Association tapped into farmers' desire for self-reliance by urging them to use their farm-made guano, make their own clothes, plant their own food, diversify their cash crops, and practice new techniques of crop rotation and erosion prevention. Most farm education, though, took place within local clubs and later suballiances where farmers compared notes and gave lectures on farming techniques. One of the hottest topics early on was the debate involving the use of manufactured fertilizer as opposed to that of homegrown manure. The debate reached such a level of sophistication at the Trinity College Farmers' Club that it made the pages of *The Progressive Farmer,* as phosphate advocates rallied behind the "progress" evident in the new technologies of manufactured fertilizer while Professor W. W. Andrews drew on commonsense thinking to tout the advantages of natural guano: "In the great economy of nature . . . after an amount is digested and the food properties assimilated, enough is left, if saved, to produce the same amount again." Hence, he argued, "It is contrary to divine nature to let things go to waste. . . . I am willing to dabble with commercial fertilizers as a luxury, but for substantial and permanent good the place of the manure bank can't be supplied by any patent compound."[17]

The Progressive Farmer furthermore urged farmers to be a part of the progressive New South—to join hands with townsfolk and industrialists to usher North Carolina into a golden age of prosperity that would decrease the state's dependence on outside manufacturing. In 1887, Polk, moved by the "restless, searching, progressive spirit of the age," desired that the Piedmont's "hill-tops should be wreathed in the smoke of furnaces, mills and foundries—its plains be made vocal with the inspiriting music of looms and spindles" and that "the exhilarating din of factories, workshops, and machine shops should dispel the silence of the wilderness, and the grand chorus of a thousand steam whistles should energize, quicken and fire its now slumbering strength." Polk noted how developing such a manufacturing base in the Piedmont would "stimulate . . . diversified farming" and increase land values.[18]

Lurking underneath this euphoria over New South progress, however, were numerous articles in the early days of the *Farmer* that criticized just about every aspect of city life. Drawing on the antielitist and antiurban barbs of rural evangelicalism, farmers and leaders in the Association contrasted the effeminizing influences of towns to the manhood- and womanhood-building agrarian life, often coupling their criticisms with attacks on fashion, professionals, and city churches.[19]

Driving such antagonism was the realization that "town fever" was striking the young people on the farms, and in response to this infection, the Farmers' Association and later the Alliance sought to restore pride in the agrarian life by bolstering its natural advantages, particularly as it pertained to the development of independent manhood and womanhood. As the Grange had done, the Association hoped that educating farmers in progressive techniques would allow them to match city dudes and manufacturers in their professional and technological achievements.[20] Moreover, as already mentioned, by the late 1880s, this animosity toward cities fueled farmers' resentment of "town hall rings," "professional politicians," and "office suckers" with "shallow brains" who fawned deceitfully over farmers and then stabbed them in the back.[21]

Along with advocating specific legislative measures that would benefit agrarian folk over against town hall and state-level "office suckers," Polk's Farmers Association and *Farmer* also joined with other soft money advocates who insisted that the problems of currency, tariff, and the money supply constituted the main source of the farmers' woes. To correct the problem, some farmers wanted "co-operation."[22] While the Alliance would promote cooperative marketing and merchandising enterprises, most farmers in the Association saw "co-operation" on the political front as the most important way to ease their burdens, since they needed to change the legislation that enabled railroads, the national bank, and the other forces of plutocracy to wreck the economic system. D. M. McKay of Harnett County, for example, wondered if he and his fellow farmers were "an *abject* class of numbskulls," since they had "delegated their right of representation to the men of other professions," who, "having a keen eye to their professional and individual advantages, benefited themselves and misrepresented the farmers." McKay concluded: "Our only hope is in that Archimedean lever, that powerful *force* which moves the world itself, *co-operation.*"[23] McKay was careful not to cast cooperation as an affront to farmers' ideals of individualism; rather, he portrayed it as a means to counterbalance the cooperative economic and political strength of plutocratic combinations.

From the start, then, many farmers in the Association looked not only to economic remedies such as diversification or self-sufficiency but also examined deep-seated political and economic shifts at the heart of the matter—shifts in the state and national political economy that for the Alliance and other soft money advocates was summarized in the language of 1776 as plutocratic "tyranny." A farmer named "Orange" articulated this sentiment well when he explored the causes of the hard times facing farmers in early 1888: "Everybody knows that something is wrong . . . [but] it is better to remove the causes of pauperism than feed the poor." At the heart of this problem was that "commerce, with its steamships, its railroads, its monopolies, its syndicates, its trusts, its banking corporations sustained by the government of the United States, has towered above every other interest and has laid them all prostrate at its feet." After identifying "political bossism" as the "greatest trust or combine . . . in this country," "Orange" then indicated the eventual form the farmers' protests would take: "The evils . . . must be remedied, and *the ballot box* is the *only power* in this country that can remedy them."[24]

4. Religion and the Rise of the Farmers' Alliance

For all of the excitement and success it generated, the Farmers' Association was not to be the predominant cooperative organization among North Carolina farmers. Nevertheless, the Association laid the groundwork for the ways in which the Alliance would address the problems facing farmers. Like the Association, in order to address the problems of credit, low commodities prices, and high overhead costs, the North Carolina Alliance stressed "progressive" farming techniques, urged farmers to be self-reliant, and embraced a number of soft money financial reforms. The Alliance furthermore adhered to the Association's goals of economic and political cooperation. Also, like the Association, the Alliance blended almost seamlessly into the rural landscape; for all its heated rhetoric against plutocrats and monopolies, it espoused economic, political, and religious values close to the heart of most rural and many urban North Carolinians. As the 1880s, however, came to a close, the antimonopolist and politically activist strains of its political agenda intensified at the expense of economic cooperative ventures and widespread conservative support. This increased assault on economic and political "tyranny," as it combined with "Orange's" insistence that the ballot was the voice of God, eventually erupted into third-party activism.

Part of the reason the Alliance was so centrist, of course, was that it luxuriated in rural evangelical soil. Without the Alliance, however, evangelicalism alone would not have produced Populism, since Populism was more than just an outlook or mind-set, evangelical or otherwise; rather, it was a movement with an agenda and an institutional structure that came together in the Alliance. For even though many evangelicals had a general idea that they needed to be politically active or curb economic and political tendencies that threatened American democracy, they had no clear social or political agenda outside prohibition. In the Alliance, rural evangelicals, however, took their ideas about freedom, justice, institutions, poverty, and America's place in the cosmos and focused them on solving the unique economic and political problems facing farmers. The result was the sacred call of Populism.

As we proceed in this chapter, then, we look at the Alliance's institutional structure, outlook, and agenda, keeping in mind the way evangelicalism shaped all three features. The first third or so of the chapter examines the way evangelical ministers, churches, and ministerial networks galvanized the Alliance organization. The rest of the chapter shows how evangelical ideas influenced the Alliance, especially through its commonsense patterns of thought, social Christianity, antielitism, patriotic millennialism, and evangelical notions of freedom or independence. Throughout, we will see that Alliance commitment to commonsense thinking and independence of conscience created a reform agenda that stressed first and foremost that men and women embody the divine principles by which God governed the religious and political economy.

* * *

In the summer of 1887, the largely unknown Farmers' Alliance of Texas swept into the state and quickly, though amicably, subsumed Polk's Farmers' Association. Local organization followed many routes. Sometimes with and sometimes without the help of a national or state organizer, a local person of some esteem, often a political leader, planter, or minister, would call together an assembly or picnic in a town hall, church, or school and explain the purposes of the Alliance. Once a fair number of suballiances had formed (locals that were the backbone of the order), Alliance members organized a county alliance that usually met once a month.

It is not surprising that Presbyterian Rev. M. T. Sealy helped establish North Carolina's first suballiance in Robeson County, for his activity epitomized the close relationship among suballiances, local ministers, and rural congregations that propelled the Alliance across the state. As a rural Presbyterian parson, Sealy also typified the unique social location the Alliance held in North Carolina. On the one hand, Sealy represented the culturally predominant religious group in his Highland-Scot, Cape Fear county, and yet, as a country pastor, Sealy also suffered with and spoke for beleaguered rural folk and was thus sympathetic to Alliance ideas about economic cooperation and political agitation.[1]

In nearby Duplin County, Presbyterian Rev. Colin Shaw similarly organized his county Alliance and, like Sealy, exhibited the mix of erudition and rural poverty common to so many Alliance organizers. Born in 1812 to a first family of the Cape Fear area, this son of wealthy planters attended the University of North Carolina and then tended a good-sized plantation while serving as pastor to a number of rural Presbyterian churches. Shaw entered the Confederate Army as a chaplain, earned the rank of captain, and in 1865 formed a guerrilla cavalry band that wreaked havoc on Sherman's army; as a result, General Hugh J. Kilpatrick razed Shaw's plantation. After the war, Rev. Shaw lived for a long period in poverty while serving a number of churches without compensation. By the time the Alliance came calling, he had, however, substantially rebuilt his estate and was a civic leader in Duplin. When he died at age ninety-two, this Alliance organizer had gained renown as an expert in Presbyterian theology and discipline, a gifted revival preacher, and, as one biographer put it, a "southern patriot."[2]

Baptists, Methodists, at least one Episcopal priest, and restorationists like those who posted the "Look to Jesus" fliers in Nash and Edgecombe counties soon followed Presbyterians like Sealy and Shaw in organizing alliances. Many, like Shaw and W. A. Graham, president of his Baptist association and son of the antebellum governor by the same name, were leading lights in their respective counties. For his part, Graham was the principal organizer for the Alliance in Catawba, Burke, and his home county of Lincoln, where he was joined by German Reformed and Methodist ministers and lay leaders, including a cadre of ministers associated with Dr. R. L. Abernathy's Rutherford College (Methodist, South). Back in the Cape Fear region, more than a dozen Baptist ministers helped Rev. Shaw organize the Alliance in Sampson, Harnett, Cumberland, Duplin, Johnston, and Wayne; among them were Revs. J. A. Oates, Jr., W. B. Oliver, and E. J. Edwards, editors of *The North Carolina Baptist*. Methodists and Quakers, too, joined Shaw and the Baptists, as did Free Will Baptist Rev. William Byrd, who was remembered as the first holiness preacher in a region that would be the epicenter of the holiness and Pentecostal movements in the Southeast.

Meanwhile, Pitt County's Episcopal priest Francis Joyner organized Alliances in Pitt, Martin, and Beaufort counties, and in Chatham and Franklin counties, Baptists, Methodist Protestants, Quakers, and O'Kellyites formed Alliances in their churches; one suballiance even honored its denomination's namesake by calling itself the "O'Kelly Alliance."

Only the Primitive Baptists rejected the Alliance outright as a secret society. Not all, however, were so convinced; one Primitive Baptist elder, A. J. Moore of Whitakers, was an Alliance lecturer, and his Williams Church was an Alliance meeting place.[3]

Not only did ministers and lay leaders participate in developing local alliances, but church connections ran through the order's leadership. Although Syd Alexander and Elias Carr, two of the old Grangers who made their way to the top of the Alliance, did not have any institutional religious leadership roles, the Alliance's driving force, L. L. Polk, was perhaps the most prominent Baptist lay leader in the state. Aside from Polk, other prominent Baptists involved themselves in the publication of *The Progressive Farmer*. Polk's son-in-law, J. W. Denmark, who was active in the administration of Wake Forest College, served as business editor for *The Progressive Farmer*, while Baptist Rev. Baylus Cade served for a time as assistant editor. Down at Marion Butler's *Caucasian*, Baptist Hal Ayer, formerly an associate editor of the *Biblical Recorder*, was managing editor. Furthermore, professors at most of the state religious colleges—Wake Forest, Trinity, Davidson, Guilford, and rural Buies Creek Academy (later Campbell College)—formed prominent suballiances and regularly contributed to *The Progressive Farmer* as well as to traveling Farmers' Institutes. The Colored Alliance was headed by J. J. Rogers, a white lay leader in the Raleigh Baptist Association, and African American (and freedman) Rev. Walter A. Patillo of Granville County, editor of *The Baptist Pilot*. Along with Thomas Dixon, other high-profile evangelists also supported the Alliance; one was William P. Fife, who, recall, bragged that "he did not know how to prepare a sermon and thanked God that he didn't."[4]

While ministers were often county organizers, this was certainly not always the case. In Edgecombe County, for example, Planter, Granger, and community leader Elias Carr organized Sparta Alliance, which initially met at the Masonic lodge in Tarboro until it moved to Carr's plantation, perhaps because it voted to include women. Rural professionals—often country doctors—also organized alliances; Dr. H. F. Freeman and Dr. Cyrus Thompson (an important Methodist lay leader) organized Wilson and Onslow counties respectively. Sometimes, though, organizers were not folk of such wealth. Quaker Hugh Johnson, a yeoman and carpenter of moderate means as well as a temperance advocate and dabbler in holiness doctrines, organized Centre Alliance in Chatham County at Centre Methodist Protestant Church; many of its participants were also Quakers or members of Centre church.[5]

Unlike Sparta Alliance, Centre Alliance included women from the start. Alliance sisters, where they were allowed to join (a decision left to the discretion of each suballiance), were usually daughters, sisters, or wives of Alliancemen. Although some Alliancemen opposed women's involvement, many noted the practical benefits of having "the ladies" attend. One Allianceman noted that "young ladies joining the Alliance will cause the young men and boys to join. . . . It will cause the young men to attend more regular, and the older ones too." As was the case in their churches, women were also far better than the brethren at raising money. Adolescents, too, sometimes attended, and some formed "juvenile alliances." The decision by Jamestown Alliance in Davie County to include both women and young folks apparently led to ulterior motives among some of its members, since it resolved that "any young man or lady caught sparkin in time of bus[iness] be fined to sweep and have water for the next meeting."[6]

This "sparkin" alludes to another facet of Alliance life: the opportunity for fun and fellowship. During weekly local and monthly county meetings, and at encampments, picnics, and public meetings, the Alliance helped relieve rural isolation. Although he proclaimed that "the mission of the Alliance is to put an end to monopolistic oppression and monetary and landed aristocracy which has been and still is in the ascendancy," this partic-ular Allianceman, not thinking the Alliance should solely concern itself with such weighty matters, did not fail to mention that if "a bachelor" was to visit his suballiance, "he could see some pretty girls, and after a short while eat some . . . good huckleberry pies and dumplings."[7]

Any white male who farmed at least part-time and believed in a "supreme being" could join a white suballiance; most were full-time farmers, though many ministers, merchants, and doctors joined so long as they farmed and had a rural residence; lawyers were excluded, as were blacks, though some-times blacks joined whites in larger public Alliance rallies.[8] Suballiances were made up mostly of small landowners, though some included tenants. Sparta Alliance in Edgecombe County drew its constituency from many sources; others, like Centre, drew from preexisting connections of church or kin (common surnames abounded in suballiances). For example, in Pitt County, local planter and county Democratic leader F. M. Kilpatrick formed Experi-ment Alliance using his church, Salem Christian (Disciples of Christ), as a base of operations. Penelope Baptist Church and School on the Burke-Catawba county line likewise emerged as an epicenter for the Alliance there, producing Alliance leaders such as J. F. Click, a leader in the South Fork Bap-tist Association who organized Burke's County Alliance, served as its first president, and edited the most important Populist paper in the western part of the state, the *Hickory Mercury*.

In like manner, the men and women of "Brother Jimmy's" Hebron Chris-tian Church formed Fairfield Alliance, so named because both it and

Hebron Christian met at Fairfield school house. After organizing Fairfield, "Brother Jimmy" rose quickly through the ranks of the Alliance, serving as the first president of his county alliance (a fellow disciple from nearby Wheat Swamp Church, J. W. Daly, was the first county secretary), then as district lecturer where he displayed the oratorical skills that had served his congregation so well. Eventually "Brother Jimmy" served two terms as president of the state Alliance.[9]

Just as church buildings and Alliances often overlapped, so did Alliance picnics and church revival meetings. At one such event, the Gates County Alliance "came together in a farmer's meeting at Warmack church to celebrate the old glorious Fourth, by having a pleasant time and showing their appreciation of the independence of our great nation." As the afternoon festivities progressed, religious and patriotic themes mingled together: "Rev. M.L. Green led off in a stirring prayer to Almighty God for our deliverance, after which A.J. Ward read the declaration of independence which was listened to with strict attention, after which Miss Emily L. Berryman read an essay on the farmers binding themselves together for their own protection. . . . Then Rev. M.L. Green . . . made a noble speech, taking in the work of Providence and this great nation's progress as tillers of the soil."[10]

* * *

Since churches often formed the basis of a Farmers' Club or suballiance, the degree to which suballiances resembled local congregations is not surprising. Local and county meetings opened with prayer by the chaplain and then the members sang Alliance songs (usually patriotic and Christian hymns), took an offering (dues), and had a period of instruction or "exhortation." Education in suballiances, like the exhortations at "Brother Jimmy's" Hebron church, was intended to be participatory. As with rural congregations, Alliance members also cared for sick or bereaved members, and they helped meet the needs of less fortunate members.

Alliances also practiced severe discipline. Getting the blackball could result from any number of offenses that might tarnish the Alliances' image or mitigate its goals, but, as in churches, public inebriation seems to have been the most common offense. At Centre Alliance, the resident Methodist Protestants and Quakers expelled one member for public drunkenness and at the same meeting resolved to discipline any member who missed three meetings in a row. The miscreant protested his ouster unsuccessfully for several months, claiming his trial was "unconstitutional." Centre Alliance also disciplined a member for violating the suballiance's resolution to buy guano only from an Alliance manufacturer. He repented, however, and was forgiven after he petitioned his fellow Alliancefolk to help him "to conduct himself in a more becoming manner."[11]

Another way the white Alliance imitated southern churches was in its relationship to the Colored Alliance. Just as with white and black evangelical institutions, the white and Colored Alliance maintained a tenuous relationship based on older patterns of paternalism and white supremacy mixed with a genuine belief that whites, blacks, and the South stood to benefit from racial harmony and black "elevation" through education and economic enterprise. While blacks—and most notably Rev. Walter Patillo—took key leadership roles in the Colored Alliance, they also deferred, as in their denominations, to white leadership in a number of matters. Reporting on the annual meeting of the Colored Alliance under Patillo in 1890, *The Progressive Farmer* noted: "The Negroes began the movement, but it has always had the aid of white leaders." The *Farmer* further affirmed that it was "glad to know that their white leaders are honest men; that as leaders they encourage their members to elevate themselves morally, mentally, and financially, and that there is no danger of the present leaders advising them to do anything wrong."[12] Like its white counterpart, the Colored Alliance hoped to educate farmers in the newest farming techniques, develop independent manhood and womanhood, and participate in cooperative action.

Informing white Alliancefolks' understanding of and attitude toward the Colored Alliance was the basic way southerners understood the proper relations among the races. Under the umbrella of "white supremacy" and the shifting post-Reconstruction rules of segregation, most whites displayed a mix of emotions toward blacks ranging from disgust to pity to genuine care, all of which reflected the close proximity in which black and white farmers lived. This ambivalence also found its way onto the pages of Alliance papers. Marion Butler's paper was, of course, entitled *The Caucasian* and subtitled "Pure Democracy and White Supremacy," by which he meant whites must rule blacks in the political sphere.[13] *The Progressive Farmer* regularly ran full pages of "darkey" jokes that were derogatory and demeaning even while it denounced lynching, though it never failed to print the most macabre details.[14] While readers often praised the efforts of Booker T. Washington and heartily supported "Negro normal schools" and other black educational facilities, they also complained about being unjustly taxed as whites to support schools for landless blacks, and many suggested the use of a poll tax to equalize taxation. Also, in typical form, the Fayetteville correspondent for *The Caucasian* desired black outmigration so that more "desirable" whites from the North would migrate to North Carolina. He denied, however, any animosity toward blacks, writing: "For the darkey . . . we have the kindliest feelings, as all southerners have. The writer loved his old 'mammy' as she was called, and can have no hard feelings for her race."[15]

L. L. Polk usually expressed a similar mix of feelings but, too, demonstrated how close the white Alliance often came to blurring the "color line." At one Raleigh speech before an audience of African Americans, Polk strikingly downplayed the category of race by saying that he was "color blind" as well as "creed blind" and "party blind" as he urged blacks to unite with whites around their common position as laborers and farmers. After denouncing racial enmity as "Satanic," he announced: "That man who comes between you and me, with the ties that bind us together, and would alienate us, is not only an enemy to your race and to my race, but an enemy to this country and the highest and best interest of us all."[16]

Alliancefolk, however, rarely crossed this "color line," as indicated by the most important cooperative action taken by the Colored Alliance: a strike by Alliance cotton-pickers in the fall of 1891. Although the Colored Alliance had established a cooperative exchange in Norfolk, by 1891 it had not posed a serious threat to white political or economic supremacy, Alliance or otherwise. That summer, however, the superintendent of the National Colored Alliance, Rev. Richard M. Humphrey, called for a general strike of black cotton-pickers to demand higher wages. In the fall, white Alliance papers resoundingly denounced Humphrey and insisted that North Carolina blacks would not strike, since they would realize that, because of low prices, white land owners could not afford to double their pay, as the Colored Alliance demanded.

Strike they did, however, against the white Alliancemen for whom they worked. As the white Alliance predicted, the strike fizzled out as white Alliancemen refused to support their black Alliance brethren. Their refusal underscored the distinction between white and black Alliancefolk in terms of both race and economic status. While the majority of white Alliancefolk were land owners of the middling sort, most blacks, except in a few counties such as Warren, were tenants or day laborers. Expressing a typical mix of outrage and sympathy toward the strikers, Methodist lay leader J. B. Lloyd, who in less than a year would help build a biracial Populist coalition in his county of Edgecombe, reminded the readers of his *Farmers' Advocate* that "the success of the white farmer means better wages for the colored farmer" and that, "at present," since farmers could not control the prices of their products, "until the whole system is changed the farmers cannot afford to pay any higher wages."[17] One year later, blacks would again challenge white supremacy; this time, however, Populists would cross the lines of race and challenge white supremacy to ensure that "the whole system" be changed.

* * *

With ministers and evangelical lay leaders at the heart of Alliance mobilization, certain evangelical patterns of thought provided the primary lens through which Alliancefolk understood the hard times they were experiencing. While Alliance farmers advocated the soft money schemes typical of the era, like many other nineteenth-century reformers, they elevated these earthly plans to apocalyptic, ultimate proportions. They were not trying to get more money or ease crop lien alone; they were attempting to put the nation's economic, social, political, and religious structures in harmony with the mind and plans of God.

Although I use the terms "evangelical" and "Alliance outlook," it would be a mistake to think these patterns of thought were monolithic or were adhered to by all Alliancefolk everywhere and at all times. The ways in which Alliancefolk (and later the Populists) constructed their outlook varied from place to place and over time in emphasis and formulation. Some elements of this thought, however, remained fairly constant. These included their basic ideas about human autonomy and liberty, the dangers of concentrated power, the importance of axiomatic, God-given principles, and God's special designs for America. Other mental constructions changed or varied. Exactly how North Carolina Alliancefolk drew the boundaries of gender and race, for example, varied by region. Also, the sense that America was experiencing economic, political, and religious centralization grew in emphasis as the Alliance faced increased resistance to its ideas in the late 1880s and early 1890s. That said, Alliancefolk nevertheless shared, for the most part, a common way of perceiving the world around them—one that combined the agenda of financial reformers and the eternal axioms of God's moral governance and patriotic millennialism. As these strands of thought came together in suballiances and political sermons across the state, the result was a clear-cut economic and political agenda backed by revivalistic zeal.[18]

How exactly, then, did evangelical ideas support the Alliance outlook? First, commonsense ways of thinking shaped the way Alliance farmers understood political economics, religion, and, most basically, the way things ought to be. More to the point, Alliancefolk had the sense that there were basic metaphysical rules or "principles" governing human relations, economics, and nature that determined right and wrong methods of human behavior and government, and that anyone, through "science," the Bible, reason, and observation, could understand and fully embody them. Moreover, they usually incorporated the concept of God's moral governance into this commonsense perspective.

As with other evangelicals, this commonsense way of thinking often reinforced conservative views in the Alliance about the proper relations among men, women (separate spheres), and children, and among whites and blacks (black subordination). As we have already, however, seen, women carved out a unique space for themselves within the Alliance, as did black farmers in the Colored Alliance. Indeed, though, part of the reason that the Alliance faced so little opposition even into the early 1890s was that it conformed so neatly to established southern norms on these points.

Too, in their thoughts about economics, even though Alliancefolk aimed to suppress monopolies and remove the "money power's" control over the nation's currency and systems of transportation, they attested to their commonsense outlook by embracing laissez-faire or classically liberal economic ideas, though with an emphasis on equity, harmony, or "fairness" based on conformity to God's laws of economic justice. Alliancefolk believed that obeying such staid laws as supply and demand, the right to private property, and ethical competition would maintain a state of harmony within the nation's political economy in which producers of wealth received just payment for their labor. Furthermore, Alliancefolk did not consider the accumulation of wealth per se a sin; in fact, Alliancefolk believed wealth accumulated by altruistic, humble folks reflected God's principles at work and would also elevate society. This basic appreciation for wealth undergirded the Alliance insistence that its reform aims were "conservative," that its ranks were filled with people from the vast "middle classes," and that its farmers were known for their inherent conservatism.[19]

Remaining consistent with this basic economic outlook, from the early days of the *Farmer* to the inauguration of the national People's Party in 1892, the Alliance stood for economy of government and opposed anything that smacked of governmental "paternalism." Unless it was intended to fund rural public education or certain public charities, the Alliance eschewed attempts to increase state appropriations or to raise taxes. Furthermore, although Alliancefolk divided over their support of fiat money (the Greenback movement had gained only a toehold in North Carolina), they were drawn to silver as the preferred means of inflating the money supply, since, to many, fiat money seemed too paternalistic. North Carolina Alliancefolk, like most all southerners, considered any movement or group that threatened private property or liberal capitalism "communist" or "anarchist."[20]

On similar grounds, the North Carolina Alliance disavowed labor radicalism and especially strikes. Although the Alliance supported the Knights of

Labor and other labor organizations as representing the economic and political interests of all producers, including farmers, they saw strikes as counterproductive, opposed to the laws of God, and immoral since they violated
the command to love one another. Most important, however, Alliancefolks'
aversion to strikes grew from their absolute confidence in the American
democratic system. Agreeing with Thomas Dixon that every American male
"represents the royal blood of universal manhood," Alliancefolk believed that
the vote, as it represented the voice of the people, represented the voice of
God, and they subsequently rested their hope of reversing the growing
disequilibrium in the economic system not in strikes but in the ballot.[21]

Despite this basic economic conservatism, Alliancefolk were certainly
aware that by the mid-1880s the political economy of the United States was
indeed in a state of disequilibrium; the laws of supply and demand and fair
competition that should have governed commodities prices, interest rates,
currency volume, and transportation rates were out of whack. As we saw with
other soft money folks, Alliancefolk believed that the root problem for these
hard times was the centralization of capital under the various trusts, monopolies, and speculators, that, along with the national banking system, had
assumed control of the nation's money supply and commodities prices. And
like Polk's Association before it, the Alliance responded to this state of disequilibrium by engaging in cooperative economic and political action.

We explore cooperative political action in the next section, but regarding
specific cooperative measures, especially in the early days, the Alliance
attempted to gain control over commodities prices and operational costs
with cooperative marketing and merchandising ventures and boycotts.
Some cooperatives were wholly local; often suballiances capitalized local
county stores and resolved not to buy from merchants attempting to under-
bid them. County Alliances also capitalized larger warehousing, manufacturing, and merchandising ventures, including a shoe factory in Raleigh and
tobacco warehouses in Granville and other counties.[22]

While cooperative marketing and warehousing ventures attempted to let
farmers gain some control over commodities prices, along with (and, un-
fortunately, often in competition with) these local endeavors, the Alliance
created a State Business Agency to provide Alliance members with manufactured items ranging from farm implements to cigars to sewing machines
through local business agents on a cash-only basis. This way, the Alliance
helped farmers circumvent local merchants and hence the crop lien system.

One of the most successful Agency projects was to contract a Durham
guano factory to produce "Alliance guano" sold solely through Alliances;
Alliances even pledged to boycott all other guano producers. Another such

powerful show of cooperative solidarity came in the summer of 1889, when North Carolina's suballiances in the cotton-producing regions participated in a national boycott of the jute binding used to bale cotton; suballiances pledged to buy cotton binding procured by the State Agency and succeeded, with the national body, in getting the jute trust to lower its prices.[23]

One conundrum in considering this cooperative activity, however, is that, at first glance, such activity seems to contradict Alliance ideals of individualism, laissez-faire economics, and limited government. This is especially the case after the Alliance began to fight for federal regulation of transportation and communication and for direct government capitalization of farmers' cooperatives. For the Alliance, though, these two strands of thought were not contradictory. Because cooperation among plutocratic monopolists had put the financial system out of whack, cooperation on the part of the producers, they believed, was necessary to bring the system back to equilibrium, be it economically through boycotts, bulking, and cooperative purchasing, or politically by insisting on legislation that benefited only one classification of people. Thus, Alliancefolk saw cooperation ultimately as a means to rural independence and as an opportunity to engage in Jesus' "law of love."

Against the charge that, politically, they advocated "paternalistic" or "class" legislation, Alliancefolk, like other soft money reformers, insisted that the federal government, as representative of the voice of the people and thus the voice of God, had to wrest control of the nation's transportation and currency away from private interests (banks, speculators, Wall Street) and put it back in the hands of the people (state and national legislatures). By such power again being in the hands of the people (hopefully an enlightened citizenry) and not in those of the "interests," economic laws reflecting the voice of God would again govern the nation's political economy. To the Alliance, therefore, such cooperative measures were, in fact, radically decentralizing and democratic.[24]

Even after the success of the guano and jute boycotts, however, by around 1890, interest in cooperative economic ventures began to wane as more politically charged antimonopolist rhetoric and calls for direct political action came to the fore. While some Alliance leaders remained committed to economic cooperation, many suballiances felt little excitement about them. Compounding this sense of apathy about economic cooperatives was the failure of major cooperatives in other states—most important, that of the largest Alliance cooperative, the Dallas Cotton Exchange. Furthermore, in spite of its short-term success, the jute boycott ended up being a bust for the Business Agency, which had purchased large amounts of cotton binding only to have the jute trust lower prices to such a degree that farmers could not afford to buy its expensive cotton binding. Perhaps most important, even if farmers could buy goods at a cheaper price from local co-ops or the State Agency, and even if they could bulk and hold their produce for better prices, these efforts still did not address the perennial problems of lack of currency and credit. In the end, for farmers deeply in arrears to the local furnishing merchant, these cooperative measures offered little assistance.[25] The remedy, it seemed, required political action intent on ending the national bank, expanding the money supply, and regulating transportation and communications.

* * *

Along with understanding the way it undergirded the Alliance's conservative attitudes toward race, gender, and political economics, commonsense thinking and the idea of God's moral governance shaped the main thrust of the Alliance reform agenda: that individuals and institutions embody God's principles. In order to reform America's economic system, the Alliance sought to bring it back into line with God's eternal laws as expressed in the Bible, the Declaration of Independence, and the basic tenets of economic liberalism.[26] For Alliancefolk, the root causes of their suffering went beyond mechanical market strategies or unfair congressional lobbying; monopolists and corrupt politicians had profaned the system to begin with because these centralizers had failed to embody the moral axioms of God, and, as a result, their corporations and political organizations lacked the internal guidance of God's principles and governance. Simply to enact reforms that would regulate industry would therefore not provide a thorough fix; a permanent change in the economic system required a change in the hearts of individuals and then through those individuals a change to political and economic organizations.

Thus, through a process of moral suasion, discipline, and education, the Alliance hoped to create an army of enlightened individuals and then to provide pathways for those individuals, acting cooperatively, to effect change in the political economy. As one Allianceman put it, "Society in our land and time is in a diseased condition" since its appointed guardians had violated God's "immutable and wholesome moral and natural laws." The only way to restore "healthful and peaceful and prosperous conditions" was through the "one true and effective remedy . . . the Word of God in life and practice." In making this claim, he was not offering some incantational formula but, rather, the application of the moral axioms of God's government encoded in the Bible: "If we would but accept this, how readily would everything find a sound adjustment in our social fabric! How soon . . . righteousness, and peace, contentment and prosperity would surely indicate the smiles of God upon a once more happy nation."[27]

Because of its commitment to this way of thinking, the Alliance emphasized over and again that the cornerstone of its mission was that its members and organization embody God's eternal *principles* of politics, religion, morality, and economics. These principles, in turn, became the standard by which Alliancefolk judged the worth of people, of reform measures, and ultimately of political parties. Thus, behind the various co-ops and political resolutions was the steady Alliance aim of instilling its sacred principles into the hearts and minds of Alliancefolk. L. L. Polk frequently reminded his vast audiences that he was present only "to discuss principles, not parties; measures, and not men. Principles come from God," he would add, "and are as eternal as the throne of justice itself. Men are of the dust of the earth, and are as transitory as the dewdrop on the morning flower."

Instilling these principles, however, required hard work. One Allianceman pointed out that these principles did not enter humans or organizations through osmosis, but, rather "to live up to the principles of the Alliance, [a] man must lead an exemplary life, and if he cannot do this, he had better abdicate before violating his obligation, thus casting reproach on himself and the order." Comparing adoption of Alliance principles to Christian conversion, he urged the "new-made convert" in the Alliance to let its principles "unfold" internally and externally so that such a convert would not be "only a member of the order, but in every sense a true Allianceman." As this Allianceman indicated, embodying Alliance principles involved moral discipline and intellectual development, for only when a conscience was pure and enlightened could it guide independent moral agents to effect social change.[28]

Three elements of Alliance life specifically reflected this aim: strict discipline, education, and, in the case of institutions, attacks on "party spirit." As we have already seen, Alliance discipline required that its members lead "exemplary" moral lives so as not to bring "reproach" upon themselves "or the order."[29] At the same time, the Alliance educated farmers not only in the best methods of guano application but in the intricacies of political economics. Between 1886 and 1892, *The Progressive Farmer, The Caucasian,* and other Alliance papers steadily replaced articles on farming techniques and recipes for sponge cake with extended lectures by Polk, national Alliance leaders, and local political figures on the contraction of currency, specie backing, and the basic contours of participatory democracy.

Not only people, however, but institutions had to conform to God's principles, so, like most evangelicals, Alliancefolk insisted that institutions, and especially political parties and religious denominations, emphasize principles rather than mere loyalty to party of denominational "titles." Alliancefolk thus heralded the phrase, "principle over party," to denounce partisan politics as well as "churchianity." Even though most white Alliancefolk were Democrats and blacks were Republicans, they nevertheless touted their lack of "party spirit," since such partisan loyalty privileged meaningless commitments to people or titles over faithfulness to divine principles. "To be non-partisan in religion and politics is the very foundation stone of the order," wrote one Allianceman, adding that, "if our order advocates principles that are contrary to either party, then of what avail would our principles be if we did not align ourselves on our principles?" A Baptist Alliance leader wrote similarly that "the greatest curse of the age is partisanship in church and state. There are thousands who are better church members than Christians—their only zeal is to build up the local church and . . . not to please God" even as "there are scores of men who let their zeal for party . . . destroy their better judgment."

Sometimes, however, all was not peaceful in this regard, especially as the Alliance became more politicized after 1889. Alliance members of underrepresented political parties sometimes faced persecution for their politics. Such episodes aside, though, even before the push for "party over principle" prompted third-party action in 1892, the ideal served, at least in theory, as a means to hold elected officials accountable to a set of demands Alliancefolk believed embodied their principles. As they spoke out, incidentally, for "principle over party," Alliancefolk also criticized appeals to sectional hostilities (the "bloody shirt") by both the Democrats and the Republicans as covers by the plutocrats to keep western and southern farmers from uniting against the monied east.[30]

* * *

As evangelical patterns of thought influenced Alliance thinking, the line between the two entities often became quite porous. As illustrated by Dixon's claim that the Alliance was the "Christian religion in concentrated form," Alliancefolk regularly proclaimed their organization the embodiment of Christ's teachings and their mission a high and holy calling—even a millennial calling—rooted in God's providential plans for the United States. This way of thinking ultimately sacralized the movement, giving the order its sense of meaning. "Who knows but this grand organization of the laboring classes of this country is the instrument under God's direction to save this Republic from anarchy and ruin," testified one Allianceman.

In fact, some Alliancefolk felt that their order not only reflected Christian principles but in fact stimulated religion itself by leading lost souls into the church or by leavening the social system with Christian principles. The business agent for Catawba County wrote that "the moral, social, and educational benefit of our order is already being felt in this community. Resolutions against drunkenness, profane swearing, etc., are having a very decided effect. Church members of different denominations are being knit together and feel like they are one brotherhood." Thomas Dixon summarized these sentiments when he asserted that the Alliance "is . . . a religious movement" that "finds its basis on the religious nature of the millions of undermasses who compose its rank and file."[31]

In identifying their principles with those of Christianity, Alliancefolk most often meant that their principles embodied southern social Christianity—especially the command to love one another—and evangelical notions of freedom or patriotic millennialism.

First, regarding social Christianity, Alliancefolk insisted that Jesus had a special identification with the "common people," "the masses," and especially the farmers and producers. This view of Jesus, when combined with producerist rhetoric and antielitism, sacralized farming and manual labor as special in God's eye. Recognizing that "the Savior of the world was called 'the carpenter's son'" who "identified himself with the common people," one farming pastor wrote therefore that "I accept this movement of the farmers as sent of God."[32]

The Alliance furthermore drew on Jesus' command to love one another (the "law of love") to assault monopoly, bribery, speculation, and other forms of "dishonest gain" not only as disruptive to the nation's economic welfare but as sins of avarice to be punished in the "Brimstone Lake State." Alliancefolk moreover condemned not only those individuals who manipulated the economic system but also entire classes that so violated the law of love, since hoarding wealth desecrated God's moral axiom to love and thus threw the economic system out of balance.

One Alliance leader, for example, raged against plutocrats "who claim to be Christians" but "think they are not responsible for the many poor children who are being over worked to get bread and suffering for clothes." He added that he was "glad that some of these old political office holders have to suffer in eternity for the punishment inflicted upon us as a nation." Asking similarly, "Are we living in a government that is actuated by the spirit of love to our fellow men?" other incriminated churches that failed to hear "the cries of suffering humanity" along with the monopolists and plutocrats who "absorb all the earning of the poor, crushing out their lives to the end that they may be made richer." This Allianceman called his order to follow Jesus, the radical reformer who "overthrew the tables of the money changers, and drove them out of the temple," adding that, "now our old temple, reared by our forefathers, is being prostituted to avarice and greed by the same kind of men, and it is time to turn their tables if we desire to preserve our liberties."[33]

As this last line indicates, Alliancefolk also believed that God established and therefore favored American individual, economic, and political liberty. Alliancefolk thus wholeheartedly drew on evangelical commitments to individual conscience and personal independence, which they coupled with patriotic millennialism to sacralize American democracy. Like most evangelicals, Alliancefolk believed American democracy rested on a nation of individuals who could exercise their own free and informed consciences.

Also, like most evangelicals, Alliancefolk usually discussed this sort of independence in a gendered way, recognizing that the development of an individual conscience was the critical component of true manhood and womanhood and hence political independence. One Allianceman wrote that, to protect "equal rights to all and special privileges to none," the nation required "men who are not for sale, men who are honest and sound from center to circumference . . . whose consciences are as steady as the needle to the pole. . . . men too large for party name to sway."[34]

Affirming that it was the purpose of the order to develop "true men" through discipline and education who could serve in public office or vote unswervingly for principle, Alliancefolk also combined this evangelical notion of gender with the idea that the rude farm life was paramount in this development and that, likewise, city life corrupted true manhood and womanhood. Thomas Dixon, for example, noted that "the city of today is destroying the character and manhood of the nation. The modern city as at present constituted does not produce men and women capable of . . . self government."[35]

Dixon's inclusion of women is significant, for within the parameters of separate spheres, a number of suballiances also developed a vision of independent Alliance womanhood. Like most evangelicals, Alliancefolk usually thought the woman's sphere involved affairs of the home, an idea reinforced by the weekly "Household Items" column in The Progressive Farmer and the "Women's Sphere" column in The Caucasian, both of which offered women recipes, sewing tips, and even advice on how "to keep a trim figure." The vast majority of Alliancefolk also reckoned that women ought neither vote nor lecture in public. Populist Ida E. Salmon of Johnston County displayed this sentiment when she wrote: "I am a school girl. . . . My papa is a true blue Populist, and I am one too, though my age and my sex will not let me vote."[36]

That little Ida considered herself, and not just her father, a Populist, however, points to the degree to which women in the Alliance, and in this case the Populist Party, identified themselves as participants in the American public sphere. Although a few Alliancemen and Alliancewomen voiced more radical notions about women working in the professions or voting, most women in the Alliance, while refusing to overturn ideals of submission and separate spheres, nevertheless pushed or relocated the boundaries of those spheres as they asserted their independent womanhood. Alliancewomen, for example, prided themselves in the fact that farming helped them develop "backbone." As opposed to dainty and dependent city girls, Alliancewomen practiced manual labor and produced their own food, clothing, and fertilizer, thereby diminishing their dependence on outside sources. With this independence they also helped save money and thus afforded their husbands greater independence. As mothers and nurturers, Alliancewomen furthermore offered themselves as examples of independence for their children and husbands to emulate and created home environments that fostered such independence.

Along with nurturing independent citizens, many Alliancefolk urged women to keep up with current political and economic issues and then to discuss them with their husbands; in doing so, they could serve as proper "helpmeets" in promoting the best use of their husbands' votes. To equip women properly for their tasks as mothers and "helpmeets," the Alliance encouraged its sisters to take part in larger Alliance meetings, read Alliance papers, and, in general, become educated like their menfolk in the intricacies of political economy.

Some Alliancewomen extended their God-given powers of moral suasion outside the walls of the farmhouse in slightly more radical ways. Balancing still on the arcs between the proper spheres, Alliance sisters sometimes gave lectures in their suballiances and in even larger Alliance gatherings; women also sometimes held offices in suballiances or wrote letters to Alliance papers, and in Onslow County, Lizzie A. Marshburn became an Alliance lecturer.[37]

* * *

As their attacks on urban influences indicate, Alliancefolk increasingly suspected that the development of farming men of firm and individual conscience faced increased resistance from economic, political, and religious centralization or "tyranny," and this trope of centralization became the organizing idea behind their economic, religious, and, especially, political reform aims. In fact, as resistance from Democrats, Republicans, and townsfolk bent on stifling Alliance aims solidified by around 1890, the Alliance linked its love of independence to God's providential designs for America so as to imagine, like the editors of the *North Carolina Baptist*, that they were no longer the free men their fathers were. As they pondered this, Alliance-folk and later the Populists increasingly saw themselves as participants in an epic struggle between liberty and tyranny.

In identifying the forces of centralization at work in America's political economy, Alliancefolk most frequently targeted monopolists' centralized control of such things as transportation costs, speculators' ("Wall Street's") control of commodities prices, and the national banks' control over the money supply, often referring to such entities as "Aristocrats," "monarchy," or the "British Crown of 1776." Similarly, they pointed out the detrimental effects of centralized populations in cities as well as the centralizing political tendencies in partyism and especially bossism (one person or committee dictating votes). This economic and political centralization was aided and abetted by an urban "churchianity" that was overly reliant on "hireling" ministers and thus incapable of developing men and women who could think for themselves and hence support democracy. Moreover, farmers believed that plutocratic centralizers, by having attained this level of control through the sins of avarice and inhumanity, had rendered ineffectual any attempts by rural folks to better their lives through progressive book farming and even, for some, cooperative economic ventures.

Again, their frustration was not aimed at an imaginary conspiracy. Farmers had for years seen their meager profits spent on exorbitant freight rates set by private railroads that got tax breaks from their state government. Year after year they had been unable to get credit or money except by paying "iniquitous" interest rates to furnishing merchants or landlords who were themselves enslaved by the national banking system, and all this, even though they produced crop yields greater than they could have conceived even thirty years earlier. It seemed prices for the products of their labor continued to drop at the will of speculators and middlemen and by the invisible hand of a contracted currency, and all the while the city folk who derided them as "hayseeds" continued to prosper. Such was this state of economic and political "tyranny."[38]

By casting the economic situation in terms of centralization and especially "tyranny," the Alliance tapped into a host of values beyond the ethereal laws of economics. For Alliancefolk, economic centralization had a trickle-down effect on personal liberty and independence. In much the same way that "churchianity" and "Romanism" doused the development of Christian manhood and womanhood by crushing individual freedom of conscience, so they believed economic centralization robbed farmers not only of fair compensation but more insidiously of their freedom to earn a living and hence their personal independence as they became enslaved to nonproducers.

Moreover, not only were individual producers enslaved, but because present and future generations would not benefit from economic independence, the entire system of democracy was exposed to decay from within, since the ideal democracy—one in which the voice of the people reflected the voice of God—rested on the presence of independent men and women.[39]

Their sense of crisis took an even more epic sense of urgency as Alliance-folk dipped deeply into evangelical patriotic millennialism. Most Alliance-folk believed wholeheartedly with L. L. Polk that, even though God had established America as "the world's last hope for civil and religious liberty," those liberties were nevertheless under assault: "Mighty forces are being marshaled which must test our virtue, our manhood, our patriotism, our appreciation of self-government and our love of liberty." Recounting the falls of Carthage, Tyre, Greece, and Egypt from loss of principle and from tyrannical rule, Polk warned that America, too, tottered on the brink of the abyss because the "inexorable and unchanging" laws of economics had become out of kilter as a result of "the unjust, partial, discriminating and wicked financial system of our government." In another jeremiad, Polk warned that there were, in his audience, "those present who . . . may live to see our God-favored land transformed into one vast mausoleum, in which shall be buried forever the splendid wreck of our past and prospective glory, and with it the world's last hope for civil and religious liberty."[40]

Although appeals to the narrative of American freedom were drenched with religious images, some Alliancefolk imagined the story of the Alliance not only as part of America's democratic struggle but as part of a more general Protestant struggle for religious and individual freedom. One Allianceman imagined his order standing arm in arm not only with the patriots of '76 but also with the Protestant Reformers, the Disciples movement of Alexander Campbell, and northern abolitionists. Another member linked the Alliance to the Quaker and regulator movements, while another likened their struggle to that of the children of Israel under the tyranny of Pharaoh.[41]

To battle centralized tyranny in all three arenas—economic, political, and religious—even though early on the Alliance stressed economic cooperation to fight the forces of economic centralization, by around 1890 Alliancefolk focused more and more on assaulting political centralization. Though Section 3 focuses more fully on the Alliance political agenda, the rationale behind the order's call to political action was to stay the forces of "class legislation" that "legitimized" this growing state of economic and political "tyranny." As L. L. Polk articulated in his presidential address at the Ocala convention: "Retrogression in American agriculture . . . is due in large measure and in most part to partial, discriminating, and grossly unjust national legislation."[42]

"Class legislation," as he liked to call it, became a shorthand way to describe both the cause and one of the effects of economic centralization. By pushing through legislation that enabled them to consolidate, control, and regulate the nation's economy, monopolists and other private interests—especially the national banking system and railroads—had "legally" secured their tyranny.

Yet, even more insidiously, while monopolists had used class legislation to control the financial system, that process of gaining control itself, especially when coupled with a growing paucity of individual independence, had created a state of political tyranny in which the American system of government was slowly changing from a democracy to an oligarchy headed by the plutocrats.

Although political conditions were not bad enough, at least at the state level, to produce much actual third-party sentiment among North Carolina Alliancefolk until 1891 or 1892, as we have already seen, the organization nevertheless grew increasingly intolerant of the way political parties, controlled by monied interests, brought out the "party lash" to persuade voters and office holders to do their bidding. To Alliancefolk, such political bossism was another form of slavery and tyranny and an indication of the degree to which the nation's political system was drifting from its democratic moorings. "My brethren, the question is," asked S. J. Veach, "Shall we, like 'dumb driven cattle' go to the polls and vote ourselves destruction. . . . Shall we allow those self-constituted leaders of the old parties to put hooks in our noses and lead us where they please?" Or, he asked, "Shall we arise in the strength of our manhood and American citizenship and throw off the shackles that bind us to corrupt partisan leaders, and come back to principle and to pure Jeffersonian Democracy? Shall we look to God, the pole star of our hope, the universal deliverer of those who put their trust in him?" As Alliancefolk like Veach thus attacked state and national political corruption and "partyism" along with local "courthouse rings" and "lawyercrats," they laid the groundwork for the Populist revolt in 1892.[43]

In order to fight class legislation, besides assaulting bossism, as early as 1886 the Association and the Alliance after it urged farmers to influence state politics by embodying and then holding political leaders accountable to divine principles. They did this under the guise of nonpartisan politics, even though most Alliance leaders, being white Democrats, assumed they would work through the white man's party. Although at first farmers lobbied the state legislature concerning matters that would immediately assist them— better roads, better service from the Department of Agriculture, a state Agricultural College—as we will see in the following chapter, by 1890 the state Alliance promoted state legislation to regulate interest and railroad rates along with national legislation to enact soft money reforms and to gain leverage in agricultural markets.

Just as they fought economic and political centralization through cooperation and direct political action, so also did many Alliancefolk assault denominational centralization as a third and equal threat to American democracy. Although the Alliance had a few denominational leaders like Polk, with their bodies and words radical restorationist Alliancefolk like Gospel Missioners W. A. Graham and J. F. Click, Disciples like "Brother Jimmy," and decentralizers like the editors of the $1.00 *North Carolina Baptist,* opposed centralization in their denominations with the same rationale the Alliance attacked it in other realms: it deprived the current generation of the freedom its ancestors had known.

Alliancefolk considered religious centralization so threatening largely because they bound religious, civil, and economic liberty so tightly together; to lose liberty in one sphere directly affected the other. If one was not able to follow the dictates of one's conscience in matters of faith, one would not be able to vote independently. In this spirit, many Alliancefolk therefore saw their order as a medicinal dose to organized religion steeped in "churchianity" and controlled by the "First Churches." Writing that "the religion of this day is defective," one Allianceman called on "the yeomanry of the land . . . full of brawn and brain," through the Alliance, to "illustrate practical Christianity, and prove the doctrine divine."[44]

As an aside, while Alliancefolk in Kansas and other midwestern states shied away from nativistic or anti-Catholic rhetoric because they found it necessary to cooperate with Roman Catholics, such was not the case in North Carolina. Although the Alliance and Populist Party did not attack Roman Catholic theology as such, they did criticize the ecclesiastical structure of Roman Catholicism as inconsistent with and even a threat to American democracy. Some, moreover, were rabidly anti-Catholic and feared an imminent invasion by Rome—the soil for such an invasion having been prepared by the centralizing tendencies of American Protestants.[45]

* * *

In extending the law of love from its role as a guide for personal morality to the status of economic law or principle, and in placing their struggle against economic, political, and religious centralization in a sacred narrative pitting the forces of liberty against the satanic forces of tyranny and oppression, the Alliance charged its reform efforts with a sense of moral purpose and zeal. As the Alliance cast hard times as a "moral plague" and their movement as "a great moral revolution," it elided moral, religious, economic, and political ideals and thus understood itself in ultimate, moral, and even eschatological terms. For Thomas Dixon, it was clear that Alliancefolk had "gone into politics" because "all social and economic questions have become political questions, and all political questions are religious."[46]

To folks like Dixon, then, the Alliance was a holy order, filled with God's salt of the earth and beholden to that radical first-century reformer, Jesus. Drawing on social Christianity, Baptist J. F. Click's *Hickory Mercury* perhaps put it best when he contrasted the "New Christ" that the monopolists and city churches proclaimed in their "churchianity" to the genuine "old Christ" upheld by the Alliance and all common-folk lovers of reform. "The nineteenth century demands a new Christ," he wrote sarcastically, since "the teachings of Jesus are too old and too fogyish. He was down on the money kings and whipped them out of the temple." Such chastisement of the wealthy, therefore, would not "do for the 19th century. The money king must be put in Paradise and the unemployed working man must be turned into hell." As the column continued, the "old Christ" became a first-century Allianceman:

> The old time Christ associated with common people and if he was on earth to-day . . . the high-toned people would not recognize him on the street. The doctrine of the equality of man was good enough for Christ to preach 1800 years ago, but in the glory of the present civilization it is out [of] place, and the new Christ must wear a plug hat, smoke 25 cent cigars, take fine whiskies freely for the stomach's sake, and faithfully vote the old party tickets arranged by the grace of Wall Street. Jesus taught . . . that heaven belonged to the poor . . . and he went about as a reform agitator, holding farm and labor picnics, and feeding the people on bread and fish. The new Christ must be a millionaire, ride in palace cars, own land enough to make a couple of states, operate several thousand miles of railroad, get up a supper worth a thousand dollars a plate, and dictate to a congress of millionaires. No, no; the old Christ was too much of a reformer, a crank, a calamity howler and was not in sympathy with the old parties, neither the Pharisees nor the Sadducees.[47]

In identifying with Jesus the agrarian reformer, and in imagining themselves the twelve disciples, the Protestant reformers, or the "Christian patriots" of 1776, evangelical Alliancefolk understood their movement to be at the heart of a sacred struggle in the twilight of the nineteenth century. Reflecting on the place of the Alliance in the firmaments, M. J. Battle compared the birth of the Alliance to that of his Messiah: "Only a short time since, the Alliance, a puny babe, was materialized: its advent was not heralded by pomp or parade emblematical, 'twas a babe born in a manger."

Battle then praised God for the millennial hope of the Alliance: "Rejoice, ye multitude! Lift up your thanks; victory is in the air. . . . Millennium is coming! Who shall say the Alliance is not a factor to hasten it?"[48]

As their religious ideas mixed with their economic and political aims, their movement possessed a sense of righteous indignation at the depth to which the nation was falling from the pristine ideals of Christ and the generations of Washington and Jefferson. Again, farmers were not just poor, they were angry. In order to urge Elias Carr to enter the 1890 congressional race as an Alliance Democrat, "Brother Jimmy" wrote to his Alliance president: "Our chains, *I feel it*, are already welded too tightly for longer endurance." Because these chains threatened the very "liberty so dearly bought and given to us by . . . the blest blood of the American Fathers," "Brother Jimmy" charged Carr to live up to "his high and holy calling as Alliance president" and run for office, adding that if he did not, that he needed to hand the "standard . . . to someone else, and long as a fold of it flutters in the breeze let me march forward to victory or a glorious death."[49]

If the Alliance called some like "Brother Jimmy" to march to a "glorious death," it gave others hope that God, working through a unified phalanx of farmers who embodied eternal principles, would bring the nation's political economy back into balance. Inspired by the idea that in America, every voter ruled as a king, one such Alliance organizer and minister wrote in 1891: "We, as an Order, must keep right on reforming and purifying the laws of our country until there will be no enemies to a just government, where peace and plenty will reign and where every man can reign as a king under his own vine and fig tree."[50]

Vox Populi, Vox Dei

"Look to Jesus"

In January 1893 Marcus Josiah Battle lost his farm. This premier Alliance-man of Edgecombe County, born to a clan that included aristocrats, manu-facturers, and college presidents, had purchased this unimproved property thirty-three years earlier for just over $33 an acre. Yet now at age fifty-five, this Civil War veteran saw his land, which had all the advantages of good soil and close proximity to roads and railroads, auctioned off for less than $3 an acre to settle his tax bill. He also lost his horse and mule team.

M. J., as he was usually known, was not alone among his Alliance friends in the Whitakers area to lose his hard-worked lands. J. M. Cutchin, who, along with Battle helped inaugurate the People's Party in Edgecombe, had lost 465 acres plus two town lots in Tarboro to a tax auction six months earlier. Dr. W. T. Mayo, who supplied the land for Bethany Christian Church and was the leader of Maple Swamp Alliance, lost 815 acres and one town lot, while the editor of *The Rattler*, Whitakers' Alliance paper, lost 241 acres to the tax man. For others in Edgecombe it was the lender, not the tax man, who did them in. The 1,700-acre "crack farm" of northern Edgecombe, owned by the widow of a Confederate colonel, was auctioned by its lien holder in December 1892 for just over $8,000, a fraction of its prewar value of $50,000.

Given such a state of destitution among even the most well-to-do and sophisticated farmers in the region (not to mention doctors like Mayo), it is not surprising that farmers were ready to seek desperate measures in order to secure relief. Battle's despair turned to indignation as he pondered, in good Alliance fashion, the damnable extravagance of fashionable tycoons, railroad men, and town-bred dudes who continued to prosper while the producers of wealth lay prostrate, all because such townsfolk, from the courthouse rings in Tarboro to the railroad lawyers in Washington City, had corrupted America's political system. As Battle looked out over his cotton fields for the last time as owner, he asked, "Why is it that the real fortune builders of this land are being so rapidly reduced to a state of bankruptcy?" He answered, "Manipulation of the finances" and added further that "the true remedy is to crush out . . . monopoly" through legislating Alliance principles, lest relief "be secured . . . by violent means."[1]

As he penned his thoughts, Battle was surprisingly subdued given his reputation as an Alliance fire eater. When it came to assaulting the plutocrats, Battle, like Thomas Dixon, forcefully melded religion, economics, and patriotism into apocalyptic assessments of economic and political affairs. Like many Alliancefolk, by late 1891 Battle considered the economic system well out of balance and counseled the application of Alliance demands. Since its demands were political, and since Battle, like most white Alliancefolk in his area, was a lifelong Democrat, he wrote that "glad would it render me to see the Democratic Party declare itself in favor of these reasonable just demands—prove itself in deed and in act, what its name implies." Yet, even as Battle hoped for such a scenario, he was bitter about the failure of the party of his fathers to enact legislation that would "give this rapidly developing land a sufficient volume of money to do the business of the country." As a result, Battle toyed with the idea of rejecting the Democratic Party outright as a means of reform, wondering aloud whether the growing third-party rumblings around Whitakers were, in fact, the "voice of God."[2]

Battle was certainly not alone in his thinking; Alliancefolk in the Whitakers and Battleboro areas had long been among the most radical in the state, advocating political action from the early days of Polk's Farmers' Association and often criticizing the Democratic Party for failing the farmers. Moreover, as indicated in their 1894 "Look to Jesus" fliers, they had no qualms about tapping into the radical, countercultural, and politically activist elements of the evangelical religion they embraced at Whitaker's Temple, Gethsemane Baptist, Bethany Christian, and other local churches. Their criticisms of the old parties, including the Democrats, intensified in late 1891 as these Alliancefolk of northern Edgecombe—a county with a black majority— began openly to threaten third-party action. J. B. Lloyd, editor of the local Alliance newspaper, waxed apocalyptic as he warned that the "manhood and virtue of the people will be tested" in the coming election year of 1892, adding: "At present the people are living under a greater despotism than

George III—and it is all due to unwise and iniquitous legislation that is spreading bankruptcy throughout the country." Demonstrating, as did Battle, an eroding faith in the party of his fathers, he noted that because the "Democrats of New England and New York are in hearty sympathy with Wall Street . . . such a party with all its sympathizers deserves defeat at the hands of the down-trodden farmers of the country, and in '92 we will bury such corruption so deep that the powers of darkness cannot resurrect it." Although Lloyd was most concerned about corruption in the national party, another Edgecombe Allianceman was worried about local centralization: "There are men in the county . . . who have set around the court house, year after year, and dictated to the great masses of Democratic voters how they shall vote and whom they shall vote for." This action, he argued, was "pushing the farmers, Alliancemen . . . clean out of the Democratic Party."[3]

Farmers beyond the borders of Edgecombe and North Carolina were also simmering, and on 22 February 1892, a congress of the leading reformers of the country, with the National Alliance and L. L. Polk at the helm, drew up the 1892 St. Louis Platform that encapsulated the demands that the Farmers' Alliance had put forth year after year. Immediately following this congress of reformers, the People's Party, in existence as a national party since May 1891, adopted the platform as its own.

Back in Edgecombe, Lloyd's revolution against national "despotism" began on 23 March as his paper called on all local reformers to meet and discuss the St. Louis Platform. In explaining the need for these "mass meetings," Allianceman "R. E. Former" reasoned: "We have talked reform and begged for it for years, now we are going to act it. . . . The powers that be by their persistent attack and false representation, their denial of all the essentials to our prosperity and happiness, have driven us to this measure." Attesting to the disintegrating ties between the Alliance and the Democracy, he argued: "True democracy and reform go hand in hand, but [the Democratic Party] of to-day can never hold again the support of our people. . . . We have only to stand true to our principles when such a tidal wave will sweep over the entire country and carry with it the death-knell of both Pharisee and Sadducee."[4]

Heeding Mr. Former's call, a mix of black and white Alliancefolk gathered at two sites and, under the leadership of Dr. Mayo, Battle, and J. M. Cutchin, adopted the St. Louis Platform and elected delegates to a state People's Party convention.[5] After Alliancefolk in bordering Nash County did likewise, Mr. "R. E. Former" warned again that the "county and state [Democratic] executive committees will learn that the patriots of North Carolina will decide for themselves who are the Democracy of this state."[6]

Even though many Alliance Democrats, including state Alliance President Marion Butler, were hesitant to part with the party of their fathers
until after Cleveland's nomination later that summer, there was no such
wavering in hostility among non-Alliance Democrats. Having feared for
years the possibility that the Alliance might split the white man's party, these
loyal Democrats lashed out against the "thirdites" in Edgecombe and elsewhere. The local Edgecombe Democratic paper labeled Cutchin and Battle
anarchists for challenging the powers that be, adding, "That these two men
belong to a Christian church we have nothing to do with. We can only say
that there is a vast difference between the socialism of the Bible, the father-
hood of God and the brotherhood of man, and the peculiar leveling views
of these two men."[7]

In response, many Populists in Whitakers refused to let Democrats speak
in front of their stores, while others, like J. B. Lloyd, escalated the war of
words: "It appears that there is a set of politicians in North Carolina who
have 'set their heads' on controlling its politics this year as they have done in
the past, but . . . the man who thinks he can bulldoze and force the masses to
vote this year, as he dictates, will learn a few things before the coming campaign is over. The people have submitted long enough to boss-rule; and they
will not be driven into the support of men who will not champion their
principles and measures."[8]

As indicated in the Democratic response to Cutchin and Battle, even as
Populists rocked the political sphere, they also ripped apart the fault lines of
race, politics, and southern identity within North Carolina evangelicalism.
While Populists tapped into more liberal components of evangelicalism to
defend American freedom, conservative evangelical Democrats utilized
commonsense thinking and the "spirituality of the church" to cast Populists
as anarchists and to demand loyalty to the "powers that be": the state Democracy and white supremacy. Casualties of the war were inevitable; evangelicals exorcised one another; congregations "shipped" their pastors; and one
group of politicized Free Will Baptists in Wilson County even founded its
own "People's Chapel."[9]

Back in Edgecombe, open warfare erupted between Democratic Elder
P. D. Gold, the leader of the state's Primitive Baptists we first met in Chapter
3, and Methodist M. J. Battle. The Primitive Baptists, despite their somewhat
radical image, were far and away the most conservative evangelical body in
the state in their support of the spirituality of the church and the Democratic Party. Rejecting the Alliance and the Populist Party because they were
"secret societies" and having had a tradition going back to Andrew Jackson
of voting the Democratic ticket, Elder Gold expertly detailed conservative

evangelical attitudes toward Populism that incidentally spelled loyalty to the party of Jackson.[10]

Citing the "spirituality of the church," Gold attacked the Populists in Whitakers—and Battle and Cutchin in particular—for sinfully mingling religion and secular politics: "Jesus did not come on earth to overthrow national governments. His kingdom is not of this world." Gold furthermore castigated Battle and Cutchin for advocating government regulation of the economy and government ownership of railroads and telegraphs: "The desire for the government to own every thing is . . . foolish and danger- ous. . . . To put all things in the government's hands is to sell ourselves as slaves to the government which would soon become the bitterest engine of oppression." Gold then reported that if one class or party took control of the levers of power (in this case, the farming class), it could oppress or enslave other groups, as the Pharaohs had done to the children of Israel.[11]

Denying he and Cutchin were anarchists (adding that they intended only to destroy "such laws as made for the hurt of our people"), M. J. Battle responded first by drawing on the law of love: "Larger equity in the division of labor in the distribution of products of labor, must obtain. Anything short of this is contrary to the teaching of the Holy Writ! This, Elder Gold, even with all of his prejudice against the People's Party, must admit." Lean- ing on the trusted tools of patriotic millennialism and the sanctity of indi- vidual liberty, Battle continued: "Elder Gold emphasizes that Scripture which enjoins submission to the powers that be; query to him: does the Bible enjoin submission to injustice, wrong? This if so, did the adherents of the fathers in his branch of the Christian church in the days of the American Revolution, in their successful effort in throwing off the British yoke, violate that Scripture? Their historians laud the action of those heroic men. Why should their descendants be denied the right of protesting against wrong and injustice?" Battle ended by warning that, even though "God's care is over all," "good government" could not "be secured without diligence—the exercise of a free ballot."[12]

As Populists such as Battle and Cutchin drew on evangelical traditions of patriotic millennialism, they merged sacred and secular worlds of morality, religion, and politics, as they wove their own struggle into the sacred drama pitting despotism against freedom. Reflecting on their rejection of these Democratic powers in Edgecombe County, "R. E. Former" wrote that his fellow farmers "have waited long and patiently on the Plutocratic Bourbons and now they are determined to throw off the yoke of their thralldom." Mr. "Former" then reported that the "common people," "whose brawny arms . . . strangled the British Lion in 1776 . . . who were chosen by Christ to give to the world the grand truths of Christianity," who "stood by Luther in the Reformatory," who "stood by Washington from Bunker Hill to Yorktown" and "who followed Lee and Grant, Jackson and Hancock . . . have crossed the Rubicon . . . with the great cry of all freemen '*vox populi; vox Dei*.'"[13]

* * *

"Seamlessness" is a term that has often been used to describe southern politics and religion. Indeed, to the casual observer, politics and religion in the period from 1877 to 1892 in North Carolina might well have appeared that way. Beginning with the "redemption" of the state government from the Republicans in 1876, white Democrats ruled the state with a fair degree of confidence. Through gerrymandering, through centralized control of local politics, and by keeping class and geographical divisions among whites at bay with appeals to the "bloody shirt" and the terror of "Negro rule," white Democratic leaders felt by 1890 that they had secured prosperity and white supremacy. In terms of religion, North Carolina boasted the highest percentage of Protestant churchgoers of any state in the Union, and the vast majority of these Protestants considered themselves evangelical; they spoke the same devotional language, sang the same hymns, and held to the same basic outlook. Moreover, despite their doctrine of the spirituality of the church, the line between white evangelicals and white Democrats proved porous, at least outside a few counties in the Quaker Belt and mountains where Republicanism was the dominant "white man's party." In the rest of the state, local, state, and national political leaders were more often than not local elders or deacons, presbytery, association, or classis presidents, and even pastors. Such were the "powers that be" in late nineteenth-century North Carolina.

One of the main reasons the Alliance was so successful in the Old North State—especially when compared to groups like the Knights of Labor and the Greenback Party—was its ability to blend almost effortlessly into this matrix of power. Although Alliancefolk rankled a few "big-business" Democrats, Alliance leaders like Polk, Carr, and Alexander were savvy Democratic insiders who supported a powerful reform wing in their party that advocated "conservative" reforms aimed at maintaining harmony between agricultural and industrial prosperity. They moreover understood, along with other reform Democrats like Judge Walter Clark, Josephus Daniels, and Confederate and redeemer governor and senator Zebulon Vance, that they rode a wave of popular, grassroots, common-folk resentment of railroads, monopolists, and other assorted "aristocratic" elites.

Again, even though some local leaders were Republicans, and even though the Alliance promoted a "nonpartisan" agenda, everyone understood that the Alliance intended to push its reforms through the Democratic Party. One Allianceman from Edgecombe affirmed: "I was a white man before I was a Democrat, I was a Democrat before I was an Alliance man.... To my mind it is as plain as a knot on a log, that white men, Democracy, and the Alliance of this State are all so entwined, so closely connected in interest, that to make a distinction between any would be impossible."[14] So even though the Alliance had a radical undercurrent, it never directly challenged the two most important sinews of Democratic rule in North Carolina: white supremacy and party fealty.

Just as the Alliance played by North Carolina's political rules, as we saw in the previous chapter, it also baptized itself in the state's religious waters. Included in its leadership was a vast army of pastors, church leaders, lay leaders, and earnestly pious evangelical Alliancewomen and Alliancemen. If socialism and communism taught by strange-looking, bespectacled folk in far-off places like Chicago seemed threatening, it seemed a safe harbor to hear beloved Pastor Shaw or "Brother Jimmy" extol the subtreasury plan or government ownership of railroads and telegraphs in the local meeting house, using references to the Bible followed by an extemporaneous sermon on the "Blood of Jesus." Its more radical ideas were rooted in the same law of love and commonsense, antielitist rhetoric that rural evangelicals had for years imagined their Lord and Savior using to cast the money changers from the temple or to condemn urbane Pharisees and Sadducees. Rural evangelical Alliancefolk fit the few conservative church folk who opposed them into their usual sacred narratives, casting themselves as the common folk for whom Jesus died and in turn imagining their enemies the citified proponents of "churchianity," ecclesial "Romanism," and Phariseeism that Jesus or Luther had opposed.

And yet, even though the Alliance did not seem to jostle North Carolina's basic religious and political connections of power, just below its surface existed a cluster of combustibles—intellectual, racial, and economic—that in the right set of circumstances might blow apart these bonds among church, state, and Alliance. In 1892 this is exactly what happened. The combustibles included many a farmer's increasingly lukewarm allegiance to the Democratic Party, desperate poverty from which there seemed no escape, and, from the non-Populist side, Democratic leaders' awareness of how tenuous their hold on the state actually was. Furthermore, as these combustibles connected with evangelicals' patriotic and sacred narratives and their tendency to think in ultimate moral terms, they developed into devastating dynamite. Many, if not most, Alliancefolk in 1892 felt that they were the last hope for American democracy against the forces of plutocratic tyranny, and they were ready to fight when the battle lines were drawn. All they needed was a flame to the fuse.

Between 1888 and 1892, the Democratic Party provided that flame as it drew the hard and fast battle lines in North Carolina between those who would and those who would not support the supremacy of the white man's party. Although the Alliance continued to exert a strong influence on the state Democracy through 1892, as that election year got under way, fearing that Alliance Democrats might support a national People's Party ticket, the state Democratic party required that all Democrats swear an oath to support the national Democratic ticket upon entering local nominating conventions. The line thus drawn, Democratic Alliancefolk who believed the state party had irrevocably succumbed to the forces of tyranny began to bolt the party.

As these Populists drew on evangelical ideas about the ways people, principles, and governing institutions ought to work, and as they coupled those ideas with a reforming sense of Christians' political responsibility and evangelical patriotic millennialism, they perceived the widespread centralization of denominations, corporations, and political parties in the 1880s and 1890s as a crisis in American democracy. They went on to condemn corporations' centralized control of pricing structures because it fouled up God's natural governance of the economic system; they likewise condemned monopolists for their undue influence in politics that had resulted in class legislation that silenced the voice of God in favoring the wealthy over the farmers and producing classes. Populists believed such influence could only have occurred, however, because the institutions of state, local, and national government were no longer governed by the rule of a consenting majority, or the "voice of People," but rather by centralized committees, "rings," "mafias," and "combines" that dictated legislation to those governed and thus quelled "the voice of God." Populists further argued that this state of affairs persisted because the two major political parties had lost the democratic and Christian principles on which they were founded. The situation was not likely to change since these parties were run now by effeminate invertebrates lacking the manhood and independence of thought needed to place principle over party. One Populist saw politicians who said "nothing will make me leave my party," as "political heathen unfit to live in a Christian civilization . . . a carbuncle on the Republic, a disgrace to human reason."[15] Such sores on the republic were not solely to blame for their disgrace, however, since the church, whose job it was to secure Christian manhood and democracy in economics and politics, had itself increasingly become oligarchical and had placed denomination-building over the proclamation of God's principles.

In leaving the party of their fathers, Populists committed an act akin to the religious separatism of the restorationist denominations to which so many Alliancefolk belonged. Leaving the Democratic Party did not mean rejecting the principles for which it stood but was rather an act intent on restoring those very principles the party had forsaken. S. J. Veach, one-time chaplain of the Alliance, wrote that both old parties had "left the landmark of old Jeffersonian Democracy and true Republicanism." An Edgecombe Allianceman remarked: "The party of to-day would not be recognized by Jefferson, Jackson and others." In April 1892, Allianceman J. T. Kennedy "arose and, placing his hand upon his noble brow (whose locks are blossoming for the grave), . . . Said he, 'for 48 long years I have cast my votes for the Democratic Party, but to-day, with the rest of my Alliance brethren, I am called a 'calamity howler,' and why should not we howl? The men whom we have elevated to positions of honor and trust, men who are (or ought to be) servants of the people, have created unto themselves the House of Lords and . . . they have turned their backs upon the people and are worshipping at the shrine of Wall street.'" G. W. Cobb, Sr., similarly wrote: "I am 61 years old; was born a Democrat and have been one ever since (that is of the Jeffersonian stripe). I am an Allianceman, true blue, and a Populist, for what Democracy there is in this country now is in the Populist Party. They are the *true* Democrats. . . . I am for liberty of conscience, liberty at the ballot box, and for the people to rule, and all the rotten eggs of the *so-called* Democratic party can't change my views. They only help to strengthen us. Give it to 'em."[16]

For Cobb, Kennedy, Veach, and others, the decision to become a Populist was fundamentally a political decision—a decision to forsake one's old political allegiances and establish new ones. While the Alliance, like the Farmers' Association before it, had always sought relief through political reform, it was not a political party; the People's Party, however, was, and thus, in attempting to understand the movement and especially the kinds of decisions key leaders like Marion Butler made over its eight-year life, it is necessary to keep in mind the specific goals of any political party: to elect office holders. In the case of Populism, the aim was to elect Populists or like-minded reformers to office who would storm national and state legislatures to restore American liberty and economic stability.

As we can see in the language these folks used to describe this decision, however, the People's Party was far more than merely a vehicle for enacting legislation. Although political campaigns in the Gilded Age aroused passions that today seem reserved only for sporting events, the decision to become a Populist, to forsake the party of one's "fathers" and "race," constituted a moral and often deeply religious decision. For those taking the leap, the consequences ran from mild chortles at the post office to rotten eggs, ostracism from family and friends, and, in 1898, even threats of death. The decision, then, to vote Populist fundamentally challenged certain aspects of the state's "powers that be" in order to preserve personal, economic, religious, and political freedom. Democrats were perhaps more correct than Populists acknowledged when the old party labeled the thirdites "Anarchists," for, indeed, they were blowing apart the social and political foundations of the state.

The Populist revolt was, in fact, devastating to white Democratic supremacy in the state. Populists not only forced the Democratic Party to assemble a new winning coalition, but they challenged the rhetorical and ideological levers it used to maintain its power as they built a biracial coalition that removed the Democrats from power in 1894. Drawing on strands of antielitist rhetoric, Populists poked fun at appeals to the bloody shirt, lampooned Democratic and Confederate heroes, exposed appeals to "Negro rule" as farcical, and refused to honor anyone who did not support their principles. They did all of this, furthermore, citing God on their side. In short, nothing of the Democrats' canopy was sacred to Populism. One particularly perceptive Populist noted that "the prestige of the Kurnel over the masses and the infallible faith in the Democratic Party of the day is shaken from center to circumference."[17]

The threat, therefore, posed by Populism to alignments of race and white Democratic rule set off a virulent counterassault in 1898. In much the same way as did the Populists, Democrats drew on evangelical thought and especially commonsense patterns of thinking to charge that God's axiomatic patterns of proper relations between men and women and blacks and whites required white supremacy which, in turn, required the Democratic rule. In order to restore this rule in 1898, Democrats launched a multifaceted and devastating "white supremacy campaign" against Populism.

Populists, who had wavered all along in their commitments to their black brothers and sisters in the movement, were unprepared for such an assault. And so while many Populists stood firm, others, especially in the East, succumbed to the arguments and returned to the Democratic Party. The result was a rout at the hands of the Democrats in 1898, followed by murder and mayhem in Wilmington and disfranchisement in 1900. Having lost a unique vision of the way the world might have been, North Carolina entered the twentieth century under white Democratic rule and limited franchise. To all appearances, the crisis of democracy prophesied by the Populists ended with tyranny triumphant.

5. "Pure Democracy and White Supremacy": The Democratic Party and the Farmers' Alliance

The Populist revolt among white farmers was a protest against the state's Democratic Party; for blacks, it was against the Republican Party. As an instance of political fratricide, the Populist drama played itself out against the backdrop of thirty years of geographical, social, religious, and cultural tensions that became politicized in 1892. As it entered the political fray, the white Alliance joined with urban reformers who comprised the reform or "progressive" wing of the state Democratic Party in order to enact its legislative agenda. But that partnership was tenuous. After an open break between the Alliance and the non-Alliance members of the reform wing over the 1890 senatorial campaign of Zebulon Vance, the path was set for open schism in 1892 as Alliancefolk remained loyal to their principles while "straight-out" or non-Alliance Democrats remained loyal to white supremacy and the party unity necessary to ensure it.

* * *

During the antebellum period, North Carolina politics played out along an east/west political divide with Whigs in the mountains and in the Piedmont (many of whom became antisecessionists) vying for power with eastern planters who, along with Piedmont Jacksonians, supported the Democrats. After the Civil War, the Republican Party built a coalition based on this prewar divide by linking blacks in the east with white antisecessionists in the mountains and Quaker Belt. Added to this Republican coalition were some Piedmont manufacturers and a few white Jacksonians in counties like Davidson who resented the way ex-Whigs had gained control of the postwar Democratic Party. With this coalition, and with the help of Reconstruction limits on white voting, the Republicans held sway in the state through much of the Reconstruction period.

While this coalition of manufacturers, eastern blacks, mountain antisecessionists, and old Piedmont Jacksonians made the state's Republican Party one of the strongest in the South, it nevertheless created interparty strife along axes of race and policy. While blacks in the east saw the party of Lincoln as their only viable option for political freedom, wealthy Republican manufacturers like Washington Duke of the American Tobacco Company were interested primarily in the party's national probusiness fiscal policies and hoped the state would foster economic growth through similar legislation aimed at attracting business. Old Piedmont Jacksonians and antisecessionist yeomen in the west, however, had little regard for blacks' rights or probusiness policies; they primarily opposed the Democrats' ironclad control over local government and election procedures—policies put into place after the Democrats "redeemed" the state in 1876 to keep Republican and black influence to a minimum. Moreover, the presence of blacks in the party, along with the party's association with Reconstruction, made many whites who might otherwise have favored Republicans' national or state platforms eschew association with the party.

Although this Republican coalition could not mount a statewide majority between the Democratic "redemption" of 1876 and the Populist fusion election of 1894, it was able to keep margins of victory just slim enough throughout this period that North Carolina Democrats necessarily resorted to centralized control and election fraud to maintain their hold on the state. In the end, for whites in the west as well as for blacks in the east, the Republican Party became a party of opposition—opposition especially to the white Democratic east's political hegemony.[1]

In order to secure "redemption" from the Reconstruction Republicans in 1876, the Democratic Party also needed to build a coalition that combined different interests and that could woo up-country white farmers and nascent manufacturers and merchants who might favor the Republicans. To do so, the Democratic Party's strategy was simple and effective: cast the "horrors" of Reconstruction under Republican rule as "black domination" and demand that whites unite in one party to ensure white supremacy. The strategy paid off in 1876, and the Democrats elected Zebulon Vance governor and subsequently maintained political hegemony until 1894.

This call for political control by whites gained its power of persuasion by tapping into deeply held, commonsense convictions about the proper relations of blacks to whites. Specifically, most whites could not fathom the idea of standing before a black judge, appealing to a black commissioner, having their local school run by a black school board, entrusting their mail to a black postmaster, or being arrested by a black sheriff. To submit to such an inversion of accepted rules of interaction brought about a deep internal revulsion among many whites who otherwise carried on cordial, though culturally regulated, day-to-day relations with blacks.[2] It is important to note, moreover, that the term "white supremacy" did not necessarily mean hatred of blacks, neither did it necessarily mean support for disfranchisement; rather, it asserted as necessary the consolidation of all political power by whites.

One wrinkle in the Democrats' white supremacy strategy, however, was that the black population in North Carolina was concentrated in the eastern part of the state. Thus, Democrats in the east were compelled to maintain strict control of county government structures to make sure blacks did not gain political power at the local level. At the same time, the Democrats, however, had to convince whites in the west that they owed it to racial solidarity to support these statewide laws that ensured white supremacy in the east, even if it meant limiting western whites' own local political power. In a move that eventually drove these western whites back to the Republican Party, to maintain white supremacy in the east, by 1877 the Democrats reworked the state constitution to put county government and election machinery under the centralized control of the dominant party in Raleigh (presumably the Democrats from that point on). Under this plan, the legislature appointed justices of the peace who in turn appointed county commissioners and election officials. This ensured white rule in eastern counties with large black populations and Democratic control in counties with a strong Republican presence in the west as well, since election officials recorded votes, could bar a voter's registration almost at will, and might fail to notice a Republican ballot box fall off the back of a wagon. In addition, the Democrats—while cutting taxes and appropriations, segregating the public school system, and prohibiting marriage between blacks and whites—also gerrymandered the infamous "black second" congressional district to isolate the majority of black votes within one congressional district.[3]

Even though the Democrats secured local white supremacy in the east and control over elections with these measures, as just indicated, this centralized partisan control quickly infuriated many western North Carolinians, who returned to the Republican Party after 1876. This new county government system also irked many farmers because local politics thereafter was often coordinated by a group of regular party loyalists and appointees who comprised "town hall" or "court house rings." Thus, while the new county government system and election laws ensured white supremacy in the east, it

solidified Republican loyalty in many western counties and further aggra-
vated urban/rural tensions.

While the Republicans remained a constant threat to Democratic rule,
North Carolina proved fairly resistant to the Greenback, Union-Labor, and
Prohibition parties that popped up across the country in the 1870s and
1880s. This was largely because the Republicans provided a legitimate party
of protest and, moreover, would-be third-party advocates feared splitting
the white vote.

The main struggle for the Democratic Party was to maintain party unity
under the banner of white supremacy. By 1890 two major factions had, however, emerged within the state Democracy: the probusiness or conservative
wing that galvanized around Senator Matthew W. Ransom and the "reform"
wing attached to Governor and then Senator Zebulon Vance.[4]

The conservative, probusiness Ransom wing, which held sway in state matters through most of the 1880s, spoke for two groups of conservatives held
together by a common commitment to noninterventionist government. A
first group included older-generation fiscal minimalists. Sometimes called
"mummies," "Bourbons," or "fossils" because their influence was growing
smaller by the 1880s, this group of conservatives still made waves in the party
by appealing to visions of a Jeffersonian, agricultural South draped in the
Confederate battle flag. More important to the conservative wing was a
second group of probusiness Democrats who, like the "fossils," advocated
governmental noninterference and fiscal economy, not out of ideological
commitments to Jeffersonianism, but rather because they feared regulation or
changes to the state's tax system might hamper business development or dis-
courage outside investment. Their plan for industrial progress was to create a
political climate hospitable to free enterprise and outside investment; in practical terms they therefore advocated low taxes, minimal regulation, decreased
appropriations, and tax breaks and other incentives for businesses or private
railroads. Important voices for this wing included Samuel A'Court Ashe,
Daniel A. Thompkins, John C. Kilgo, president of Trinity College, Democratic
strategist F. M. Simmons, and stump master Charles Brantley Aycock; its electoral strength was in the Piedmont and in coastal commercial towns. The
conservative Ransom wing also supported the Cleveland or gold-standard
wing of the national party that touted strict, laissez faire capitalism and a low
or nonexistent tariff. The wing also held firm to white supremacy.[5]

Opposing the Ransom wing was a coalition of urban and rural reformers,
including members of the Farmers' Alliance, that comprised the "reform"
wing of the party. Although this wing was also committed to industrial
progress and laissez-faire economics, it did not want progress in the indus-

trial sector to be purchased at the expense of the agricultural sector or the well-being of workers. The reform wing therefore advocated an even playing field for all economic competitors—manufacturing, commercial, and agricultural. Guided by the need for economic harmony, reform Democrats believed that for business to succeed, agriculture, too, had to be strong, and producers needed fair compensation for their labor. All sectors working together in harmony, they argued, would provide a healthy, prosperous business environment and stave off the threat of "class war" or unionization.

Specifically, creating an even playing field meant curbing the abuses by businesses on the one hand and extending economic opportunity to farmers and laborers on the other. Tapping into common-man, antielitist, anti–Wall Street rhetoric, the reform wing thus attacked the unfair advantage the state's tax structure gave certain industries and decried the exploitation of farmers and workers. The reform wing especially abhorred the undue influence railroads had in government and thus favored government regulation in order to ensure fair rates and to put an end to the bribes and perks railroads paid to their "hired help" in the legislature. Hoping to open more individual economic opportunity by increasing the money supply, the reform wing also adopted soft money measures such as free silver, and it opposed the national banking system. The wing furthermore wanted to increase appropriations to public schools and the university system, since education evened the economic playing field and helped produce wealth. By the late 1890s it also supported child labor regulation and other labor reforms as well as the demands of the Farmers' Alliance. The reform wing, however, stopped short of any reform, such as fiat money or government ownership of railroads, telephones, and telegraphs, that smacked of "paternalism."

As the reform wing gained power through the late 1880s, its leaders reflected a new generation of Democrats poised to take control of the party in the 1890s. Backed by the strong grassroots support of farmers and reveling in the personal popularity of their figurehead, Zebulon Vance, leaders such as Josephus Daniels, editor of the *State Chronicle* in the 1880s and the *News and Observer* in the 1890s, state supreme court Judge Walter Clark, and the leaders of the state university and the Farmers' Alliance (most important, S. B. Alexander and L. L. Polk), gained increasing sway in formulating the party's platform and ticket, and after 1896, this wing of the party galvanized around the Bryan or silver wing of the national party.

These reform Democrats, it is important to note, were nevertheless savvy politicians wholly committed to party unity even at the expense of reform, and thus, like the conservative Ransom wing, the reform wing was wholly dedicated to white supremacy. Under the constant fear that the Republican

Party would find a way to drive a wedge into the Democratic Party, the reform wing cooperated with conservatives on electoral tickets and platforms, often supporting measures and candidates opposed to their reform agenda. Furthermore, because state Democrats craved the federal appointments held for most of this period by Republicans, loyalty to the state Democracy also entailed loyalty to a national party desperate for success; hence, reform Democrats also supported conservative goldbug Grover Cleveland for president in 1884, 1888, and 1892. In fact, during the 1898 white supremacy campaign, reform Democrats fought for disfranchisement by arguing that, with the threat of black rule gone, they would be free to advocate their reforms without worrying about splitting the white vote.

Again, what held these two wings together was their absolute commitment to white supremacy and its corollary, party fealty. As a result, by the late 1880s commitment to party for white Democrats was something akin to the unquestioned commitment to clan or church, and this commitment to party superseded any particular legislative agenda. In this spirit, Governor Alfred Scales launched the 1888 campaign by charging his fellow Democrats: "Let everything subserve to this great question. White men must rule. That is the question that rises high above all others."[6]

* * *

Into this political landscape stepped the Alliance. As we saw in the previous chapter, the Alliance believed that at the heart of the farmers' financial crisis was a steady centralization of religious, economic, demographic, and political power enforced by class legislation that had produced a state of tyranny in America's political economy. As political action increasingly got the lion's share of its attention in the late 1880s and early 1890s, under the ideals of nonpartisanship, the Alliance initially attempted to blame all parties equally for this political curse. It is not surprising, however, given the overwhelming predominance of Democrats in the white Alliance, that Alliancefolk usually singled out Republicans for blame.

As had been the case with the Farmers' Association, numerous folks in the Alliance were politically active from its beginning, although many of their political aims early on involved local or, at best, state interests. Centre Alliance in Chatham County, for example, entered the political fray with a whimper in the summer of 1888 when it petitioned the state legislature to restrict bird-hunting. Perhaps evincing its Quaker constituency, again in December of that year Centre Alliance demanded restrictions on bird-hunting and recommended laws against "carrying concealed weapons and [laws] making drunkenness a crime."[7]

With a slightly broader political vision, Polk's Farmers' Association helped to established an Agricultural and Mechanical land grant college in 1887, largely with the help of Democratic progressives such as eventual Populist R. Joseph Peele along with Josephus Daniels, Walter Hines Page, Judge Walter Clark, and Thomas Dixon, Jr.[8] Building on the success of the Agricultural and Mechanical College, in the late 1880s Alliancefolk increasingly petitioned the state legislature to aid the plight of the farmers. Suballiances passed resolutions to bring fiscal economy in the state, lessen the legislative advantages for railroads, introduce some form of prohibition, and end the state's convict lease system, which provided convicts as cheap labor to railroads (for Alliancefolk, this created an unfair labor market). White farmers also demanded a more equitable distribution of the state tax burden, often assaulting tax breaks for railroads and businesses and at other times calling for a poll tax aimed at landless blacks, justified typically by the state's expenditures for black schools. The Alliance also wanted the state Department of Agriculture to regulate commercial fertilizer, and some farmers urged the legislature to establish savings, postal, or real estate-based banks. Although sometimes Alliance farmers sought revisions in the crop lien law, in terms of state-level financial reform, after 1889 they focused on legislating a 6 percent interest cap to help debtors. This interest cap, along with a state railroad commission to set shipping fees and end political corruption by the railroads, became the two main components of the Alliance's state-level reform agenda by 1890.[9]

As Alliance education and the 1889 jute boycott focused attention on national issues, and as economic cooperation, book farming, and state-level legislation often failed to bring relief, by 1890 Alliancefolk also targeted class legislation at the federal level. Hence, they adopted soft money ideas (especially silver), assaulted the national banking system and monopolies, and especially called for federal control of railroads. Downplaying the importance of economic cooperation and marking a growing commitment to direct political action, "XXX" of Whitakers wrote: "Our redemption is to enter the halls of legislation and scourge the rascals out and secure laws that will unfetter us. . . . Freemen whose sires once threw off the yoke should not be enslaved again."[10]

As we can see in "XXX's" thinking, to "scourge the rascals," the Alliance cast legislation such as silver and banking reform as a struggle for individual freedom against the assaults of plutocratic tyranny. Regarding the national banking system, for example, Alliancefolk insisted that, with the present system, a private institution serving the private interests of the "banking class" rather than the federal government itself or "the people," controlled the money supply of the nation. This state of affairs, in turn, constituted a departure from natural economic law and established a state of economic tyranny. That this was done legally furthermore reflected class legislation and thus political tyranny.[11]

In order to stay such tyrannical plutocracy, by 1890, the national financial reform that most excited Alliancefolk was the subtreasury plan, a bill to create government-subsidized warehouses in which farmers could deposit a portion of their crop to hold for better prices. Moreover, farmers could borrow notes from these warehouses, or "subtreasuries," using this stored crop as collateral. Introduced by C. W. Macune at the 1889 annual meeting of the national Farmers' Alliance, the subtreasury system not only provided control over prices but a source of credit to get around the crop lien system. Where other ventures of this sort had failed because of undercapitalization, federal subtreasuries would be backed by the U.S. Treasury. Although this legislation was attacked by its detractors as paternalistic, unconstitutional, or as "class legislation," Alliancefolk replied that such legislation on behalf of farmers was necessary to counterbalance the class legislation enacted by the money power that had knocked the economic system out of kilter in the first place. One Allianceman put it succinctly: "The system is exactly the reverse of centralization."[12]

* * *

Even though it feigned nonpartisan commitment, again, just about all white Alliancefolk understood that political reform was to be accomplished through the white man's party. In order to enact its state and national reforms, the aim of the state Alliance up until 1892 was therefore to work within the reform wing to control the state Democracy and thereby pass state legislation to aid farmers and to send congressional representatives to Washington who would enact soft money reforms. This commitment to the party of Jackson made sense, given that the vast majority of white Alliancefolk were Democrats and that their leaders, including L. L. Polk, were Raleigh insiders and party stalwarts.[13]

That is not to say that the Alliance contained no Republicans, but none were in conspicuous positions of leadership, except within the Colored Alliance, and even its white supervisors were Democrats. This dissociation between white Alliancefolk and the Republican Party in part reflected the Alliance's poor representation in the mountains, and, even though the Alliance was quite strong in such Republican strongholds as Davidson, Montgomery, Guilford, and Forsythe counties, it is unclear whether Alliancefolk there attempted to pass reforms through the Republicans (and these counties yielded very few Populist votes). Aside from these geographical issues, the disparity in policy between the Alliance and the Republican Party gave reason enough for the two entities rarely to cross paths. The Alliance wanted to expand currency, get rid of the national banking system and protective tariff, and, to a certain extent, regulate business, all of which were antithetical to the Republican agenda. Moreover, at the state level, Republicans, when not appealing to business interests, were obsessed with election reform and with changing the county government system, or they were busy just hating the Democrats. In short, the state's Republican leadership and the Alliance spoke different languages and focused on different issues.

The geography and agenda of the Alliance and the Democratic reform wing, however, blended exquisitely. As far as geography went, the Alliance blossomed in the rural Piedmont and eastern areas where the Democratic Party was strongest; thus, most Alliance county organizers and local presidents like W. A. Graham, J. M. Mewborne, Marion Butler, and the firebrands in Edgecombe and Nash were also political leaders closely identified for twenty years with the white man's party. Beyond these geographical and familial connections, the Alliance had a clear ideological affinity with the reform wing of the state Democracy, as Marion Butler pointed out in 1890: "The platform of the Alliance is in harmony with pure Jeffersonian Democracy; and there can be no conflict between the Alliance and the party, save when and where the party is dominated and controlled by corrupt and monopolistic influences."[14] In terms of practical measures, Alliance and reform Democrats (like all good Democrats) favored lower taxes, a lower or nonexistent tariff, and fiscal economy. They also agreed on educational appropriations, railroad regulation, free silver, some kind of change in the national banking system, some form of prohibition, and antimonopoly legislation. Importantly, suballiances rarely questioned the Democrats' centralized county government and election laws and neither did they threaten white supremacy.

Finally, Alliance and reform Democrats shared two common enemies: the Republicans and the Ransom/Cleveland wing of the Democratic Party. Both the Alliance and reform (and not so reformed) Democrats blamed the Republican Party for the nation's economic instability and for the political corruption and tyranny in Washington City. In their eyes, the Republicans authored iniquitous tariff legislation, opposed regulation, and were funded by robber barons. Moreover, Republicans had crafted and continued to support the national banking system, oversaw the contraction of the money supply, and supported the gold standard. Thus, not only did the GOP represent "black Reconstruction rule," but it symbolized northeastern Yankee

greed. The purportedly nonpartisan Alliance never blushed as it implicated
the Republicans in this political and economic iniquity or steered Alliancemen away from the party of Lincoln, which Alliance President Elias Carr
termed "iniquitous" and whose wiles, he believed, threatened to "jeopardize
the white man's party in the state."[15]

Fighting the Republicans was simple enough for reform and Alliance
Democrats; it required absolute commitment to the state and national
Democratic Party. Fighting the Ransom wing, however, was much trickier
and eventually fractured the union between Alliance and non-Alliance
reform Democrats. While reform and Ransom-wing Democrats usually laid
aside ideological differences for the sake of party unity, conservative Democrats worried that Alliance Democrats might jeopardize that unity for the
sake of their principles. Even as early as 1887, the way in which the Alliance
was "religiously" committed to its reform principles worried many conservative and not-so-conservative Democrats. Especially after the Alliance—a
national organization—replaced Polk's homegrown Farmers' Association,
many Democrats worried that "outside leaders" in other parts of the country might try to dictate the voting patterns of Alliance members, turning
North Carolina farmers into a political machine that would weaken their
own wing's sway over the state party or, worse, split the white vote. So while
Ransom Democrats such as Samuel A'Court Ashe and his Raleigh *News and
Observer* gave a warm reception to Polk's Farmers' Association, it wasted little time in assaulting the Alliance. These criticisms caused only a minor rip-
ple in Alliance commitment to the Democratic Party, however, since
reforming Democrats had been subjected to Ashe's barbs before and
regarded them as an affirmation of the verity of their own cause.

As opposed to Democratic conservatives like Ashe, non-Alliance reform
Democrats like Daniels and Vance championed the Alliance openly, though
in private correspondence, many of them, too, expressed concern that the
principles to which the Alliance adhered so dearly might eventually jeopardize Alliancefolks' party fealty. Rather than attacking the Alliance directly,
however, these Democrats worked cautiously behind the scenes to promote
"conservative" leadership in the Alliance.[16]

As would become more evident between 1890 and 1892, Democrats of
both stripes were right to worry; many Alliancefolk did indeed carry a political algebra in their heads that differed significantly from that of non-
Alliance reform Democrats—a different political algebra that did, in fact,
threaten party unity. For while they stood for the same legislative agenda
and tapped into the same antielitist sensibilities, two important factors
divided Alliance and non-Alliance reform Democrats. First, Alliancefolk

were utterly rural; membership required it. Quite simply, urban reform Democrats like Governor T. J. Jarvis and Daniels, who were disqualified from Alliance membership by both profession and urban address, were out of touch with the day-to-day grind of rural poverty. When push came to shove, most non-Alliance reform Democrats, lacking the existential knowledge of the endless cycle of rural poverty, proved unwilling to stand by the farmers if it meant sacrificing party unity. Second, and perhaps most important, reform Democrats lived outside the crucible of Alliance education, a crucible that from 1886 forward, on a week-by-week basis, "iterated and reiterated" reform principles among its members. While most urban reform Democrats held firm to commitments to white supremacy and party loyalty in 1892, many rural Alliance Democrats, living the day-by-day reality of rural poverty, schooled in Alliance political economy, and utterly committed to their order ("Christianity in concentrated form"), were more than willing to put Alliance principle over party.[17]

* * *

Until an open break between Polk and Senator Vance over the subtreasury plan in 1890, these underlying tensions between Alliance and non-Alliance reform Democrats were submerged in the fight against Republicans and the Ransom wing. With their legislative focus on state matters, both Alliance and non-Alliance reform Democrats understood that they needed each other to secure control of the state party in order to enact pressing state legislation that was opposed by the Ransom wing and the Republicans.

The Association and Alliance initially advocated "conservative" action to influence the state legislature with its agenda. This meant that in the 1886 election Polk made no formal calls to influence primaries, though his Farmers' clubs and *The Farmer,* as we have already seen, issued resolutions to the 1887 legislature while Alliance insiders worked with reform Democrats to lobby for and secure the state Agricultural and Mechanical College.[18] Not until the election of 1888 did the Alliance enter the political sphere in full force, joining with the reform wing to place a farmer at the head of the state ticket and to control the 1889 state legislature. That year, however, the Ransom wing, which oversaw the lion's share of federal appointments, vowed to fight Alliance influence in the state party that might jeopardize Cleveland's reelection. The wing therefore openly attacked Polk and other Alliance leaders as "hayseeds" who ought best to leave the business of government to those who knew what they were doing.[19]

Using antielitist themes, Polk, warning that the Alliance would not "be intimidated or frightened by the cry that 'the farmers are going into politics,'" played the Ransom wing perfectly that year, portraying it as a bastion of haughty elitists and greedy town-bred dudes.[20] To avoid the accusation that the Alliance was practicing "partisan politics"—which it was—local Alliances, especially if they contained Republicans, only discussed their involvement in local Democratic primaries after Alliance meetings had officially adjourned. White Alliancefolk thus drew a distinction between Alliance activity and individual, independent political activity. The two entities were connected, however, by principles; individual Alliancemen were independently voting their consciences that reflected Alliance principles.

And, indeed, local Alliancefolk had a great deal of success in nominating farmers in 1888 for the General Assembly, and Alliance President Syd Alexander's prospects for heading the state ticket seemed promising. When it came time to enact "the science of government" at the state Democratic convention in May, however, the Alliance and reform bloc withered in the face of the powerful Ransom machine and its mighty sword of federal appointments. Although reform Democrats put up a stiff fight for Allianceman Alexander, Ransom's "railroad candidate" Daniel Fowle won the gubernatorial nomination on the twenty-third ballot. Moreover, Alliance demands, which stressed a railroad commission, received little attention in the state platform. The only Alliance leader to find his way onto the state ticket was Baptist minister G. W. Sanderlin, candidate for state auditor.

Even though Republicans nominated an Allianceman for governor and offered to end the convict lease system and to provide for road construction, the GOP apparently garnered little Alliance support. For the Alliance, the battle for political influence took place primarily *within* the state Democracy. This commitment to the Democracy was evident as Polk stumped for the Democrats throughout the state after the convention. Samuel A'Court Ashe, in fact, confessed that his nemesis was "a power for Democracy."[21] After Democratic victory in November, however, under strong pressure from the Ransom machine, the party again snubbed the Alliance by thwarting Syd Alexander's bid for the U.S. Senate. To make matters worse, several prominent Alliancemen voted to return Ransom—a goldbug—to the Senate, in exchange for political patronage and privilege.

Because farmers dominated the state's lower house, however, hope ran high that the "farmers legislature" might enact Alliance reforms. Resolutions from local alliances advocating silver, greenbacks, interest caps, lower taxes, and so on, poured into the 1889 General Assembly. One farmer remarked: "Our farmers have been fighting the bagging trust and monopolists of all kinds and they are zealous and enthusiastic in the cause of the Alliance, for they see no other way to be redeemed from their deplorable condition. If the

Farmers' Alliance and our Legislature do not work up something for our good we may as well give up."[22] The lower house did work up a number of Alliance reforms—most important, a bill to set up a state railroad commission. The upper house, however, summarily quashed almost all of the bills. And this, despite Alliance Democrats' willingness to follow party discipline in support of non-Alliance measures, including changes to the state election laws that added byzantine registration requirements aimed at disfranchising blacks. The farmers did pass a few bits of legislation in 1889 such as an end to the convict lease system, but by March, the Alliance had precious little to show for its efforts, and the blame, it seemed, lay with the Ransom machine with its patronage and railroad backing.

* * *

Coming off the heels of this disappointment, the Alliance intensified its commitment to political action, and, as a result, the mid-year elections of 1890 marked a turning point in the political strategy of the Alliance and subsequently its relationship to the Democratic Party. Rather than begging for scraps at the political table as it did in 1888, by 1891 the Alliance was the most powerful political force in North Carolina Democracy; it dominated the 1890 elections and passed the most aggressive reform platform, including a railroad commission, in twenty years of Democratic rule.[23]

Two factors precipitated this more aggressive posture. First, having been snubbed by Ransom Democrats in the 1888 nominating conventions, senate race, and General Assembly of 1889, the state Alliance put in place aggressive measures to obtain Alliance control of local Democratic nominations to ensure Alliance strength and discipline at the convention and in the legislature. Second, in 1889 the Alliance embraced a detailed national political platform. These organizational and disciplinary changes, when coupled with the massive growth of the Alliance, gave the order the ability to take command of the state Democracy but also hardened the division between conservative and Alliance Democrats and strained relations between Alliance and the reform wing, laying the groundwork for the eventual break between the Alliance and reform Democrats in 1892.[24]

Both of these shifts were symbolized by the Alliance "Yardstick." Applying the "Yardstick" involved an Alliance pledge to support only those (Democratic) nominees sworn to uphold the national Alliance's 1889 St. Louis Demands and the usual state demands. The "St. Louis Demands" included government ownership of railroads and railways (replaced by government "regulation" in the Ocala demands a year later), an end to the national banking system and "alien ownership" of public lands ("alien" meaning

both foreigners and corporations), prohibition of speculation on agricultural futures, free silver, an increase in fractional paper currency, and the
centerpiece: the subtreasury plan. State reforms included a railroad commission, 6 percent interest cap, increased appropriations for public education, and congressional support for the subtreasury bill. The Alliance did
not demand that candidates belong to the order; doing so would have made
the Alliance seem too much like a machine and disqualified some of its most
qualified supporters. By using the "Yardstick," however, to elect men who
pledged to support the cause, Syd Alexander spoke for Alliancefolk across
the state when he remarked that farmers would "see that they [Alliance
principles] are enforced, and then 'taffy' and 'love' for the farmers and
laborers will give way for measures of real benefit." Confident in their
Alliance "Yardstick," local Alliances leapt into the fray.

Despite Alliance pledges not to create a third party, conservative Ransom-
wing Democrats did not appreciate this newfound political energy and
assailed Alliance leaders and especially Colonel Polk, now president of the
Southern Alliance. As these conservative Democrats assaulted the Alliance
leadership and as reform Democrats let Alliancemen have the lead in that
wing's agenda, the state party ultimately bifurcated into two new factions:
"Alliance Democrats" (which included non-Alliance reformers like Daniels
and Vance who supported the cause) and "straight-out" Democrats dominated by Ransom conservatives who opposed Alliance control of the party.

Straight-outs not only recognized the real possibility that they were losing control of the state party, but they especially resented having to pledge
to support a set of demands—the "Yardstick"—not of their making. These
demands ran contrary to the concerns of urban business types not only
because they smacked of government intervention but because they seemed
to point the state in a backward direction, threatening to plunge it into rural
lethargy and hayseed idiocy. By supporting such an outlook, straight-out
leaders feared the party might lose many of its most important business
leaders to the Republican Party. They were also concerned that the Alliance's
more general principles, rooted in a national organization that included
Yankees, thirdites, and Republicans, failed to include white supremacy.
Straight-outs thus worried that the Alliance might not only split the white
vote by alienating business-types from the party but might also inaugurate
a third party. Either way, the Alliance threatened to turn the state over to
Radical and black rule.

Although sometimes the straight-outs attacked the Alliance and its platform in general as socialist, paternalistic, backward, and what not, they were
far too aware of the strong, grassroots Democratic support within the

Alliance to engage in a frontal assault that might drive the rank-and-file from the party. Their strategy, then, was to divide Alliance faithful from their leadership, especially Colonel Polk. With unending pursuit, conservatives like Ashe attacked Polk's Civil War record (Polk had been honorably acquitted at a court martial for desertion), joked about Polk's diphtheria cure, and generally cast Polk as a man of vaulting ambition who used the Alliance as a means to sate his appetite for power. Ashe averred that the Alliance president "was a failure as a soldier . . . as a farmer . . . [and] as Commissioner of Agriculture," and when he "went into journalism," he "was a failure at that," too. Ashe concluded, "He was born to failure as his lot and inheritance in life, and it will be so to the end."[25]

Though few Alliancefolk faced the fire that Polk did, at the local level Alliance aspirants for office sometimes faced similar slander by local straight-outs. After the Democratic nominee for Congress in the "black second" fell ill, J. M. "Brother Jimmy" Mewborne became the last-minute Alliance-backed, Democratic candidate. Mewborne then faced charges of having voted for Republican Garfield (who, like Mewborne, was a member of the Disciples of Christ), being a closet Republican, and, in general, being a tempestuous hay-seed not worthy of the office. The treatment Mewborne received in the second district left numerous Alliancefolk there embittered toward the Democratic Party, and that bitterness festered into the coming years.[26]

Such vitriolic attacks by the straight-outs, however, backfired and only strengthened Alliance grit. For Alliancefolk schooled in Protestant marty-rology, these assaults added fuel to the internal fires of righteous anger by justifying the verity of the Alliance cause and by drawing sharper lines between the forces of good and evil.[27] It helped, too, that in most congres-sional districts the Alliance Democrats, once organized, simply outnum-bered and overwhelmed the straight-outs, especially in the east. Overall, Alliance candidates won six of the state's nine Democratic congressional nominations in 1890, and of the remaining three Democratic nominees, only one was a genuine straight-out, and even he, along with the other two moderate straight-out nominees, pledged to support the Alliance planks except for the subtreasury plan or government ownership. In the local con-ventions for the state legislature, most of the eastern and Piedmont rural districts easily fielded Alliance candidates, though straight-outs held most of the urban districts.

While an open and clean break with straight-outs in 1890 helped strengthen Alliance resolve and ultimately Alliance success, again, the adop-tion of a national platform and use of the "Yardstick" strained the relationship between Alliance and non-Alliance reform Democrats. While they battled side by side, as the election year wore on, and even as non-Alliance reform Democrats championed the farmers' concerns in public and acknowledged the necessity of relinquishing leadership of their wing to the order, many of them nevertheless resented Alliance aggressiveness in taking control of the party and expressed disdain for the acrimony the Alliance was generating. Like the straight-outs, reform Democrats worried, too, about the degree to which Alliance Democrats were glued to their principles, since such dedication to principle might threaten party unity and hence white supremacy. At one point, state Democratic Chairman E. Chambers Smith tried to persuade one reform Democrat, who was friendly to the Alliance, to "arrange for barbecues," hoping that some nicely smoked swine flesh might strengthen Alliance support for Democratic unity. In doing so, Smith confided his frustration that "it is difficult . . . to get the Alliances to take an active, square part with the Democrats. They will mostly vote the Democratic ticket, but they seem to oppose, as Alliances, allying themselves squarely with the Democrats."[28]

Even though Alliance and reform Democrats were able to submerge these differences in 1890 in order to maintain a united front against the straight-outs and the Republicans, the campaign to return Zebulon Vance to the Senate that year and in 1891 temporarily split Alliance and non-Alliance reform Democrats and also highlighted this central tension between party loyalty and principle. Vance, as Confederate and Redeemer governor and "friend of the farmer," was undoubtedly the most popular and powerful Democrat in the state. Vance had championed the Alliance since its inception; he was personal friends with Polk and most of the other Alliance leaders, and, in fact, he had introduced the subtreasury bill in the U.S. Senate. Because Vance was up for reelection to the Senate in 1891, the Alliance applied the "Yardstick" to him in the summer of 1890. To its shock, the senator rejected the subtreasury plan as unconstitutional and impractical. In response, *The Progressive Farmer* scathingly editorialized Vance as a traitor for having submitted a bill to the Senate he no longer endorsed. In turn, reform Democrat Josephus Daniels (who supported the subtreasury plan) in his *State Chronicle,* along with the straight-out *News and Observer,* joined forces in excoriating the *Farmer* for dishonoring the state's most honored citizen.[29]

As the battle increasingly pitted Polk against Vance, Alliancefolk themselves divided, with many supporting one or the other and just as many undecided. Alliance and non-Alliance Democrats eventually returned Vance to the Senate after he vaguely pledged to support "financial measures intended to help the farmers," but the debacle marked an open wound between many Alliance leaders and Democratic Party loyalists within and without the Alliance. For Alliancefolk who opposed Vance, no candidate, no matter how beloved, stood above Alliance principles. As representing eternal axioms, originating in the divine mind, these principles stood in judgment over any aspect of Vance's or any other candidate's life. Alliance ideals stood moreover above Vance's image as an icon of the Confederacy and the practical consideration that Vance wielded a great deal of power in the Senate. To those reform Democrats within and without the Alliance who supported Vance, however, such an affront to his honor and his ability, as well as to the unity of the party, was appalling. Vance was the state's most important political leader and revered southern patriot; attacking Vance was akin to attacking not only the party but the South, its codes of honor, and white unity.[30]

Even though the battle over Vance increased the antagonism between some leaders of the Alliance and of the Democratic Party, very few Alliancefolk contemplated third-party action in 1890, even though the powerful Alliance in Kansas had established a state People's Party that summer. While a few firebrands or folks in heavily straight-out areas like Wilmington might have toyed with the idea, most Alliancefolk—even those most disconcerted with the Democratic straight-outs—considered such a notion unthinkable or at least premature.[31]

Yet, even though few Alliancefolk were willing to go as far as the Alliance in Kansas, many were nonetheless willing to indict the Democrats at the *national* level (along with the Republicans) for bringing about a state of tyranny in Washington—a notable shift in Alliance rhetoric. For even though the reform/Alliance wing of the Democratic Party held sway in North Carolina and in many other southern and western states where free silver was popular, the northeastern, goldbug/Cleveland wing still dominated the goals and agenda of the national party. Attacks on the national leadership of the party emerged, therefore, in 1890, and they intensified in 1891 as Congress stalled on the subtreasury plan and rumors that Cleveland would receive the 1892 nomination loomed large. A few North Carolina Alliancefolk even threatened that, if reformers were unable to gain effective leadership of the national party, an open break might be in order. Even though he would run for Congress as a Democrat a few months later, J. M. Mewborne, for example, suggested to Elias Carr in the spring of 1890 that "neither of the two great political parties satisfy me as regarding efforts made in the interest of labor."[32]

Despite these grumblings Mewborne, like most Alliance Democrats in 1890, was ultimately unshakable in his support for the white man's party. Mewborne, though willing to cite the party's faults, recognized that a split between the Alliance and the party of Jackson would limit the Alliance's ability to achieve its political goals. Furthermore, he retained a steadfast familial attachment to the party, writing in one place that the Democrats were the "giant oak of the forest" and the "splashing sparkling whale of the briny deep" in comparison to the Republicans, "the scraggly prickly pear of the desert" and the "slimy tadpole of the stagnant pool."[33] Assuring local Democrats that his order offered no threat to the state Democracy, another Allianceman confessed that, even though, in his suballiance, "attachment to right is stronger than . . . love of a meaningless party name," the "principles" of the Democracy among his fellow Alliancefolk were "inborn, inherited of fathers who received fixed notions of finance and liberty at the hands of that immortal apostle and preserver of equal rights [Andrew Jackson]."[34]

* * *

By November 1890, Alliance, reform, and even straight-out Democrats put their squabbles aside and worked together (with the help of the new 1889 suffrage law) to achieve impressive victories. Democrats won all but one congressional race—the black second—in which African American Henry Cheatham narrowly defeated "Brother Jimmy."

In the state legislature, experienced Alliance and reform Democrats carefully mobilized to hold discipline tight and fend off straight-out attacks. This mobilization and discipline paid off, for when compared even to the most progressive southern Democratic legislatures in the 1890s, the accomplishments of the 1891 "Alliance legislature" were stunning. The centerpiece was a railroad commission (headed by Alliancemen) that had the power to investigate tax evasion, forbid rebates and other favors to legislators, and regulate freight and passenger rates. The legislature also increased appropriations to public schools and the state university and appropriated funds for a Normal and Industrial School for Women (now UNC-Greensboro), an Agricultural and Mechanical school for blacks (North Carolina A&T), a normal school for blacks (Elizabeth City State), and additional school facilities for physically challenged children in Morganton. The legislature moreover passed antitrust legislation against the fertilizer trust and appropriations for a state orphanage and for a state geological survey to attract industry and bolster agriculture, mining, and forestry. Holding firm, however, to governmental minimalism, Alliance Democrats rejected free textbooks and regulations that would ease the working conditions of women and children. Holding firm to white supremacy, Alliance representatives joined their fellow Democrats in rejecting the Australian secret ballot, in better gerrymandering the black second, and in denouncing Henry Cabot Lodge's "Force Bill" that threatened federal intervention to ensure fair elections. Only two

Alliance measures failed to pass: a change to crop lien laws and the imposition of a 6 percent cap on interest rates. Straight-outs joined with Republicans to defeat the latter measure in the state senate.[35]

Despite these two failures, Alliancefolk celebrated their access to state power and pondered what 1892 might bring. One Forsythe County Alliance Democrat concluded: "We did a good thing in the November election; we have only struck the first lick. . . . Keep up our demands for relief until 1892 when, if we are not heeded, we will surprise the natives of this nation by electing such a host of Alliancemen as will make our enemies call for rocks and mountains to fall upon them to hide them from the face of the next president and congress."[36]

6. Crossing the Rubicon:
The Populist Revolt of 1892

For white Alliancefolk in North Carolina, Populism was a revolt against the Democratic Party—a product of the closeness of the Alliance to the white man's party and of increasing and unresolved tensions between the two. Few white Republicans in the mountains and Quaker Belt became Populists; the Alliance never built the strong constituency or political connections with the GOP there that it had with the Democrats in the east. Furthermore, since the Republicans constituted a party of protest against the Democrats in these regions anyway, a new party opposing the Democracy had little practical value locally or nationally. Thus, as far as most whites were concerned, the Populist revolt represented a fratricidal struggle among fellow southerners and Democrats holding to many of the same ideas and yet animated by deep social, cultural, and religious fragmentation. Among black Populists in the east, the decision to side with the third party reflected frustration with the Republican Party and an Alliance vision that whites and blacks could perhaps join together in a struggle against plutocratic greed and tyranny.

Tensions between Alliance and non-Alliance Democrats reached the breaking point in the winter and spring of 1892, when the state Democratic Party required that all delegates to the local and state conventions pledge to support the national ticket regardless of who was at its head. In light of this requirement, Alliancefolk who thought they controlled the state Democracy realized that urban and non-Alliance Democratic reformers would not jeopardize patronage or privilege on behalf of the farming interests. For Baptist and Populist editor J. F. Click, by requiring that individuals pledge blind allegiance to the national party, the Democrats of the state had "reached the point of impudence." He added, "If the would-be leaders of the Democratic Party want to draw the dead-line, we can stand it if they can."[1]

As this "dead-line" was drawn between Alliance reform principles and party fealty, with righteous indignation, Alliancefolk and even some urban reformers likened themselves to Protestant reformers and the patriots in '76 and so formed a third party dedicated to their principles of reform. This elevation of "principle over party" that had for so long kept the Alliance from making "an active, square part with the Democrats," ultimately propelled Populists from the Democratic Party with righteous anger in a prophetic denunciation of the temporal "powers that be." As one Populist fire-brand and Methodist class leader put it: "We . . . are *out* and *out* for our own principles and our own nominees. Call it 3rd or 4th party or what you please—the day of compromise is past. We act from principles and God defends the right. . . . We will sink or swim upon the merit, justice and holiness of our cause."[2]

* * *

It did not take long for the elation over the success of the 1891 Alliance legislature that winter to turn to talk of third-party revolt against the *national* Democratic Party by the summer. While most white Alliancemen and Alliancewomen remained confident that the organization could enact its state demands through the state Democratic Party, this growing dissatisfaction with the national leadership of the Democratic Party stemmed from two issues.

First, Alliancefolk bemoaned the inability of Alliance-backed Democrats in Congress to pass needed reforms. Alliance and reform Democrats had ordered their congressional representatives in 1890 to reverse two decades of Republican dominance in the nation's capitol by passing the subtreasury bill and enacting changes to the nation's monetary and banking structures. Even though Democrats had a majority of 128 in the House, Washington gridlock stultified any such attempts.[3]

Second, as frustration with congressional gridlock set in, by the spring of 1891, it was clear that the national Democratic Party intended to name Grover Cleveland its presidential nominee. Although the Alliance had supported Cleveland in 1888, by 1891 Cleveland was the bane not only of the Alliance but of many southern and silver Democrats for his gold monometallism and his general coziness with the northeastern commercial establishment. While a few Alliancefolk supported Cleveland as a "friend of the farmer," many boldly threatened to bolt the party if "King Grover" received the nomination. One Alliance Democrat confided that "Mr. Cleveland must

be shelved. . . . I am opposed to a third party, but if Cleveland is nominated
. . . then I am for a third party."[4]

This animosity toward Cleveland and the national leadership of the
Democratic Party revealed a few subtle shifts in the outlook of the order.
First and most basically, many Alliancefolk increasingly believed that the
Democratic Party's national leadership was captive to the same forces of
tyranny and centralization that had already infected and destroyed the
Republicans. Although these tropes of centralization had long been present,
Alliance Democrats increasingly indicted the national leadership of both
parties as equally iniquitous. "Let us . . . stop so much talk about Democratic
and Republican Parties," announced one Allianceman; "the Alliance was
established to remedy the rottenness of both."[5]

Moreover, their denunciations of Cleveland illustrated Alliancefolks'
dismissal of the tariff as a critical issue and furthermore revealed their
growing support for silver, for even though the Association and Alliance
had always supported free silver, the issue came to the fore in the early
1890s and eventually overshadowed the subtreasury plan. Not only did
numerous farmers believe the reform would bring needed relief by increasing the money supply, but as attention turned toward the national election
of 1892, free silver appeared to be an issue on which southerners and westerners could unite in order, initially, to wrest control of the national Democratic Party from the Northeast and then eventually to mount a third-party
assault.[6]

In addition, in 1891, the Alliance, at both the national and state levels, continued to strengthen the political education and mobilization program it
had begun two years earlier. As Polk and other Alliance leaders in Washington continued their lobbying efforts and nationwide speaking tours, they
also centralized the dissemination of Alliance information and education
by forming national and state press associations and by inaugurating a
national lecture series that brought Polk, Texan Ben Terrell, Georgian Tom
Watson, and Kansas Populist "Sockless" Jerry Simpson to large Alliance
rallies in the winter and summer of 1891. Too, although the North Carolina
Alliance had already divided its lecture circuit along congressional bound-
ary lines, at Polk's insistence this became the norm for the country. By
organizing the Alliance along congressional district boundaries, overseen
by district lecturers embarked on a new campaign to educate Alliancefolk
on how to play party politics, Polk helped position the Alliance to control
congressional nominating conventions nationwide in 1892. Alliance rallies,
picnics, and mass meetings organized along congressional district boundaries could not mask their political intentions.

In North Carolina, the Alliance also made clandestine efforts to mobilize black political support by enlisting the help of Rev. Walter A. Patillo to work among members of the Colored Alliance. Many members of the Colored Alliance in the second district, it appeared, had abandoned the Republican Party in the congressional race of 1890 to vote for Allianceman J. M. Mewborne. White Alliancefolk therefore hoped that, with black support, they could win a congressional seat for an Allianceman in the second district in 1892. To the alarm of local Democrats, in 1891 the Colored Alliance agreed to vote for any party, including the People's Party, that supported Alliance demands.[7]

Even though few Alliancefolk threatened third-party action in early 1891, Democrats continued to fear the Alliance would go that route, and those fears intensified after the inauguration of the national People's Party in Cincinnati in May of that year. Although the Farmers' Alliance had a leadership role in the inauguration of the third party, conspicuously absent from this Cincinnati meeting were both southern delegates (only Texas, Alabama, and Arkansas were represented) and Colonel Polk himself. For even though Polk was suggesting support for a national third-party ticket among friends, open advocacy for the third party not only jeopardized the Alliance's nonpartisan outlook but also its relationship to the state Democratic Party. In public, therefore, Polk reported that he "neither advocated nor opposed a third party movement."[8]

The difficulty for Polk and other southern Alliancefolk was that the birth of the People's Party brought the problems of loyalty to party and race, as well as to the Alliance's nonpartisan commitment, squarely into the open. Southern Alliancefolk, while generally despising Cleveland and Harrison alike, recognized that schism in the Democratic Party made the possibility of black or Republican rule in state matters all too real, and many also realized the potential futility of enacting national reform without the infrastructure of the old parties. Thus, while many Alliancefolk might have been ready to support a national Populist ticket, they had yet to work out the implications of such a move for state politics. Most Alliance leaders and moderate Democrats still hoped the national Democratic Party would exercise good judgment and steer away from Cleveland to preserve the relationship between the party and the Alliance that had succeeded so well in the election of 1890.[9]

While leaders like Polk, Carr, and newly elected state Alliance President Marion Butler exercised caution, in the spring and summer of 1891 talk of national third-party action nevertheless raced through suballiances and local Alliance papers in response to the Cincinnati meeting and more general concerns about the leadership of the national Democratic Party, which brought on the typical—though especially escalated—war of words between more radical Alliancefolk and conservative Democratic leaders. Most white Alliancefolk, though, would still have agreed with J. F. Click of the *Hickory Mercury,* who, on the eve of the election year, laid out his hope of working through the Democratic Party in contractual terms: "The Democratic Party of North Carolina rests under moral and political obligations to . . . secure, in good faith, the incorporation of the Alliance principles of the state platform into the national platform of the Democratic Party in 1892." He then warned: "The people are watching as well as praying and intend that they shall be honestly dealt with. Our leaders are not bosses, but the people are, and their wishes must be obeyed. They bear the burdens of government, and will, at the next Presidential election, if it is made necessary to the preservation of their sovereignty, repudiate even the Democratic Party at the polls. If the Democratic Party would reign, it must deal in good faith with the people, standing steadfastly by principle and adhering strictly to its promises. *Vox populi vox Dei.*"[10]

* * *

The Democrats decided they would reign—with or without the help of the Alliance—once, in February 1892, the People's Party, in St. Louis, put forth its platform and planned a nominating convention that July in Omaha. As projected at the Cincinnati convention nine months earlier, representatives of numerous reform organizations met in St. Louis on 22 February 1892 to put together the political strategy and platform that they hoped would cull out the "reform elements" in all the national parties into a single political party. As opposed to the situation in Cincinnati, the Alliance took command of the meeting, and Marion Butler led a large delegation of Alliancemen from North Carolina. The convention adopted in its platform the basic reform agenda the Alliance had been pushing for several years: government ownership of railroads and communications, the abolition of the national banking system, an end to "alien" land ownership, and legislation aimed at increasing the money supply, including free silver and the subtreasury plan. It also supported a graduated income tax and various labor planks.

Beyond its platform, however, this "Second Declaration of Independence," or "St. Louis Platform," represented a stark departure from the platforms of the Democratic and Republican parties not so much in its demands but in its sense of crisis and political purpose. More than simply proposing a legislative agenda, the document, penned by Minnesota Populist Ignatius Donnelly, was a clarion call for true reformers to cling to principle and bolt the two old parties in order to preserve American democracy. For after "invoking upon its action the blessing and protection of Almighty God," the preamble to the Declaration, which comprised a full two-thirds of the document, announced: "We meet in the midst of a nation brought to the verge of moral, political, and material ruin." As opposed to the Democrats who attacked certain political ideas and policies of the Republican Party, the St. Louis Platform blamed this impending ruin on both of the two old parties. Waxing apocalyptic, the "Second Declaration" identified a "vast conspiracy against mankind" intent on "the destruction of civilization, or the establishment of absolute despotism." Meeting on George Washington's birthday, this restorationist document sought "to restore the government of the republic to the hands of the 'plain people,' with whom it originated."[11]

While state Alliance President Marion Butler and many other Alliance leaders exercised caution regarding the St. Louis Platform, Polk, goaded on by many Alliancefolk and friends, ignored the order's nonpartisan stance and urged North Carolina suballiances to ratify the St. Louis demands and support a *national* Populist ticket. Thomas Dixon, for example, wrote to his old friend, "I'm convinced you should strike *now* the death blow to *the old* parties. Give it to them between the eyes. Make your plans well and strike to kill when you do strike. They are both rotten and now is a good time to begin the funeral."[12]

As more cautious Alliance leaders pondered their next moves, both reform and conservative Democratic leaders determined that the Alliance would not push the state nominating convention toward support for a national third-party candidate and thereby forsake national patronage and privilege. Thus, the state Democratic Committee, under the leadership of reform Chairman E. Chambers Smith, barred anyone who would not pledge to support the national Democratic ticket from local nominating conventions, though, as would soon become apparent, Smith was willing, nevertheless, to let the Alliance set the party's state agenda.[13]

Even though Polk, state President Marion Butler, and other key Alliance leaders in North Carolina still wanted to find some way to work with the *state* Democratic Party, "Smith's dictum," as it came to be known, set off a firestorm of protest against the state party and provoked the first major Populist exodus from the white man's party in March and April. Using the mental rubric of tyranny and centralization that Alliancefolk had applied for five years to monopolists, plutocrats, Romanists, and the two national parties, W. R. Lindsey, the first state chairman of the People's Party, wrote: "Nothing is made plainer than the naked tyranny of this rule ["Smith's dictum"]. . . . A man on entering a political convention, there sells out, body and soul. He has lost his identity as a thinking, rational and moral

being and has become a part of a machine. He has surrendered his conscience . . . his sense of right and justice . . . his country and patriotism. He
has surrendered all things which go up to make a free man. . . . This, if [it is]
not destruction of liberty, soon will be."

Comparing Chairman Smith's tyranny to that of "the Pope of Rome" and
adding that "we see the fiery tongue of the serpent here," Lindsey echoed the
sentiments of Baptists who believed they were not the free men their fathers
were: "We verily thought that political conventions were deliberative bodies. . . . You [the Democracy] spit upon the very first principle of democracy
which you pretend to value so highly. Your conventions then are not to voice
the will of the people but the will of a few dictators." Pulling deeply from
commonsense and democratic ideals, Lindsey concluded:

> Whatever of civil rights and of Republican liberty we have left is due to those
> voters who have not sold out, body and soul, to any party. It is high time that
> the people smash these fetters of the party bosses and every man stand out
> open and unshackled on his own individuality. . . . What is a Democrat? It is
> one who is willing for the majority to rule. It takes in every man, white or
> black, or all political opinions, and whatever this majority may say is the guide
> of action for every man, so far as his individual judgment and conscience will
> permit. This is true Jeffersonian Democracy. It prescribes no man on account
> of his opinions. It binds no man's individual conscience or judgement.[14]

As Alliancefolk like Lindsey and a few other urban reformers began their
revolt against the Democratic despots, as reflected in the St. Louis Platform,
their general concern about centralization sharpened into an acute sense
that they were experiencing a crisis of democracy with apocalyptic consequences. This sense of crisis, rooted in patriotic millennialism, accounts for
the eschatological fervor with which Populists attacked the Democratic
"heathens" who worshipped the man-made idols of party rather than the
eternal principles of God. One Populist, for example, wrote that the third
party's platform "embodies the essential principles of democracy and in
them is found the only hope for a dying republic." Attacking the "two
headed dragon" of plutocracy, another Populist warned that, under its
tyranny, "the tree of liberty will wither" and the "light of Christian progress
and civilization will be darkened." Regarding the coming election, he
warned: "On this conflict rests the hopes of the world. Let victory be gained
and all will be gained—hope, home, freedom, Christian integrity and happy
country. Let the battle be lost and all will be lost."[15]

As they anathematized the Democratic Party at all levels, Populists
charged that the old party had departed the principles of Jefferson and Jack-

son, and this charge revealed the central rationale for Populist revolt: reform required a new party to embody the principles necessary to bring the nation's political economy back under God's governance. Populism was thus a restorationist movement. As Marion Butler articulated on the eve of the election: "When a party no longer represents the principles you believe in it is your duty to leave that Party," since "principles are eternal" and "parties are but a means for securing these principles." Drawing even more on evangelical imagery, another farmer wrote: "The Old Democratic party must be regenerated—born again, with a new set of nurses on board and christened the People's Party."[16]

In rejecting the Democratic Party's immediate past, the People's Party hearkened to the undying principles evident in an older time—principles it hoped to reassert in the present. As a restorationist movement, therefore, the People's Party was neither reactionary nor progressive. Older bourbon reactionaries were a dying breed in North Carolina and consistently proved to be the Alliance's harshest critics. The adjective "progressive" could best have been applied to urban Republicans as well as to both probusiness Democrats who championed a road to progress paved by unregulated growth in industry, transportation, and commerce, and reform Democrats who linked progress to improving the educational, economic, and social advancement of the common folk within the confines of white supremacy and fiscal economy.

So while the Populists supported mostly the same progressive reform agenda and laissez-faire economic liberalism that reform Democrats did, in outlook and attitude, in the ways they made decisions regarding candidates and in their sense of democratic crisis, they were worlds apart. Reform Democrats held firm not only to white supremacy but to ideals of political expediency, including the necessity of being linked to the national party in order to sustain national influence and enjoy the fruits of patronage. They moreover found the Populists' sense of impending doom a limitless source for scorn and ridicule.[17] So even though both the Populists and reform Democrats wanted to change society so that it might better embrace the twentieth century, reform Democrats and other southern progressives found their salvation in looking forward while clinging to the old yoke of white supremacy. Populists, however, found their hope in looking backward while disregarding the specter of "Negro rule." The bottom line was that Populists, believing that implementing God's axioms was the only way to secure harmony in the political economy, placed principles of love, democracy, commonsense, liberal economics, and patriotic millennialism above party. As one Populist wrote, "*Cowards vote of Party, but it takes men of moral courage to vote for principles, independent of party.*" Drawing a firm line between the forces of right and the forces of evil, another Allianceman wrote, "No man can serve two masters. . . . He who is not for us is against us." Never given to "mob" action, as members of a political party, Populists aimed to secure these principles with the "the white-winged ballot"—the means by which God could speak to the problems the farmers faced.[18]

*   *   *

By May, on the eve of the state Democratic convention, not all Alliance Democrats were ready to charge the gates of hell. Even Polk, who would likely head the Populists' national ticket, wavered in advocating a state People's Party ticket despite his and the *Farmer*'s support for the national third party. While Alliancefolk like Polk hesitated, others wanted to delay third-party action or opposed it outright. Elias Carr, for one, cited party loyalty as the primary reason for rejecting the third party: "I am an Allianceman now and forever but not a third party man by any means," he wrote to Polk.[19] While fear of black and Republican rule in North Carolina always lurked behind cries of Democratic loyalty, other Alliance Democrats believed that only an established party like the Democrats could enact Alliance demands. Some Alliancefolk worried that Alliance withdrawal from the Democracy would turn the party over to the Ransom wing. Still others strove to keep the Farmers' Alliance and People's Party separate entities, arguing that only a nonpolitical organization like the Alliance could rid the Democratic Party of corruption so that it could enact reform, while some Alliancefolk believed that the disharmony the People's Party brought to the Alliance was evidence enough of its diabolical origins.

In response to those who considered insurgency rash, imprudent, and ultimately counterproductive to the aims of the Alliance, third-party supporters argued that by leaving the Democrats, the party of Jackson would flounder and its conservative elements merge with the Republican Party. As the two old parties would thus unite as an "Aristocratic Party" or "the Plutes," the reform elements would form the party of the masses and prove victorious by uniting the West and South against the corrupt East.[20]

As the campaign year wore on, and especially after state Alliance President Butler converted to Populism in August, the majority of these loyal Democratic Alliancefolk, hearts heavy, left the order, pointing out that third-party advocates had essentially assumed control. Especially for those Alliance Democrats who were in deep sympathy with the aims of the Populists, the elision of the Alliance with the third party caused deep despair.[21]

A few Democrats nevertheless remained in the Alliance, most hoping to strengthen the reform presence in their party. Alliance State Business Agent and South Fork Baptist Association President W. A. Graham was one. Graham sympathized with the Populists and even refused to stump for the Democrats where his Baptist and Populist friends, whom he considered the "best men" of their counties, were running for office. The Lincoln County patriarch considered third-party politics futile, however, believing that the Populists could never win national office and hence the Democrats remained the best choice for enacting Alliance demands.[22]

There was no such division, however, on the part of straight-out Democrats. Immediately after the first mass meetings in March initiated the People's Party, both reform- and Ransom-wing straight-outs alike, including ardent Alliance advocates like Josephus Daniels, blistered Polk along with third-party bolters for betraying their race and state. At the local level, Alliancefolk with third-party leanings believed the Democrats hoped to "exterminate" the Alliance by barring members from local conventions. One Alliance Democrat in the second district reported that Republicans were similarly barring members of the Colored Alliance from local nominating conventions since many vowed political independence.[23]

After this initial assault, however, non-Alliance Democrats came to their senses and, realizing the real threat of widespread defection, were ready to make broad concessions to the Alliance to ensure stability and support for the national ticket. And concede they did: the Alliance dominated every aspect of the 1892 state convention that May. Former Alliance president Elias Carr easily won the gubernatorial nomination, and in terms of specific demands, the Democrats essentially duplicated the platform the Alliance had so vigorously supported in 1890. Even though the convention pledged to support the national ticket, confidence was high that Alliance Democrats could thwart Cleveland's nomination and put forth a reform platform. State Alliance President Butler, for one, was convinced the national Democratic Party would not be so foolish as to alienate the South with a Cleveland nomination.[24] In terms of actual policy, the state Democratic Party and Populist Party platforms differed little. Their main difference was at the level of the sacred. Populists spoke of an immanent crisis in democracy while Democrats feared a crisis in white supremacy.

The willingness of the state Democracy to placate the Alliance was a temporary blow to third-party organizers. After *The Progressive Farmer* endorsed the state Democratic ticket, all seemed well, at least at the state level, for unity between the Democracy and the Alliance.[25] This unity, however, like Colonel Polk, was not long for this world. In late May, to the surprise of everyone, including the editors of *The Progressive Farmer* themselves, Polk boldly pledged loyalty to the People's Party and resigned the

Farmer as state organ for the Alliance so that it could advocate the People's Party without damaging the Alliance's nonpartisan commitment.[26] The uproar over Polk's move had hardly begun, however, when the great agrarian reformer succumbed suddenly to a ruptured tumor in his bladder and passed away on 11 June. Shortly afterward the *Farmer* returned as the state Alliance organ, and peace again reigned until the national Democratic convention in early July. Not only did Cleveland receive the Democratic nomination, but the national platform opposed free silver and completely disregarded the subtreasury and other Alliance demands.

Even for many of the most partisan Alliance Democrats, this pill was too much to swallow, and a second Populist exodus from the state Democracy followed. One Pitt County Allianceman wrote: "We had hoped no People's Party ticket would be put in the field for state and county tickets, but from the present denunciatory attitude of some who would like to be considered Democratic bosses—it seems inevitable." "Brother Jimmy," likewise a late convert to Populism, stated: "I did have hope that these [reforms] could be obtained through the Democratic Party, but since that body has met and presented its nominees, and last and least its platform, every vestige of hope vanished from me."[27]

While state Alliance President Butler voiced utter disgust for Cleveland's nomination and attempted for a month or so to put together a cooperative arrangement between the state Democratic and national Populist tickets, he, too, eventually became a Populist and thus severed what "formal" ties remained between the Alliance and the Democratic Party. Although he had no official position in the party, as president of the state Alliance, Butler quickly became the Populists' most important leader as he helped mold a powerful third-party presence in the Cape Fear region. His star on the rise, Butler was poised to control the Southern Alliance and Populist Party, becoming national Alliance president in 1893, a Populist senator in 1895, and president of the national party in 1896.[28]

* * *

As Populists accused Alliance Democrats of putting loyalty to party over loyalty to principle, both sides were well aware that loyalty to the Democratic Party also entailed loyalty to the white race. Though few Populists would vocalize such a radical position, state Populist President W. R. Lindsey regarded the Democrats' fear of "Negro supremacy and radical rule" ridiculous, asking, "Are we not all under bondage to certain capitalistic tyranny, passed and voted upon and now sustained by both parties alike?" Noting then that "white and black alike are now under the same bondage," he added, "we don't intend to crouch under the party lash."[29]

Lindsey was right to point out that behind all the rhetorical posturing between Democrats and Populists loomed the "party lash" of race, for as soon as the People's Party formed and especially after it put forth a state ticket in August, Democrats labeled Populists traitors to the white race who threatened to split the white vote and thus pave the way for black or Republican rule. After Edgecombe County Populists put two blacks on the local ticket, the editor of the local Democratic paper's response was typical: "Come out white-men come out. The civilization of whiteman must not be scotched. . . . No Negro leaders no black domination. Come out, come out."[30]

In response to such charges, many Populists like Lindsey derided the Democrats for emphasizing issues of race rather than the more pressing concerns of financial reform, and they couched their assaults within a number of rhetorical strategies. One was to attack the Democrats themselves as too cozy with blacks, pointing out the Democrats' penchant for seeking or buying black votes and reminding Democrats of Grover Cleveland's black appointments. Other Populists argued that blacks would never gain a majority in the state, noting that Democratic gerrymandering, centralized control, and black "docility" in general prevented this supposed menace. Still other Populists argued that Democrats would themselves split the white vote by supporting Cleveland. Populists additionally urged voters to dismiss appeals to the "bloody shirt," believing they had no relevance.[31]

As their rhetoric indicates, Populists, like Alliancefolk, displayed a full range of racial attitudes. On the one extreme, some demonstrated outright disgust in leaving the party of white supremacy and did so only out of passionate loyalty to Alliance principles.[32] On the other hand, some whites openly called for blacks to join them in procuring needed relief and in removing the Democrats from power. For some of these whites, issues of class superseded those of race. One Populist from the east wrote: "What is good for the white laborer in the South is equally as good for the colored laborer, and why should they not vote the same way. . . . As long as the toiling masses remain divided because of appeals to race prejudice and party line, so long will they be at the mercy of organized capital."[33]

Most white Populists, though, probably considered appeals to black voters a matter of expediency; nevertheless, whatever the reason given, and despite their ambivalence toward social equality with blacks, to their credit, white Populists willingly set aside categories of race and disregarded what for most of their fellow Democratic southerners was a cardinal axiom—

white supremacy. J. F. Click wrote in his *Hickory Mercury* that the "smallest *nothing* God ever made, is the man who believes his principles are right in the sight of God and man . . . and says he is afraid such a thing, put into practice, would put God's people under Negro rule." Another ridiculed the Democrat who will "swear that white supremacy overshadows all else" and therefore "shut his eyes and vote his children into slavery more galling than any Negro ever suffered."[34]

This commitment to overturn the category of race attests to Populists' utter commitment to the principles on which their movement was founded. In dedication to these principles, Populists faced rotten eggs, slander, and even physical threats. When Harnett County Baptist minister, educator, and county superintendent of education J. A. Campbell voted Populist in 1898, a local paper ominously warned him: "He who was not for white supremacy [in the 1898 election], was for Negro domination, and he who favors Negro rule is not the man to fashion or mold the minds and characters of the youth of the country. Our people generally are determined that those who allied themselves with the enemies of white supremacy in the late election feel the terrible weight of their hand of retribution."[35] By the same token, their unwillingness to part with commitments to white supremacy caused many Alliancefolk to resist third-party insurgency.[36]

Race in the campaign of 1892 was more than a rhetorical, cultural, and intellectual issue, however, for to the surprise of Republicans and to the consternation of Democrats, blacks gave massive support, especially in the east, to the Populist ticket. Because most historians have relied on county rather than precinct returns in assessing Populist voting patterns, they have often overlooked this high level of black support, since resistance to Populism among blacks and other Republicans in urban precincts obscured these high levels of rural black support. In rural precincts, black Republican support for Populism in 1892 was in many cases unanimous. In addition to voting the ticket, blacks sometimes furthermore took roles in county organization and in mobilizing black voters. Some counties placed blacks on ballots, and blacks were present at Populist rallies and in local Populist nominating conventions at the invitation of white leaders. In short, we must understand the Populist revolt in North Carolina as a biracial movement.[37]

The reality of black support, however, raises a number of critical yet unanswerable questions. While the motivations of white Populists in enlisting black support were mixed, assessing what motivated blacks to bolt the Republican Party in favor of Populism remains elusive, since, beyond a few scattered comments in white newspapers, virtually no records exist indicating black

Populists' reasoning. From white accounts, though, three factors appear to have motivated black voters.

First, the third party offered the real possibility of casting the hated Democrats out of office and thus securing election reform. Populism was thus a means to an end.[38]

Second, the Republican Party was itself divided between "lily white" reformers who supported silver and hoped to attract poor whites into the party and "black-and-tan" probusiness stalwarts who hoped to build the Piedmont into an industrial empire with the help of black voters in the east. Blacks, too, divided in their support of these two wings. Those urban or middle-class blacks who believed upper-class whites were their best friends allied themselves with black-and-tan stalwarts to secure protection against the violence of "poor whites." Others blacks, including those in the Colored Alliance, believed an even economic playing field and fair elections were the means to racial uplift and so, oddly enough, sided with the lily-white faction. After the black-and-tan faction gained control of the party in 1892, many rural blacks joined whites in the lily-white faction to support the People's ticket as a protest against the black-and-tan faction. During and after the election, in fact, the lily-white faction supported silver and urged fusion with the Populists.[39]

Third, the Colored Alliance appears to have lent its support to the People's Party because of its reform principles and especially silver. As mentioned earlier, in 1890, some black Alliancefolk bolted the Republican Party to support Alliance Democrats. Moreover, Colored Alliance leaders like Reverend Patillo had been working within the Colored Alliance to procure black political support for Alliance demands through the Democratic Party, and as early as 1890 the Colored Alliance had vowed to take independent political action in order to secure reform if the two old parties rejected Alliance demands. In a few instances, black Alliancemen made it clear that they had voted the People's ticket out of dedication to principle. In Bertie County, for example, according to one white Populist, "good, honest colored men" in his township "came into our convention and pledged to vote with us from township constable to the President of the United States purely on the ground of our principles" in order to "redeem our once free and happy country from the grasp of plutocracy." In Halifax, one black, lifelong Republican vowed no longer to bow to the "party lash" and to vote, rather, only for silver candidates.[40]

White Populists responded to this black support with the same ambivalence they showed toward Democratic assaults on their loyalty to race. While many Populists embraced a biracial coalition with genuine excitement, others found the prospect repulsive.[41] Again, most Populists probably followed Marion Butler in seeing the coalition as a matter of expediency. Butler, for example, favored whatever means necessary to secure Populist victory; if it meant securing black votes, then so be it. Butler, however, usually opposed placing blacks on local ballots, since it might have alienated more white voters statewide than it secured in one county.[42]

Beyond this typical ambivalence, the most significant reaction to black voting by white Populist leaders was to ignore it. Page after page of Populist correspondence and Populist newsprint discussed the ebb and flow of Populist success as if this massive black voting bloc never existed. Perhaps these Populists, like many of their historians, were simply unaware of the numbers. Perhaps they were aware but chose not to advertise the fact in order to avoid more Democratic condemnation. Either way, white Populist leaders across the board wholly ignored black voters and paid dearly for it in 1896 and 1898. In 1896, by engineering fusion agreements with the Democrats, Populists turned their backs on black supporters and drove most of them back to the Republican Party. In 1898, when the Democrats made a violent frontal assault on both black and white Populists, white Populist leaders were caught off guard and had neither the time nor ability to construct a biracial coalition capable of withstanding the charge.

If blacks left little written record of their Populist involvement, they nevertheless found a voice with their votes. In the first and second districts, where the majority of black counties were, black voters left the Republican Party and voted the People's ticket en masse. In Wilson County, for example, black Republicans in three townships threw unanimous support behind the Populist ticket in 1892. In Hyde County, black Republicans in four of five townships voted unanimously for the People's Party that year, constituting at least 60 percent of the county's Populist votes. The same patterns occurred in townships in Edgecombe, Johnston, and Nash counties in the east.[43] Even toward the west, in Chatham County—the only county to give Populists an actual majority in 1892—blacks again voted the People's ticket in huge numbers.[44] In looking at these returns, it becomes clear that without this silent black vote, the North Carolina People's Party would have amounted to merely a blip on the political scene, as it did in Virginia and South Carolina. Butler, whose *Caucasian* masthead read "Pure Democracy and White Supremacy," owed his high place among Populist leaders to black support.

* * *

The electoral battle that erupted after the Populist state convention in August was the most divisive North Carolinians had seen in years. Newly elected state Democratic Chairman F. M. Simmons reported that opposition to the Democracy "had assumed the form of a craze."[45] Religious papers warned partisan church members to stop consigning each other to hell and worried openly that the election would dampen evangelical ardor and inflame partisan hatred to the point that it would rend churches asunder.

While the Democrats hollered white supremacy, Populists expressed their true manhood and womanhood in a religious frenzy of support for their new party, prophesying wide margins of victory. Although Populists never lacked confidence and ardor, a number of factors nevertheless hampered their path to the white city. Perhaps, most important, the Republicans, under the leadership of the anti-Populist business or black-and-tan faction, put forth a state ticket that split the anti-Democratic vote. Populists were further hampered by rumors that they supported a clandestine vigilante group called "Gideon's Band." To make matters worse, the Populist presidential and gubernatorial candidates were less than ideal. Presidential candidate James B. Weaver, a Union general and former Greenbacker, was unpopular in the South to begin with, and his decision to tour the state with radical Populist and suffragist Mary Lease helped seal his doom among conservative Democrats. The Populists' gubernatorial candidate, Goldsboro physician W. P. Exum, quickly became a liability as well for his use of profanity on the campaign trail (for which he was once arrested), for his half-hearted commitment to the party, and for wounding Democratic stump speaker extraordinaire C. B. Aycock with a knife following a heated debate.[46]

Despite these setbacks, Populists maintained their vaulting sense of confidence into November. Victory, however, went to Carr and Cleveland. The final—and highly contested—results of the 1892 election were 135,519 for Carr (127,763 for Cleveland), 94,684 for Republican gubernatorial candidate D. M. Furches, and 47,840 for Exum. The Populists elected three state senators and eleven state representatives.

In assessing voting patterns in the 1892 election, Populists found strength in the first, second, third, and fourth districts in the east and in western foothill counties like Catawba, Lincoln, and Cleveland. Populists, however, drew few votes in traditional Republican strongholds like the Quaker Belt and mountains, demonstrating the party held little appeal for white Piedmont Republicans.[47] Besides the evidence of large black support for the third party in the returns, Populist votes came overwhelmingly from rural districts, and though some rural districts proved resistant to Populism, urban areas across the board showed precious little third-party support. In Wilson County in the east, for example, highly urban Wilson Township, which contained the southern boom town of Wilson, returned only twenty-five Populist votes (0.02

percent) out of 1,371 cast in the township. The adjacent nine rural townships, however, returned a combined 1,252 third-party votes, or 54 percent of the entire number of votes cast in the those rural townships.[48]

Even though urban areas in the west such as Hickory and Statesville yielded a few more Populist votes than did those like Wilson in the east, this urban/ rural divide was significant enough there and in other counties to suggest a few social characteristics of Populism. First, and most obviously, Populists were overwhelmingly rural. Their legislative concerns and political culture were born of rural social conditions, rural evangelicalism, and the organization and ideology of the Farmers' Alliance. Townsfolk rooted in other concerns and social problems had little resonance with Populism; thus, the People's Party reflected, in part, the social tensions brought about by North Carolina's increasing urbanization—tensions also reflected in Populist antagonism toward "town-hall rings," "First Churches," and urban plutocrats and monopolists near and far.[49] Second, rural Populist voting patterns, as well as rural Democratic ones, often concentrated geographically, which would seem to indicate that ties of church, kin, and fellowship held a strong sway in voting patterns.[50] Finally, the large returns in rural areas help explain Populists' confidence despite their meager overall showing. Again, taking Wilson County as an example, Populists cast only 34 percent of the county vote, yet in three rural townships—Gardner, Saratoga, and Taylor—Populist support amounted to 72 percent, 79 percent, and 84 percent respectively. On the ground level, then, many farmers observed almost all of their neighbors join the cause and hence got the impression of widespread support despite the stealthy weight of urban voting. While their rallies, speeches, and parades exuded confidence and excitement, the elusive juggernaut of southern urbanization defeated Populism statistically at the polls.

* * *

Immediately after the election, M. J. Battle expressed the mix of defeat, resignation, and hope that pervaded Populist sentiment: "God does not slumber, nor is He slack in His judgements. The cries of His people are being heard; they will be answered. The People's Party is an outgrowth of discontentment, and unrest, begotten by injustice, wrong. The attempt to crush it, stamp it out by a resort to still greater injustice, wrong, will prove as abortive as the addition of fuel to quell a flame."[51] Indeed, the judgment of God was not long in coming, for Battle, along with his fellow Populists, could see the writing on the wall: the combined Populist and Republican vote in 1892 had exceeded that of the Democrats.

7. Religion and the Populist Revolt

To its followers and detractors alike, Populism evinced the ethos, language, and crusading spirit of a religious movement. Democrats and Republicans, for example, ridiculed the way Populists on the stump assumed rural financial problems had apocalyptic consequences; Populists, on the other hand, considered their rallies safe places for women and children because of their paucity of swearing and inebriation, and they welcomed sobriquets such as "calamity howler." "We may thank the enemies of the people for the very appropriate name of 'calamity howler,'" Populist J. F. Click remarked, reminding his readers that in the "Good Book . . . God sent his prophets, holy men and women to warn nations, cities, and individuals of danger to come. These were 'calamity howlers,' and happy were they who heeded their warnings." In fact, state party President W. R. Lindsey took pride in being called a "red-eyed calamity howler."[1]

Certainly not all Populists were evangelical "calamity howlers," red-eyed or not; Populism was first and foremost a political movement attracting a wide range of folk, and as with any movement, it had a core of true believers and a periphery along for the ride. Since this political movement was rooted in North Carolina rural culture, however, even those rural folk who avoided church membership were touched by evangelicalism's shadow and therefore resonated with and embraced many of its basic patterns of thought. So, even when evangelical Populists were not at the fore in organizing local Alliances and Populist clubs, their traditions nevertheless commanded the language that gave meaning and a sense of angst to the movement.

As we saw in Section 1, this evangelical tradition was, however, fragmented by opposing vectors of thought regarding the place of the church in politics, the place of the church in relation to accepted customs of gender and race, and the right equation for balancing individual autonomy and centralized ecclesiological concerns. In other words, North Carolina evangelicalism had produced a range of options when it came to one's relationship to the church and society. Because all sides of the political contest drew on this same evangelical tradition, these various vectors of thought not only stimulated the Populist response but also emboldened those detractors of Populism who hoped to cast the third party as a threat to peace, white rule, and ultimately the way things were.

Although denominational affiliation is a poor indicator of who became Populists, Populism was most attractive to those evangelicals living tenuously in, but not quite of, southern society: rural evangelicals who cared enough about southern (and American) society to want to save it and yet who separated in their minds the way things were from the way things ought to be. These religious "kickers" and generally cantankerous zealots like M .J. Battle and "Brother Jimmy," after engaging religious tyranny and bossism in the forms of Roman Catholicism, centralized denominational control, and urban "churchianity," were mentally and emotionally seasoned to make war against the economic and political centralization festering in the plutocratic camps. These "calamity howlers" thus comprised the core— the "true believers"—of the movement. Prominent as local organizers, lecturers, and especially writers in Populist newspapers, these religious radicals put into words what so many farmers felt as they looked out over their crops rotting in the field because it did not pay to harvest them.

In Populism, then, long-standing religious traditions that had throughout the 1800s engendered a reforming impulse once again, out of the crucible of the Alliance, propelled another political movement that challenged not only the southern political status quo but inadvertently the rules of southern racial politics. Unlike religious-political movements that would pop up in the twentieth century—such as the religious right of the 1980s and 1990s that used the political system to further its specific religious agenda—Populists wanted not merely to use but *to preserve and sustain the American democratic system itself.* In this sense Populists were heirs to a millennial tradition that saw America as the tool of God to bring a divine system of democracy to the world. When Populism died—or, perhaps more correctly, when white supremacy murdered it—this vision, in many ways, for North Carolinians and other southerners died too.

In the end, the political and economic goals of Populism fused with evangelical goals of eternal life in the arms of Jesus and the establishment of the millennium to produce a movement baptized in a religious fervor matching the ultimate, eschatological certainty and seriousness of the ideals and hopes that propelled it. J. F. Click epitomized well this sense of ultimate concern when, in the heat of the 1898 white supremacy campaign, he summarized his reasons for supporting free silver as an axiomatic rule of divine governance. Reiterating what being a Populist meant for him, he wrote:

> To continue ... the present gold standard ... means abject slavery to your children and their posterity. It means damnation to your children whom you have tried to teach to reverence God as the great Ruler of the Universe. When your children realize that this claims to be a Christian nation and that the religion of the Lord Jesus reigns, they will be loath to accept such Christianity and such religion that underlies a government that has no humanity in it, and that would oppress the poor, those Christ ... wanted ... free from want and misery which is brought upon them by uncivil, immoral and unjust laws, instigated at all times by the devil himself.

He argued further that the money question "is not only a political question, but, underneath it all is a great moral principle that is too vital to be trifled with, and that you will be held morally responsible to God and man and your children and future generations for the way in which you deal with this question." Click ended by warning: "Unless they repent, hell will be full of editors, politicians and even professed Christians for the ignorant and reckless manner in which they have exercised the rights delegated to them by God Himself, in the way of giving the people just and civil laws."[2]

The rest of this chapter fleshes out the details of exactly how and why evangelicals divided in their support for the Populist and Democratic causes and ends with an episode that illuminates the way both sides thought about this religious and political crisis—a paper war between two Methodist lay leaders—Dr. Cyrus Thompson, a Populist leader and president of the state Alliance, and Josephus Daniels, a reform Democrat and editor of the Raleigh *News and Observer*.

* * *

By tapping into the countercultural traditions within an evangelicalism at the center of southern culture and society, the Populist revolt awakened passions between Populists and Democrats rarely seen in political contests. While Populists fought for their principles tooth and nail because they involved matters of ultimate religious and moral concern, for Democrats, white supremacy, reflected in party loyalty, likewise revealed their intimate attachment to sacred patterns of behavior or proper relations. With whites on both sides clinging to southern and commonsense ways of thinking—

Democrats to the way things were and Populists to the way things ought to be—North Carolina plunged into a political maelstrom lasting for six years.

Given the typical assumption that southerners did not mix politics and religion, it is stunning to witness the degree to which all sides of the political fray in 1892 tapped into religious dialogue and the degree to which the election fragmented the church in North Carolina. The organ of the North Carolina Methodists, for example, remarked: "Some very good men are ready to consign to eternal punishment all who do not agree with them both in religion and politics. We heard a very good man consign a certain political party to hell and every man who voted for its nominees." "We are now in the midst of one of the most bitter and exciting political campaigns," wrote the Democratic editor of the Disciples of Christ's *Watch Tower,* who then recalled that "not long since a young man, a professed Christian, said in the presence of the editor of this paper that he would not allow a person of a certain political party to sleep on a bed in his room. A Christian lady said if she believed a certain minister belonged to a certain party she would never hear him preach again."[3] The upstart *North Carolina Baptist* also experienced these tensions. While one of its editors joined the Populists, the others did not, though one later embraced the Prohibition Party. The paper, however, expressed sorrow and despair over the ensuing religious fratricide: "It is fearfully sad to note the readiness with which many church members lay conscience, honor, and God's word aside and trample morals in the dust in their eagerness to carry some point, gain some wished-for advantage, secure some hesitating voter."[4]

As these statements suggest, both Populists and Democrats claimed they were fighting on God's side, with Populists clinging to a vision of God fighting for the oppressed and with white Democrats fighting for God's order against the forces of political and racial anarchy. Drenching her movement with biblical overtones, Populist Alice Mull wrote that the "cause" of the "laboring classes . . . is a just one and if God be for us, who can be against us." *The Progressive Farmer* similarly warned: "There can be but two political parties to claim the suffrage of the people, the one having truth, justice and right on its side; the other the love of money, office and corruption. . . . With God for the acknowledged leader of the former and the devil for the latter, all good people ought to know which will win" and thereby "save our republican institutions and common Christianity from decay and death."

Populists many times considered it a sin even to affiliate with the Democrats. One wondered how anybody "professing to be a Christian can vote the Democratic ticket"; another wrote that the Democrats represented "the abomination of desolation" and were "stenches in the nostrils of decent people"—a party crying "lustily to Baal." Still others accused Democrats of "idolatry," "harlotry," "heathenism," "iniquity," of being the "whore of Babylon" and "of the Devil."[5]

Evangelical Democrats, too, could hurl the vitriol. One Democratic Presbyterian in a moment of heated debate proclaimed the third party to be "of the Devil," arguing that Populists, by ignoring the separation of church and state, had "all mixed religion and politics so much that you all can't tell which is which." Conservatives such as Elder Gold of the Primitive Baptists regularly labeled the Populists "anarchists" and "communists," and C. T. Bailey, editor of the Baptist state organ, openly attacked the People's Party as "demagoguery" for its elision of church and state.[6]

Drawing on conservative views of church and state, such evangelical Democrats were especially upset about the degree to which ministers were active in the Populist campaign. Even though some Alliance ministers did not want to exert undue influence on their congregants in political matters, many ministers openly stumped for the Populists and likewise ran for and won public office. Such ministers concurred with *The Farmers' Advocate's* sentiment that "the question of politics—the science of government . . . involves both moral and religious principles and if more of the ministers took an interest in the politics of the country we dare say that there would soon be a changed condition of affairs."[7]

Not only did local ministers take up this call, but some of the state's most visible and cantankerous evangelists did so as well. W. P. Fife, for example, stumped for the People's Party in 1894, combining revival meetings and political speeches. Although there were very few holiness folk in the state in 1892, a handful of the most important holiness leaders supported the People's Party, and when the holiness movement exploded in 1896 in the Sampson County area—the area, incidentally, of greatest Populist strength in the state—the revival's leader, Rev. A. B. Crumpler, opened the 1896 third district Populist convention in prayer. Thomas Dixon advocated the People's Party early on and was a staunch, though at times ambivalent, supporter of the third party. Although Dixon worked behind the scenes and in sermons to promote the third party between 1892 and 1896, he voted for his friend Grover Cleveland in 1892 (he later repented) and opposed Bryan in 1896 because they disagreed on the money question.[8]

Sometimes when ministers were unwilling to heed the call, Populist congregants proved ready to give their pastors "shipping papers" for failing to endorse the party. Thomas Dixon, Sr., a loyal Democrat, for example, was "shipped" by one of his Cleveland County congregations. Democratic congregants were likewise willing to extend the "right foot of fellowship" to pastors advocating the third party. After the venerable Presbyterian Alliance organizer Rev. Colin Shaw of Duplin County began to stump for the Populists, he was unceremoniously "shipped" by his congregation of Alliance-folk loyal to the Democracy. Back west, Methodist Protestant Rev. G. E. Hunt was similarly ousted from his Davidson County congregation because of "Democratic trickery in church as well as state." According to Hunt, the Democrats, who "oppress the poor," "do mean things," throw rotten eggs, corrupt the registration books, and buy votes, "threatened to dismiss pastors who voted against the Democratic Party."[9]

* * *

The election of 1892 was so heated because the issues being debated tapped into intellectual, cultural, and social traditions and conditions at the very heart of what it meant to be Christian, southern, American, and black or white. Yet trying to follow these seams in evangelicalism to see if they indicate Populist voting patterns can be tricky.

A few patterns, however, emerge. All told, geography was, again, a critical factor in determining Populist support, as was the rural/urban line. Regardless of denominational affiliation, very few townsfolk or farmers in traditional rural Republican strongholds became Populists.

Hearkening back to the three categories used in Chapter 1, however, there were some perceptible religious patterns in Populist voting in areas of strong Populist turnout that illuminate the Populists' ideological and cultural outlook.

Rural folk associated with denominations of a restorationist bent (save the Primitive Baptists) and a more decentralized ecclesiology (officially or unofficially) were among the most vocal and active Populists. Such self-proclaimed "kickers" affiliated the Quakers, Free Will Baptists, Methodist Protestants, and Disciples of Christ like J. M. Mewborne, along with like-minded rural Baptists, Presbyterians, and Methodists, constituted the spiritual center of the movement.

Included in this group also were a smattering of holiness folk. Although holiness advocates stood in many ways outside southern culture with their women preachers and ecstatic worship habits, they nevertheless carried, because of their roots in northern antebellum perfectionism, a drive to reform society. Thus, despite their otherworldly premillennial eschatology, North Carolina holiness folk in the 1890s were broad-minded in their outlook and perfectionist ideals, which, when linked to their anticentralization and common-folk emphases, dovetailed well with the reform ethos of Populism. Moreover, their general dismissal of southern cultural convention meant that ideals of party loyalty or white supremacy held little sway in their thinking.[10]

While the representation of these rural restorationist groups in Populism no doubt reflected, in part, their predominantly rural social location, Populism's intellectual ethos—its cluster of knee-jerk reactions—also resonated deeply with these restorationist evangelicals. From the time they were children, these restorationists had been taught sacred myths identifying their groups as heirs to a tradition that had championed religious toleration and freedom of conscience; they believed, moreover, that their insistence on human liberty had helped establish and continued to undergird American liberty. They therefore saw themselves as trustees of America's sacred mission, and in the one or two decades prior to the 1890s, many had embraced the politically active side of evangelism as they had promoted prohibition or discussed how to apply the law of love to the suffering they saw around them within and without the Alliance.

To denominational restorationists who owed their heritage to fighting religious tyranny, and to members of the larger denominations who were presently fighting against denominational centralization, the tropes against plutocratic tyranny in Populism not only had a familiar ring but were woven into general story lines pitting the forces of Jesus against the centralizing, demonic forces of tyranny in all three spheres—religious, political, and economic. Although, due to the paucity of black sources, my focus here is on white evangelicals, if the thinking of black Georgia Populist leader Rev. L. H. Holsey is any indication of North Carolina black evangelical Populist thinking, African Americans, in a similar manner, tied together themes of religious and political tyranny.[11]

Expressing this idea of a Populist war against plutocracy in all three spheres, a Baptist "P.P. Girl" from Sampson County, for example, revealed her Gospel Mission outlook in a letter to *The Progressive Farmer* that castigated the North Carolina Baptist Convention for dictating from a committee how much each church should pledge in its missions giving: "Just give yourselves up to the 'Board,'" she chided, "and let them direct you, what you shall do, where you shall go, and above all, let your salary pass through the hands of the members of the board and you are a true apostle with the right kind of spirit." She then compared this denominational centralization to the political centralization under "King Grover," and, after referencing her disgust at the visit by Cardinal Satolli of the Vatican to Washington, went on to argue that Cleveland's administration would result in political monarchy and religious Romanism that would "abolish all our free religious rights to worship the true and only living God which is in Heaven."[12]

While a "P.P. Girl" had clear landmarker tendencies, other landmark Baptists of the state, and those advocating the Gospel Mission movement in particular, maintained a somewhat ambivalent relationship to Populism. Although Populism attracted a number of anticentralizing, Gospel Mission-minded Baptists like a "P.P. Girl" and J. F. Click, it attracted none of its primary leaders. Even though the anticentralization strains of Populism closely resembled those of landmarkism, many Gospel Mission churches were urban, and many of its leaders were urban pastors. The urban constituency of the Gospel Missioners may therefore help to explain why this group, as a whole, apparently ignored Populism.[13]

Yet, perhaps more important, the paucity of landmarkers in the Populist ranks also indicates, as in the case of the Primitive Baptist hostility toward the third party, that a localist outlook per se was not the guiding force behind Populism (Gospel Missioners were not only anticentralizers but, like the Primitive Baptists, were fighting for local control over churches and especially the disbursement of money). While the two issues—anticentralization and local control—were similar, they were not exactly the same thing. The anticentralization of Populism was an ideological aversion to institutional centralization because it limited individual autonomy; local control was sometimes an intellectual and other times a more practical call for local jurisdiction over ministerial choices and especially the disbursement of funds. Local control was often advocated by wealthy church benefactors who did not care to bow a knee to professional ministers or by rural folk who believed no one beyond their immediate vicinity ought to have a say in their affairs. Again, in contrast, Populism displayed a broad, though restorationist, outlook as it linked itself to national circles of ideas and reforms. Populists set out to erase the lines between blue and gray in order to construct a national movement that would influence the political economy not only of North Carolina and the South but of the nation and world. Holiness folk, who, like many Primitive Baptists, were also religious outsiders, therefore resonated with Populism, since they, too, belonged to organizations with broad national and international ties.

Turning to Populism's religious detractors, as we saw earlier with Elder Gold and other Primitive Baptists, rural folk who eschewed the mixing of church and state and disliked the "paternalism" of Populist demands made up one group of third-party antagonists. These Democratic evangelicals urged farmers to be self-reliant and not to expect government "handouts" in the form of the subtreasury and other reforms that would soften their manhood. Such "paternalism" was anathema to their vision of fiscal conservatism, economic liberalism, and manly independence. For example, one

Democratic Primitive Baptist criticized farmers "who waste their time in going to pic-nics, sitting around stores, whittling good's boxes, reading news papers, and abusing the government for not giving them more money." Attacking the "greed" and lethargy apparent in such abuse, this writer argued, "A little more energy and a little less extravagance will place us in a better condition." He then confessed that he was "very much elated" over the Democrats' victory in the state and national campaigns of 1892, because "for the past three years I have had impressions to pray for the oppressed poor, and I think that prayer has been answered. . . . I feel like saying 'Blessed be God who giveth us the victory.'"[14]

Populism's most visible evangelical detractors, however, were not the Primitive Baptists but the urbane leaders of the largest denominations. These leaders, particularly faithful Democrats like John C. Kilgo, president of Trinity College, as well as C. T. Bailey and his son, Josiah, sequential editors of the Baptist state organ, the *Biblical Recorder,* regularly excoriated the third party for assaulting the "powers that be." While the Democratic or Republican denominational leaders of the Disciples of Christ, Methodist Protestant Church, Christian Connection, and Reformed Church refrained from directly denouncing the Populists (though, if Reverend Hunt is correct, Methodist Protestant Democrats had prevented him from taking a charge in 1893), Baptist, Presbyterian, and Methodist leaders harassed the Populists repeatedly. Populists returned fire by criticizing Kilgo, the Baileys, and other denominational leaders as traitors to Christ and leaders of an urbane "churchianity" that assisted the forces of plutocracy, likening them to Roman Catholic inquisitors, Sodomites, and King George (Kilgo's close relationship with the Dukes provided ample evidence in this regard).[15]

As with the Primitive Baptists, mainline Democratic evangelicals often focused their assaults on the way Populists mixed religion and politics and thus drew on the more conservative side of evangelical thinking about political involvement. Moreover, these denominational leaders, who in their religious spheres criticized or censured religious "kickers" who opposed the denominational centralization integral to their vision of intellectual, cultural, and numerical denominational progress, were primarily urbanites and therefore removed from the day-to-day rural poverty from which Populism derived much of its motive force. As would become more apparent in the 1898 white supremacy campaign, these denominational leaders, as men of considerable social and political power (Josiah Bailey eventually became a powerful U.S. senator), also held a vision of southern economic progress based on urban, industrial growth that, in their minds, required Democratic rule. Democratic rule, in turn, required white supremacy, and these denominational leaders, based on commonsense ruminations about proper relations or for mere reasons of political expediency, helped win Democratic supremacy in 1898.

* * *

In the fall of 1895, with the white supremacy campaign still three years away and with a Populist-Republican legislature in control of the state government, these religious tensions between mainline leaders and Populists came to a head. The catalyst was a speech by incoming state Alliance President Dr. Cyrus Thompson concerning the place of the church in reform (Thompson was succeeding two-term Alliance President J. M. "Brother Jimmy" Mewborne). During the speech, Thompson inflamed Democratic evangelicals by stating: "The church to-day stands where it has always stood, on the side of human slavery and not on the side of liberty." The paper war that ensued between Thompson and reform Democrat Josephus Daniels over the following six months showcased the way the intellectual, religious, and social forces played out in Populism.

Dr. Thompson was born to Onslow County planter Franklin Thompson in 1855. As befitted a child of status, Cyrus—or "Cy," as he was known to friends—attended the best private schools and then in 1872 set off for Randolph Macon College, where he especially enjoyed studying moral philosophy and Greek. Thompson was a deeply committed Methodist who, in spite of his fiancé's concerns that he was filling his college years with discussions of medicine and other "worldly topics" in a "cloud of tobacco smoke," filled his letters to her with heartfelt piety, and he studied the New Testament daily in the original Greek. After graduating from medical school in 1878, he put his interests in politics and philosophy and his patrician background to work by entering public service. Like his father, Thompson became a faithful member of the Democratic Party, serving as a state legislator in 1883, a state senator in 1885, and a county commissioner from time to time. (Thompson eventually ran unsuccessfully for the U.S. Senate in 1896 and for governor in 1900 as a Populist; he was elected Populist secretary of state in 1896.) As an Alliance organizer, district lecturer, state president, and Populist lecturer, Thompson gained a reputation as perhaps the best stump speaker in the state, rivaled only by Democrat Charles Brantley Aycock, who debated the good doctor repeatedly through the 1890s (Aycock became Democratic governor in 1900).[16]

In 1895, with Populist-Republican fusion at its peak of power and the Democrats bleeding and on the run, Thompson addressed an Alliance rally held at a local church on a Sunday afternoon in Cary, just outside Raleigh.

Thompson drew from antielitist and politically activist elements of evangelicalism to implicate city preachers, along with all advocates of mere "churchianity," in the decline of American freedom and civilization. Attempting to demonstrate the degree to which the church, as a human organization, repeatedly departed from the democratic principles of Christ and thus reinforced cultural, political, and social oppression in supporting the "powers that be," Thompson made his extemporaneous remark regarding the church and slavery.

The Democratic press, led by Daniel's *New and Observer,* expressed outrage at the statement, arguing that by assaulting the church, Thompson, as a typical third-party anarchist, was assaulting the very foundation of law, order, and peace in Western civilization. Announcing that "the churchgoing people of the state and all who believe in the power of Christianity to save, have never been more indignant at the utterance of a public man than they now are with Dr. Cyrus Thompson, the leader of the Populists," Daniels, a former ally of the Alliance, averred that Thompson's "crusade on the church" was a "sin" and "a crime against society."[17] The attack by Daniels, who was also a Methodist lay leader (both he and Thompson were, oddly enough, lay delegates to the state's Annual Conference in 1896), prompted state- and even nationwide Populist, Democrat, and evangelical commentary on Thompson's statement.

In the ensuing paper war, Thompson launched an extended discussion of the way he and other Populists connected not only issues of church and state but more generally their religious ideas to their reform goals. In brief, Thompson understood history as an eternal dialectic between organizational tyranny and individual liberty. For Thompson, the antithesis of individual freedom or freedom of conscience was slavery, by which he meant "subjection to the will of another, and the consequent destruction of rights and the failure of individual development."[18] And while institutions, be they civic, religious, economic, or political, should, in subjection to the ultimate authority of God's eternal axioms, promote individual freedom, such human institutions and their accompanying civilizations, he believed, typically centralized power and produced states of tyranny though coercion or ignorance. Thus, common folk everywhere faced the threat of being enslaved by the powerful.

For Thompson, then, individual freedom, no matter where it existed, was constantly threatened by the forces of institutional centralization. "If we have been a free people, we recognize the constant tendency to loss of liberty," he warned; "eternal vigilance is its price. Liberty, like the manna that fell from heaven, because it is perishable, must be contended for every day."

For the American democratic system, he added, "Peaceable it may be regained or preserved only by the wise use of the ballot."[19]

Regarding the institutional church, specifically, Thompson drew on the classic Protestant and restorationist idea that early on—at least by the time of Constantine—the church had departed from Christ's emphasis on a free and individual reception of God's grace as it forced individuals to convert at sword point or to swallow church/state-approved doctrine. Casting Christ himself as the champion of "the individual," of "conscience," and of "individual right and human freedom," Thompson argued that, as the early church became a fashionable belief system among rich and powerful Roman city folk, it "resorted to the . . . method of authority. . . . Whoever impugned its tradition and doctrine met cruel persecution." For Thompson, this "Constantinianism" was "the only course left to those who would lord it over their fellows, the enemies of human freedom."

This coercive and hence tyrannical alliance of religious and temporal authority thus produced a "dark age" of ignorance, superstition, and monarchy—in short, "a long millennium of unbroken oppression." Furthermore, because this Constantinian heresy was perpetrated by aristocrats "in the cities, centres then as now of wealth, power, and corruption" rather than in "the rural districts," the church, "dominated by the rich and consequently powerful," became an instrument of oppression as it "ceased to bear a message from the poor to the rich, and became the irresistible messenger of the rich to the poor."[20]

Moreover, according to Thompson, even though religious reformers from John Hus to John Knox engendered movements promoting human liberty, the churches these reformers founded, just as did those they left, drifted toward tyranny. Calvinists, for example, had replaced "the tyranny of councils" with "the tyranny of texts" to suppress the "slightest expression of dissent." In the end, then, wherever common folk struggled for freedom, the church labeled their "discontent and agitation . . . an expression of anarchy." Thompson added that the church "has thrown its influence with the powers that be, no matter if the powers were Monarch, Master, or Mammon."[21]

In implicating the church, Thompson did not assail the teachings of Christ or "Christianity" itself. "Against *Christianity*," he wrote, "I said nothing. In behalf of Christianity, Christly living, I was pleading." This distinction was critical for Populists, as this pattern of thinking was the basis of Populism's restorationism. What was at fault with the institutional church (or with the Democratic or Republican parties) was not that it had bad "governing principles" but that its leaders had failed to embody those principles and had thus led their organizations away from their foundations.

Thompson stressed repeatedly that if the church had embraced "the free spirit of Christ and its moral influence" it "would have aided instead of retarding the progress of human freedom."[22]

Indeed, the church had witnessed waves of reformers who helped inaugurate new periods of freedom. Thompson's favorites included pre-reformers like the Albigensians, John Hus, John Wycliffe, and Savonarola, as well as Protestant reformers like Luther, Wesley, and modern-day reformers including the leaders of the holiness movement within his own Methodist denomination. Thompson was careful to point out, however, that such radicals worked from *without* the church, in *separate* organizations (third parties), intending to restore the lost teachings of Christ. Where Christians stood on the side of liberty, argued Thompson, it constituted "triumphs of Christianity . . . *over* the church, not triumphs *of* the church."[23]

Thompson's critics, including Daniels, were unable or unwilling to make this distinction. Drawing on the "spirituality of the church," they cast the institutional church as the basis and defender of peace, civilization, the "powers that be," and, ultimately, the status quo. Evaluating Thompson's attack on the church, the *Atlanta Constitution* argued, for example, that Thompson "turns his back on his Bible and sneers at the churches," claiming that he was "on the road to anarchy" and that "he weakens his influence with the better class of his order and of society in general by going out of his way to attack the churches." Evangelical Populists, however, understood exactly the restorationist distinction Thompson was making. In response to the *Constitution*, Francis B. Livesey defended Thompson by demonstrating that the Alliance president employed commonsense reasoning to upend the status quo from the vantage of God's eternal axioms, arguing that "the popular leader who turns his back upon the perverted use made of the Bible by the churches is a defender of the Bible, a perverter of anarchy." He then continued: "Men who believe in Christianity, but not in churchianity, are increasing in number. From the leading thinkers down to the humblest toilers the conviction is growing that the churches do not represent Christ."[24]

In a critical piece of argumentation that linked religious liberty to political freedom and American millennialism, Thompson connected the religious freedom achieved in the Reformation to the political and educational freedom brought on by the Renaissance and Enlightenment. Hence, even though the church censured such champions of freedom as Galileo and Joseph Priestley, the sixteenth through nineteenth centuries witnessed a powerful wave of religious and political reform that, according to Thompson, resulted in the expansion of individual freedom and culminated in the birth of the United States of America—an idea that was the foundation for

Dr. Cyrus Thompson. From
Cyrus Thompson Papers #715,
Southern Historical Collection,
Wilson Library, University of
North Carolina at Chapel Hill.

the patriotic millennialism so critical to Populists' sense of both impending crisis and civic duty.[25]

But in America, Thompson believed, the pendulum was again making a fateful swing. Although America's political and religious liberty had engendered a great Christian land of freedom, the present conditions of economic, political, and religious centralization brought about by the two old parties, "churchianity," and plutocratic monopoly, threatened to undo this state of freedom. In that context, Thompson argued that the church was again siding with the forces of centralization in its failure to preach the gospel of love and permeate society with the truths of Jesus Christ. Citing a number of contemporary examples, ranging from the Methodists' censure of holiness preachers to effeminate city preachers enslaved by the donations of their wealthy benefactors, Thompson indicted the church in the present democratic crisis and in particular criticized its tendency to side with the "powers that be" under the guise of the "spirituality of the church": "Just as the church may lose the spirit of its head and accept the lordship of Constantine or Mammon . . . so a republic may be robbed of the fruits of democracy and its citizens . . . become slaves of increasing aggregations of wealth and power . . . such is the rapid tendency of the times and of the country in which we live." Thompson then wondered aloud: "What becomes of democracy, of civilization, of Christianity in this last Western empire, the hope of the freedom and righteousness of the world?" He answered by calling on the church, and especially its ministers, to follow John the Baptist, who "inspired His [God's] prophets to meddle with politics and to say that national evils were consequent upon national sins" and Jesus who "was himself the model of indignant rebuke of sin in high places." Thompson then urged the church to follow the lead of North Carolina farmers who, in order "to check these destructive conditions and tendencies" had come "together on grounds of purest patriotism and Christianity."[26]

Across the state, other Populists lent their voices in hearty agreement with Thompson's assessment. *The Caucasian* wrote: "Dr. Thompson knew he was speaking the truth." J. F. Click wrote in his *Hickory Mercury:* "The truth must be told, let it hurt whom it may."[27] Another wrote: "Some of our 'best' preachers have strayed almost as far from the real font of the teachings of Christ, as the Democratic party has from the principles of Jefferson and Jackson. If the ministers had preached the gospel straight and had condemned the sins around them, this government would never have grown as corrupt and oppressive as it has. Some of our preachers must get religion."[28]

Conservative evangelicals and Democrats in North Carolina, however, were quick to condemn not only Thompson but also the People's Party for his "famous statement." E. A. Yates of Durham wrote that, although he had "nothing whatever to object to his [Thompson's] politics," nevertheless, "in the opinion of all right thinkers [he] has perpetrated a wrong upon himself, upon his children, upon the church of God and upon Christian civilization." "Unless he purges himself of it," he added, "it will haunt his mind in the dark hours of affliction, and trouble his soul in the dying hour." The *Biblical Recorder* reported that "Dr. Thompson's remark is not true, so far as the 'Baptist Church.'" The *North Carolina Presbyterian* attacked Thompson's idea of "churchianity," writing that "the Church cannot exist without Christ. . . . *There is no such thing as a Christless Church.*" The Methodist *Christian Advocate* reported further that "the man who goes about the country and cries out against the Church and destroys the confidence of the public in her leaders is an enemy to mankind—an emissary of the devil."[29]

Thompson's argument prompted such a reaction for a number of reasons. First, it exposed the southern evangelical tension between the more conservative and more radical views of the relationship of the church to the state. On the conservative side, Baptist E. A. Yates, who admitted his disgust for politics and reluctance even to vote (even though he wrote a commentary on Thompson's speech for Daniel's Democratic *News and Observer*), criticized the Alliance president's remarks as representative of the merger of politics and religion that plagued the People's Party. "The church is necessarily . . . a conservative power, and therefore an antagonist to all disorder, anarchy, and nihilism," he wrote. Echoing the sentiments of Elder Gold and the *Atlanta Constitution,* Yates confessed that the church "can but align itself with the powers that be, for 'they are ordained by God,' whether the government be Populist, Democratic, Republican, Kingly, or what not."[30] Thompson, like most Populists, however, drew on evangelicalism's active stance toward politics by equating Christian duty with political action.

Second, besides marking the line between conservative and activist positions on church and state, the debate emphasized the way evangelicals connected individual freedom to political independence and hence rejected party fealty. For Thompson, Christian freedom meant more than the spiritual freedom to access God without the necessity of human mediators, creeds, or institutions; it was also a tutor for the economic and political freedom exercised in all Protestant countries, best exemplified in the United States. So whether it was a comparison to the regulators, Luther at the Diet of Worms, or Jesus against the Pharisees and Sadducees, such thinking sacralized the political independence of the Populists as they left their old political parties that had succumbed to the forces of tyranny.[31]

Finally, the term "slavery" loaded Thompson's statement with racial overtones. The Civil War having been fought only thirty years earlier, most of his listeners had grown up around human slavery, had fought—at least in part—to protect it, and had justified doing so through Christian apologetics. Although Thompson only rarely mentioned African slavery in his extended discussions, commentators observed that he was not just attacking the church in general but the southern church in particular and thus, in effect, southern social and racial norms. So, even though, like most Populists, Thompson was reluctant to assault white supremacy directly, he was nevertheless willing to assault the southern church's support of chattel slavery as one more example of its general complicity in human slavery. In one article, for example, Thompson pointed to the church's defense of "domestic slavery" and its rejection of the Emancipation Proclamation in 1863 and then noted that "if the sentiment of the southern church has ever changed upon this question, I know of no expression to that effect by conference or convention; and . . . I do not remember even to have heard a prayer in any church thanking God for the liberation of four million slaves."[32] So while Thompson did not specifically advocate "social equality among the races," he disregarded, as did most Populists, lines of racial/political taboo and in doing so, assaulted the intellectual supports of white supremacy.

If Thompson indirectly attacked hierarchies of race, he more directly attacked southern conventions of gender. Although crossing gender boundaries for Populists never assumed the central place crossing boundaries of race did, the power of gender to shape political attitudes was never far below the surface. As in the case of Mary Lease in the 1892 election, Populists faced from time to time the charge that they were upsetting proper relations between the sexes. In practice, as we saw with "a P.P. Girl," Populist sisters maintained much the same gender constructions they had in the Alliance; "a P.P. Girl" identified herself, as did little Ida in Chapter 4, as a Populist, not as a mere supporter of male Populists, though her sphere did not involve actual voting.

Even though they held to such an idea of separate spheres, evangelical Populists, entrenched in the language of individual autonomy and liberty, nevertheless discussed a woman's sphere as liberating and likewise opposed social constructions they thought enslaved women. Speaking, then, for many Populists, Thompson wrote that "the church cannot boast to have honored and elevated womanhood while it silences, even in North Carolina, the tongue[s] of women of intelligence, eloquence, and intense piety, and sees, without effort to remove, the existence of economic conditions that make of women the slaves of 'sweat-shops' and force thousands to choose between starvation and lives of shame. Ask the women of the crowded tenements what honor the church bestows upon them." Another Populist and Quaker concurred that the southern church had "aided in perpetuating the ignorance and slavery of woman in that she has not been accorded the right and privileges accorded her in the Bible." A few years later, J. F. Click, in his *Times Mercury*, openly fought for women's suffrage.[33] Although, as with attacks on white supremacy, not every Populist would go as far as Thompson or Click in denouncing hierarchies of gender, that these Populists did so, again, in the eyes of Democrats, represented a subversion of southern norms. In the 1898 white supremacy campaign, the Democracy of North Carolina was more than willing to exploit this point as it sought to silence forever any voices that opposed its supremacy.

* * *

In the end, Thompson not only outlined the ways in which evangelicalism and Populism were entangled but demonstrated the radical overtures of a movement that, though thoroughly rooted in southern evangelical culture, threatened to turn that culture on its head. Expressing the desperation of Battle, Cutchin, and other Populists in the language of evangelical apocalypticism, Thompson wrote: "The few who control the currency and create panics at will have the power to . . . sweep away without compensation the accumulations of all classes and the concrete toil of millions." He continued:

"However legalized, the result is none the less heartless robbery, progressive impoverishment, and certain slavery. For when men lose their property, they lose their independence, and when through loss of the fruits of past or present toil, they are brought into subjection to the will of another, what are they but slaves?" In the end, Thompson worried that "the small land-owner is being swept away in democratic America by the same cruel process that crushed out the proud yeoman of England." Thompson then sighed and expressed a sentiment with which M. J. Battle would no doubt have resonated in January 1893: "This is a sad picture. . . . I sit by my fireside and . . . look silently into the eyes of my children. Such is the doom that startles the farmer, holding many acres or few. And what promise does it hold for industries built upon his? Such is the prospect of the country. The rural population see it and feel it. Do you wonder that they are restless?"[34]

8. Victory, Defeat, and Disfranchisement, 1893–98

While a few Democrats and Populists hoped to mend the breach created by the 1892 election, and while churches hoped their members would settle back into fellowship with one another, it soon became evident that this was not to be the case. The hostilities that flew during the 1892 campaign, and especially the "abuses," "rotten eggs," and election fraud perpetrated by the Democrats lingered long in the hearts of Populists, and so in 1894 they struck up a fusion agreement with their former Republican nemeses to remove these Democratic perpetrators from office. Before their defeat in the white supremacy campaign of 1898, Populists realized many of their dreams during the height of their power between 1894 and 1896. Despite their strength and vision, however, these Populists were never able to command their party's destiny. As dedication to their principles of reform clashed with the pragmatic realities of party politics, the People's Party fragmented over fusion decisions between 1896 and 1898. With all the factions within the People's Party claiming to stand for principle over party, Populists often battled Populists with as much intensity as they battled the old parties, feeling they were fighting for the very life of their ideals. In such a condition, the party was no match for a solid Democratic front hell-bent on shackling together a coalition built on white rule. Ambivalent always toward the black Populists among them, white Populists were unable and in some cases unwilling to counter the Democratic assault that in 1898 spelled their doom.

* * *

While M. J. Battle called down the judgment of God after the 1892 election, most other Populists were busy denouncing widespread Democratic election fraud. Corruption was especially bad in the east, where Democrats, well trained in keeping black voting to a minimum, turned their prowess on white and black Populists. To Populists and to many Alliancefolk, seeing former allies in matters of family, religion, and politics committing such atrocities was especially hard to swallow. This fraud therefore initiated a deep-seated hatred for the Democratic Party that not only prevented many Populists' return to or fusion with the party of Jackson but eventually drove them into fusion with the party of Lincoln. Rhetoric between Populists and Democrats often became ugly and personal, as when, in the heat of battle, Marion Butler called his former ally, Josephus Daniels, "a supercilious idiot, within whose skull there is but a thimbleful of brains."[1]

The Democrats' machinations in 1892 also led Populists to adopt election and county government reform as major campaign issues in 1894 (recall that the Democrats had put county government policies in place in the 1870s to maintain white supremacy in the east and curtail Republican power in the west). Populists wove these reforms into their general assaults on centralization and tyranny as they continued to insist that the ballot was the sacred means of God's moral governance. "The ballot box should be as sacred as the Ark of the Covenant," wrote one Populist minister. "The hand that touches it . . . should be withered by all the pains and penalties which attaches to the crime of high treason."[2] Thus, while Populists continued to advocate state-level reforms such as good roads, increased appropriations to education, and a 6 percent state interest cap, election and county government reform emerged as the glue that could join them to the Republicans, who had pushed these measures for years.

If election fraud was not enough to alienate Populists and many Alliancefolk permanently from the Democratic Party, the Democracy's actions in the 1893 legislature deepened the divide not only between Democrats and Populists but also between Democrats and the Alliance. Although the 1893 legislature tossed a few scraps to the farmers, a group of Democrats rushed a bill through the legislature revoking the state Alliance's charter, charging that the order had violated its nonpartisan guidelines by giving financial support to the third party. This action unleashed a firestorm of protest among Alliancefolk, many of whom had remained loyal Democrats. "If the earth was raked, the sea scum and Satan's habitation scraped," wrote one such Allianceman, "there could not be another such a piece of diabolical premeditated legislation found on record."[3]

Meanwhile, by midsummer it was clear that the nation was heading into a devastating financial depression. In an emergency session of Congress, Grover Cleveland repealed portions of the Sherman Silver Purchase Act

(1890) that had provided for a limited coining of silver. The action only further alienated many North Carolina Democrats from the national party's leadership and confirmed for many Alliancefolk what the Populists had charged in 1892: that the national Democratic Party was captive to Wall Street and irrevocably corrupt. Even Senator Vance, who died in April 1894, broke with the president, though he resisted attempts by Populists to enlist him in their cause.

Taken together, these factors helped precipitate a third exodus of Alliance and reform Democrats from their old party as new Populist Party Clubs appeared across the state in 1893 and 1894. Among the defectors were a number of prominent Democrats, including former state Democratic Chairman Spier Whitaker and race-baiting, flamboyant William H. "Buck" Kitchin from Halifax County, both of whom quickly assumed prominent roles in the state Populist Party.[4]

With this new influx of members, by 1894 the Populist Party in North Carolina was cresting in terms of passion and leverage. To turn that passion into legislation, however, the Populists needed help from the Republican Party. Because the 1894 election mostly involved state offices, Populists and Republicans put aside their differences on such national matters as money and the national bank and aimed to defeat the hated Democrats and then blunt their power with election and county government reforms. As one Populist put it, fusion with the Republicans ensured "the defeat of what has become the most unscrupulous, most tyrannical party that ever existed upon the face of the globe."[5] With fair elections in place, both Populists and Republicans were confident that, in 1896, they could compete in a "square fight" based on their respective principles.

Fusion agreements on the state, congressional, and local levels varied in detail but had the same basic intention. Both parties maintained their institutional identities while electing joint tickets with candidates intent on cooperation in the state legislature (Republicans also agreed to support the Populists' 6 percent interest rate cap, along with many other measures, including congressional support for silver, which many North Carolina Republicans supported anyway). As the campaign opened against the "intolerant, stalwart Bourbon spirit that has molded a slavery of opinion among the controlling classes and anyone who has the independence of thought and character to think or move out of groove," Populists exhibited the same excitement and acid rhetoric they had in 1892. "The one great and powerful party is dead. It came to a violent death at its own hand," wrote one Populist: "How art the mighty fallen.... By this time it stinketh in the nostrils of the people. There is nothing left of it except the smell of brimstone and Wall Street."[6]

And, indeed, how the mighty had fallen. The threat posed by Populist-Republican fusion could not have come at a worse time for the badly riven state Democratic Party. Although the Republicans were also divided between the same black-and-tan and lily-white factions as before, the prospect of defeating the Democrats galvanized the GOP behind the lily-whites and their pro-fusion stance. Factionalism within the Democratic Party, however, when coupled with widespread animosity toward Cleveland and a reluctant and largely ineffective Governor Carr, zapped whatever strength the party might have mustered to fight the fusionists.

As anticipated, therefore, the fusionists routed the Democrats in November; in Marion Butler's words, "North Carolina has splendidly vindicated the manhood of its people in the crushing defeat of the 'machine.'"[7] Populists elected five congressmen (six once the contested Democratic victory in the sixth district was overturned), the Republicans one, and the Democrats two from the second and third districts, where three-way races hurt the fusionist cause. Fusionists elected their state ticket, and the state house consisted of 47 Populists, 32 Republicans, and 41 Democrats, while in the state senate there were 22 Populists, 16 Republicans, and 12 Democrats. Fusionists achieved this success, moreover, in spite of massive Democratic election fraud. As in 1892, Democrats and Populists divided along an urban/rural axis, and blacks voted the Populist or fusion tickets in large numbers.[8]

According to Josephus Daniels, Democrats were "thunderstruck" after the election. Democrat J. G. Martin wrote to Matt Ransom: "The thought of *North Carolina* being in the hands of Republicans has stunned me. . . . In national affairs it is not so crushing—but in the State—great heavens, it is *awful!*"[9] Although the Democrats had never been wanting for leadership, not until 1898 did a new crop of leaders emerge who would oversee the Democrats' resurgence through white supremacy. In the interim, though, the state party floundered, able to rely only on its political experience and dilatory tactics to hold the fusionists' legislative onslaught at bay.

These tactics, however, could only delay the inevitable. The 1895 legislature overturned landmark Democratic legislation going back to the 1870s constitutional changes that had helped the party maintain its dominance through the two previous decades. The legislature enacted an election bill that provided for equal representation of all political parties among election judges and registrars, curtailed the ability of registrars to challenge registrants, simplified the registration process, used different colored ballots to prevent stuffing and other fraudulent measures, outlawed bribes, vote buying, and intimidation, and required that all ballots be saved for recounts. Furthermore, the legislature passed a compromise bill that created popularly elected county commission boards with equal representation of all parties. Under the law, three of five commissioners were elected, while a judge would appoint up to two more of different parties on petitions of two hundred free-holders. This later clause was included at white eastern Populists' insistence in order to prevent "black rule" in their counties. In addition, the legislature increased school appropriations, passed the 6 percent interest rate cap, restored the original Alliance charter, and increased appropriations to various charities and to the university. The fusionists furthermore sent Populist Marion Butler to the U.S. Senate for six years to replace Senator Ransom and Republican Jeter Pritchard to serve the remaining two years of Zebulon Vance's term with the understanding that Pritchard would remain in office if the fusionists won again in 1896. In the end, Marion Butler assessed the 1895 legislature as "the tangible result of a political state revolution . . . the expression of a rebellion on the part of the people against . . . the Democratic Party."[10] Yet this revolution was short lived, for even though Populist-Republican fusion in 1894 and 1895 marked the high point of Populist power in North Carolina and perhaps in the country, it also contained the seeds of Populism's internal unraveling.

* * *

The 1896 election marked a turning point in the national political party structure as the reform wing of the national Democratic Party, under the leadership of presidential candidate William Jennings Bryan, assumed control of the party. It also marked the high point of Populist influence nationally and in North Carolina as Democrats bent their candidates and platform to appeal to Populists. Disagreements over state and national fusion arrangements, however, fractured the People's Party and, in North Carolina, alienated its black voter base, for despite an era of good feelings between Republicans and Populists in the 1894 election and 1895 legislature, with the presidency on the line in 1896 tensions quickly developed between the two parties over national legislative agendas and prospects of patronage. Moreover, reform-minded Democrats, their pride now bruised, hoped to fuse with the Populists on a national silver ticket or state ticket. By November, North Carolina Populists fused with the Republicans on certain state, local, and congressional tickets, though all three parties ran separate candidates for governor and some counties eschewed fusion arrangements altogether. On the national ticket, however, both the Democratic and People's parties nominated Democrat William Jennings Bryan for president, but each nominated different vice-presidential candidates: Georgia firebrand Tom Watson for the Populists and banker, railroad baron, and ship magnate

Arthur M. Sewall of Maine for the Democrats. The result of these arrangements was Republican victory for gubernatorial candidate Daniel Russell,
Populist dominance in the North Carolina congressional delegation, Populist-Republican fusion victory in the state legislature, and presidential
victory in the state for Bryan, though goldbug McKinley won the general
presidential election.[11]

How did such a menagerie of fusion options arise? As the election year of
1896 unfolded, the senator and soon-to-become national party president
Marion Butler reminded Populists that while fusion with the goldbugs in
1894 had secured free elections and had therefore paved the way for Populist
success in state congressional races, without a silver president, a silver Congress or Populist state legislature could do little to reform the financial
system. Thus, even though many Republicans in North Carolina were pro-
silver, and even though there was a strong national silver faction of Republicans, Butler refused to entertain prospects of fusion with the Republicans
on the state or national ticket, believing the Republican Party was determined to nominate a goldbug for president. Butler intended, rather, for the
Populists to nominate a nonpartisan silver man for president who would
draw reformers from both old parties; Butler and his supporters did not
intend at this point to fuse nationally with the Democrats or any other party
but believed they were taking the high road of principle over party, that is,
fusion on the principle of silver that would secure a president amenable to a
Populist- and silver-dominated Congress.[12]

In the meantime, however, Butler had met secretly with reform Democrats over the previous year to discuss fusion possibilities while refusing
Republican overtures. As a result, in early spring of 1896 a group of Populists
began a heated assault on Butler and his supporters from within and without North Carolina, claiming the senator was attempting to fold the People's Party into the Democratic Party. Most of these "mid-roaders" (who
believed they took the "mid road" between the two old parties—that is,
refused to fuse) believed fusion would water down commitment to the
party by yoking believers with unbelievers. For mid-roaders, if the Populists
refused, however, to touch the unclean Democrats, God would give them
the victory and the party would "rise again with healing in its wings."[13] This
sentiment outside North Carolina was especially strong in Texas and Georgia, where Tom Watson became the "mid-roaders'" spokesman. (The name
"mid-roader," like the claim to fight for "principle over party," was slippery,
however, since at different points both factions adopted the terms to desig-
nate their positions.) Back in North Carolina, as Butler's forces countered
mid-roaders by calling them closet goldbugs and Republican dupes, the

state party rent asunder between pro- and anti-Butler factions. Though the actual party institution did not split until early 1897, these tensions festered throughout the remaining short life of the party.[14]

With pro- and anti-Butler factions in their corners by early summer, campaign options became even more complex once the Democrats nominated Bryan in early July and once state Democratic Party presented a proreform platform centered on silver. With Bryan's nomination, any hope of drawing silver Democrats out of their party to support a "non-Partisan" silver candidate seemed futile. Butler, therefore, faced two options: (1) fuse with the Democrats on the principle of silver at the national level and likely win the election but weaken or obliterate the People's Party (or, as mid-roaders rightly argued, dampen the motivation of rank-and-file members), or (2) set aside the current election and put forth a straight national ticket that had little chance of winning, choosing instead to fight another day with a party still unified behind its banner and principles. Complicating the dilemma further, schism threatened the national People's Party over the decision, since mid-roaders from Texas, Georgia, and other parts of the South scorned Bryan while western Populists favored a joint nomination. To negotiate all these twists and turns, Butler orchestrated a *via media* between the two options at the Populist national convention on 22 July. He first oversaw the nomination of mid-roader Tom Watson as the vice-presidential nominee and, having appeased the mid-roaders temporarily, orchestrated the joint nomination of Bryan. An initial peace hovered about the convention under rumors that Bryan would dump Sewall for Watson.

Back in the trenches, however, Bryan's nomination met with a cool response. Anti-Butler forces in North Carolina rebuked the national president for selling the party down the river, while even many Butler supporters claimed they would vote for Bryan only if he jettisoned Sewall. Amid confusion and schism, Populists nevertheless managed to put forth a full slate of candidates, including W. A. Guthrie for governor and ex-Republican gubernatorial nominee Oliver Dockery (1888) for lieutenant governor; complementing the ticket was the usual platform of state and national reforms. Earlier that summer the Republicans had put out a separate ticket headed by lily-white and former Greenbacker Daniel Russell.

With a Republican gubernatorial candidate in the field, the Populist state executive committee eventually worked out national fusion agreements with Democratic electors while maintaining a separate state ticket and at the same time allowing local fusion with Republicans. Even though official Populist speeches and newspapers hailed Bryan as savior of the masses, many Populists expressed disgust for Bryan and considered him the lesser of two evils; other Populists even advocated a new national ticket. Notably missing was the usual Populist exuberance over its prospects; in its place was confusion, lethargy, and, among a few, a sense of impending doom for the party. To make matters worse, Watson publicly criticized Butler for his handling of the national election and was rumored to have called for Populists to support McKinley, while Guthrie, who was perhaps a reluctant Populist himself, publicly broke with the Populist state leadership and advocated fusion with the Democrats instead of the Republicans on the state and local tickets two weeks before the election.[15]

What exactly propelled such a breakdown? In North Carolina, these "mid-road"/anti-Butler and pro-Bryan/pro-Butler factions split along a number of competing axes of thought. One axis involved pragmatic party politics. North Carolina Populists bent on maintaining the reforms passed in the 1895 legislature knew that doing so required fusion with the Republicans on the state level, since everyone expected wholesale disfranchisement if the Democrats regained state power. On the other hand, those like Butler and his supporters who opposed Republican fusion on the state level were quick to point out that, since the Republicans were committed to the gold standard at the national level, in practical terms, securing a Republican vote for a local or congressional fusion candidate also meant securing another vote for goldbug McKinley.

At the deeper level, however, at least three other axes of thought motivated the different sides of this schism. The first was a gut-level commitment to free silver. As silver had been steadily rising in the Populist panoply of reforms, it symbolized the resentment North Carolina farmers felt toward the northeastern financial establishment; to vote for a goldbug like McKinley, or even to support him indirectly through state Republican fusion, was wholly anathema to countless Populists. Wrote one such Populist: "The man who will vote for goldbugism is an enemy to his God, his country . . . and his own children. . . . To vote for the single gold standard is to vote for the slavery of the American people—white and black alike."[16] Opposition to Republican fusion on the state level, therefore, had less to do with favoring fusion with the Democrats and more to do with being unable to stomach a goldbug like McKinley.

Second, as mentioned earlier, animosity toward the Democrats made the prospect of fusion with these mongrels a pill too bitter to swallow for many Populists. It was therefore not a disregard for silver or the national agenda but a gut-wrenching hatred of the Democrats that fueled the mid-road position in the Old North State. One Populist wrote along this line: "What! Talk of co-operation with the Democratic Party when they have ridiculed

us, abused us, and insulted us in every way imaginable? No!" Another
Allianceman wrote, "We still remember 1892. Their cursing, abuse, and
roughs and rowdies who ran our men out of town and rotten-egged our
leaders, are too fresh in the memory of true Populists to vote that ticket
now." Other Populists like J. M. Mewborne, a mid-roader, worried that if the
Democrats regained power they would again corrupt the political process.
With a free ballot, the voice of the God, he argued, would mend the fractured economy with or without silver. Mid-roaders, therefore, in southern
parts of the country, as historian Robert Durden has correctly assessed, were
not more ardent Populists; they simply hated the Democrats more than did
those like Butler who supported Bryan.[17]

Finally, race inevitably came into play for both whites and blacks. The
election and county government reforms enacted in 1895 increased ex-
ponentially the black vote in North Carolina and thus gave blacks new political power and in the second district all but guaranteed Republican victory.
For many white Populists, especially in the east, this was an unwanted by-
product of fusion, and, as attested to in their opposition to a fully democratic county government law, they also fretted about black representation
(or "domination") in local government, Populist or not.[18]

With this in mind, those white Populists who saw the influx of black voters
as a positive development generally opposed national Democratic fusion,
because they feared rightly that such an arrangement would drive away black
support. For example, when rumors of Democratic fusion were running rampant in April, the chairman of the Populist Party in Bertie County, which had
a large black population, urged Butler not "to go back on ourselves and our
party and worse still, those honest colored men" who had joined with the
Populists.[19] Contrariwise, white Populists who opposed any hint of "black
rule" and had held their noses while fusing with the party of Lincoln in 1894,
generally rejected Republican fusion. This racist sentiment could, however,
act as a free radical. Populist Harry Skinner, for example, a devout white
supremacist who turned down the 1892 Populist gubernatorial nomination
for fear he would split the white vote, was one of the most vocal mid-roaders
and detractors of Butler; ironically, he eventually became a Republican.[20]

Among black Populists and Republicans the fusion dilemma was equally
perplexing. At the Republican Convention in May, many blacks supported
black-and-tan Oliver Dockery for governor. When pro-fusionist, lily-white
Daniel Russell, who had a notorious reputation for opposing black leadership in the party, got the nod, many black Republicans threatened schism.
In a rump convention in early July, black Republicans, in another odd turn
of events, endorsed Populist W. A. Guthrie for governor prior to Guthrie's

actual nomination. Before the Populists fused with the Democrats on the national ticket, then, black Republicans of all factions were pledging to support the Populist ticket to protest Republican gubernatorial candidate Russell. After the Populists fused with the Democrats on the national ticket, however, black Republicans firmly committed to the Republican ticket.[21]

Black Populists shared many of the same concerns and perplexing axes of thought that white Populists did in the 1896 election, expressing both a deep commitment to silver and other financial reforms while nevertheless insisting that the gains made by the 1895 legislature be preserved.[22] The written record of black Populists, however, falls loudly silent after Butler secured national fusion with the Democrats. Though some blacks continued to vote Populist, vast numbers returned to the Republicans. Blacks, regardless of their economic destitution, put the color of skin over the color of money and with good reason refused to touch the unclean Democrats.

In the Republican victory that November, even though fusion arrangements across the state generally conformed to party discipline, Populists experienced heavy losses, falling from 17 percent of the state's votes in 1892 to only 9 percent in 1896. On the bright side, Populists elected five congressional representatives who accompanied two silver Republicans, a Democrat, and second-district African American Republican George White to Washington City. Populists also held a few state positions.

The extent to which white anti-Butler, mid-road Populists supported the GOP is unclear, but black Populists left the People's Party with a vengeance, adding to the Republicans' spectacular victory. The state Republicans gained not only black Populist votes but black votes in general from changes to election laws in 1895. In 1896, the number of votes cast increased by close to fifty thousand, and 87 percent of registered blacks voted. In the sixteen counties with black majorities, voting increased by over 15,000 votes. Overall, North Carolina held its only truly free election since before the war.[23]

When all was said and done, the election of 1896 radically altered the political landscape of the state and nation. On the national scene, McKinley's victory in the momentous "battle of the standards" initiated more than three decades of Republican dominance. Bryan's nomination also changed the complexion of the Democratic Party and its constituency. In North Carolina, the Republicans regained power in the state and, as long as the People's Party remained intact, there seemed little reason to doubt they would maintain their position. To make matters worse for white supremacy, North Carolinians elected eleven black state legislators and a black congressman from the second district. Moreover, numerous local black officials won office and the threat of black Republican appointments hovered in the air.

In the end, having lost the bulk of its black constituency and torn by infight-ing, the People's Party came limping out of 1896 election; the Republicans were firmly in command.

* * *

In the early months of 1897, Populist infighting became worse as the party faced institutional disintegration after a number of anti-Butler Populists sided with Republicans in the state legislature to return silver Republican Jeter Pritchard to the Senate, as had been part of the 1894 fusion agreements. For whatever reason, Pritchard had fallen out of favor with many Pop-ulists—mostly those aligned with the Butler wing—under the wrong impression that he had turned his back on silver; hence, Butler urged the Populist caucus in the state legislature to support Cyrus Thompson for the Senate. Because Pritchard might have promised them appointments, or simply because they considered it the honorable thing to do, a group of state legislators ignored Butler and, under the leadership of Harry Skinner, bolted the Populist caucus to help the Republicans defeat Thompson. Such a visible break in party discipline not only embarrassed Butler but under-scored deep divisions within the party. Moreover, Governor Russell aggra-vated these tensions by siding with Butler against his fellow Republicans. Always a maverick, Russell advocated reforms that were contrary to Repub-lican policy and more in line with Populism. By March, badly riven and without strong gubernatorial leadership, Populists and Republicans accom-plished little in the 1897 legislature and were ill prepared for the coming Democratic blitzkrieg.[24]

But the vultures were not circling just yet. In the winter and spring of 1898, in fact, many rural Democrats in the east and numerous reform Democratic leaders such as Josephus Daniels felt that the time was right to strike some sort of state-level fusion arrangement over silver with the Pop-ulists. Such plans were furthermore backed by the national Democratic Party and Bryan, who urged state-level allegiance between Populists and Democrats in order to elect silver men to Congress.[25]

With Democratic (and Republican) overtures abounding and with Bryan himself urging cooperation on silver, in early 1898 state Populist leaders attempted to leave an open door to Democratic fusion and at the same time not alienate mid-road Populists who threatened to join the Republicans. As they tried to work through this political labyrinth that spring, Populists aligned with Butler made a general offer—though one clearly aimed at the Democrats—for cooperation on Populist terms to support silver candidates (presumably Populist) in 1898.

Despite its careful wording, this overture plunged the People's Party
again into what was quickly becoming a bottomless pit of turmoil. Even the
Farmer, which had always supported Butler, criticized the senator for such
overtures. At the state convention, Populists constructed a tenuous peace
while maintaining the aim of fusion with any party that would answer the
call. The Populists put forth the usual demands and urged the maintenance
of the reforms put in place in 1895. As in 1896, their schemes ignored the
powerful black voting bloc that had established the party in 1892 and 1894.[26]

When the Democrats met a week later, despite calls for Populist fusion
from Josephus Daniels and other reform Democrats (which were met with
jeers, boos, hisses, and the cry, "it makes me puke"), the stalwarts (or
"lawyercrats," as *The Caucasian* put it), led by state Democratic Committee
Chairman F. M. Simmons, "respectfully declined" the Populists' invitation
for fusion and sent out an invitation of its own. Admitting their folly in supporting Cleveland in 1892, they offered Populists full reinstatement in the
Democratic Party now thankfully controlled by Bryan (a proposal met with
cheers and hymn-singing). Along with pledging to support silver and other
reforms, the party then vowed to uphold fair election laws to assuage fears it
intended to disfranchise. Foreshadowing the carnage to come, however, the
Democrats denounced black office holding and pledged to enforce "rule by
the white men of the state." By appealing to race, the Democrats, not the
Populists, had now established the terms of the coming campaign.[27]

As they had in redeeming the state from the "black Republicans" in 1876,
the Democrats launched a full-scale white supremacy campaign in 1898
aimed at intimidating blacks and uniting white voters behind loyalty to race
and manhood. Whether out of economic or class concerns or sheer racism,
Democratic leaders wanted control over the political direction of the state
and the Democratic rank-and-file supported the cause. By the eve of the
election, Populists faced threats of death; armed red shirt thugs patrolled
voting places along the South Carolina border; Marion Butler was warned
not to travel in the east for fear of assassination, and a train carrying Governor Russell from his hometown of Wilmington to Raleigh was boarded by
red shirts who would have lynched the governor had he not found refuge in
the mail-baggage car. Victory was capped off by murder and mayhem as victorious whites in Wilmington, not satisfied with political dominance alone,
drove black office holders and leaders out of town, killing at least twelve
innocent black citizens in the process. As historian Edward Ayers has so
poignantly written: "So it was that North Carolina, the Southern state with
the highest voter turnout, the most vital black political organization, and
the most evenly matched party system in the region throughout the 1880s

Marion Butler. Courtesy of the
North Carolina Office of Archives
and History of the North Carolina
Department of Cultural
Resources, Raleigh, North
Carolina.

and 1890s, underwent the most violent convulsion to restore unquestioned
and unblemished white power."[28]

The aims of the white supremacy campaign were twofold. Having lost
control of the legislature through the combined voting of blacks and whites,
the Democrats first needed to eliminate black votes. This they accomplished
in 1898 with violence and intimidation, and, after winning the 1898 election,
Democrats secured a more permanent solution in the 1899 legislature by
reversing the fusionists' election and county government reforms and by
passing a constitutional amendment referendum requiring a literacy test to
vote, a move intended to disfranchise most blacks. The referendum, ratified
by popular vote in 1900, protected illiterate whites with a clause exempting
those from the literacy test whose father or grandfather had voted prior
to 1867.

The Democrats' second step in securing power was to convince the majority of white Populists (and any white Republicans who might be so inclined)
to rejoin the Democratic Party. To accomplish this goal, Democrats used a
number of strategies. As outlined in the Democratic Convention, Democrats
first admitted their error in supporting Cleveland and attempted to draw
Populists back into the fold under commitments to silver, railroad regulation, antimonopolism, and especially education reform.

Democrats next appealed to Populists' white manhood by urging them to
unite with the white man's party and put an end to an escalating "black

domination" in politics and especially "domination" of white women brought on by Republican rule. Regarding domination in politics, Democratic orators and newspaper editors trumped up the numbers of black office holders in the east to argue that Republican rule had brought about an inversion of proper race relations. Democrats emphasized, for example, that whites, and especially white women, regularly submitted to black juries and justices of the peace while white children attended schools supervised by black school boards.

Furthermore, Democrats portrayed this supposed "black domination" in politics as symptomatic of a more sinister lack of restraint among blacks not born into slavery. "Uppity" black men, they insisted, who had not learned by the crack of the whip the proper relations between blacks and whites, sought white position and, worst of all, white women. To hammer this point home, Democratic editors fabricated weekly tales of "black brutes" victimizing young white virgins to illustrate the lawlessness prevailing under such a state of inverted race relations. Women, too, took an active role in the propaganda machine, marching in white robes and giving speeches intended to inflame white manhood by emphasizing and symbolizing the threat to virginal purity posed by "black brutes" and Republican rule. On the stump, Democrats insisted that a Democracy unified by white supremacy was alone capable of putting blacks back in their places. Restoring proper relations among the races, therefore, required Populists to place issues of race above all else and join with the Democrats to end the black menace. Democrats further insisted that by removing the specter of race, Populists could champion their reforms without the fear that they might split the white vote.[29]

In addition to intimidation and death threats, Simmons and the Democratic machine enlisted the help of mainline evangelical leaders, most of whom were long-standing opponents of Populism, to champion the cause of white supremacy as a means of maintaining God's axioms for race relations. Along with securing the support of state Presbyterian leader Rev. Alexander McKelway and Primitive Baptist leader E. P. Gold, Simmons sweetened the pot for many Baptists and Methodists by assuring Josiah Bailey, editor of the *Biblical Recorder,* and John C. Kilgo, president of Trinity College (Simmons's alma mater), that appropriations to the state university would stand indefinitely frozen should they choose to assist the cause (recall that Bailey and Kilgo had for many years led the charge against "state aid" to the state university). Bailey, in response to these overtures, not only advocated disfranchising blacks but also poor whites for good measure, framing disfranchisement with a clarion call for increased appropriations for public secondary education (a rationale used by many reforming or progressive disfranchisers in 1900, since voting required literacy).[30]

Exploiting and exacerbating existing tensions among North Carolina evangelicals, these church leaders stumped at white supremacy rallies, heralding the Democratic cause as a means to rescue society from the racial and social convulsions brought about by Populist and Republican anarchy. A trustee of Trinity College, for example, opened one large white supremacy rally by calling on God to "look down upon this vast assemblage of people who are gathered here in the interest of peace and good government towards all men." He continued: "Let us feel this day the vibrations of our coming redemption from all wicked rule, and the supremacy of that race destined not only to rule this country but to carry the Gospel to all nations and maintain Civil and Religious Liberty throughout the world."[31]

Certainly not all North Carolina evangelicals, and not even all leaders and newspapers, supported white supremacy. Though not necessarily sympathetic to either Populism or black suffrage, some eastern papers, such as the Disciples' *Watch Tower* and the *North Carolina Baptist,* nevertheless decried the Democrats' white supremacy rhetoric and especially the misinformation regarding "black domination," which they believed wrongfully stirred "racial strife." The *Baptist* advocated black civil rights, yet admitted, with typical evangelical ambivalence on issues of race, that it did not believe blacks were educated enough to vote just yet, though it hoped, through education, that blacks would attain the sober judgment required for this task. Other religious papers simply ignored the election altogether or called for voters of all three parties to vote their consciences or for "morality."[32]

For their part, many evangelical Populists and ministers fought valiantly, though often with the usual ambivalence, against white supremacy and against those ministers who advocated it. Brother J. L. Burns, for example, the Disciples' state evangelist and founder of Bethany Church in Whitakers, along with lay leader J. J. Rawls, faced rotten eggs for their Populism and for their opposition to white supremacy. One Populist wrote, "Elder J.L. Burns is well known to me as one of the best Christian gentlemen I ever knew, and these attacks on him with rotten-egg Democracy have roused within me a spirit of resentment that is hard to control."[33] *Caucasian* editor Hal Ayer and other Populists resoundingly castigated Bailey, Kilgo, and other denominational leaders for conspiring with Simmons to support white supremacy. Ayer also chastised Christians who sat idly by while Democratic deviltry was rampant: "How is it possible for the defamation of an honest state government, the slander of women, the vile insulting of one-armed soldiers [a reference to Burns], red shirt riding, the threats of violence and the inciting insurrection among a CHRISTIAN PEOPLE . . . [to] go unrebuked and undenounced by people who claim to be Christians? All this is going on to-day in North Carolina. The devil dances a daily hornpipe over such Christianity as that."[34]

While the devil might have been dancing in 1898, historians ever since have been debating what else might have motivated the Democratic leaders and voters to pursue white supremacy as a means to regain control of the state. Some, including C. Vann Woodward, have argued that the campaign was driven and financed by conservative, probusiness, and railroad interests that wanted an end to Populism. For them, the economic benefit of ridding the state of Populism was the goal. Populists like Butler certainly believed this was the case, arguing throughout the campaign that the Democrats' ultimate aim was not to disfranchise blacks but to enslave all farmers and producers to the plutocrats. His *Caucasian* reported, "The Railroad Attorneys and monopolist hirelings will soon be on the stump in North Carolina howling, nigger! nigger!! nigger!!! It is behind the 'nigger' that these enemies of humanity hope to rob the people in the interest of monopoly." *The Caucasian* concluded, that when the Democrats "cry 'nigger,' they lie. The gold syndicate and the railroads are the 'nigger in the woodpile.'"[35]

Other historians have argued to the contrary that a gut-wrenching racism born of postemancipation angst drove Democrats to disfranchise and segregate. This was no doubt the case for many rank-and-file Democrats and Populists in the east, who responded positively to the white supremacy arguments and especially to the fear of "black brute rapists." One Populist displayed such revulsion when he wrote to Marion Butler that the "Negroes are fussing for rule and power and must be put into subjection, and any course we may pursue that does not lead in that direction consistently will divide . . . Pops or make Democrats of them." Regarding the specter of black rapists, J. M. Cutchin, the stalwart Populist leader from Whitakers, criticized the race-baiting tactics by Daniel's *News and Observer,* but added, nevertheless, "that the man, black or white, who rapes an innocent, virtuous girl, the man who stoops to this level of a brute, who thus puts himself outside the pale of civilization and humanity, forfeits the right to civil trial and deserves lynching."[36]

In the end, probably both historical views are right. A variety of social, economic, and racial factors motivated Democratic leaders, while unquestionably a deep-seated racism motivated voters, rioters, lynch mobs, and red shirt thugs. It is necessary, however, to recall that in the east, *many blacks were in fact Populists.* Therefore, whether white supremacy was aimed at Populists or blacks is something of a moot question for the first and second districts, since it was aimed at black and white Populists alike.

Whatever it was that motivated the Democrats, few Populists could have imagined such a violent battle that summer and fall, even though they had warned for years that the Democrats intended to disfranchise those who opposed their rule. Badly divided themselves, Populists, though sometimes valiant, could not mount an effective countercharge as they worked out fusion arrangements on a county-by-county basis, sometimes with the Democrats and sometimes with the Republicans, while also battling internal demons of despondency and schism.[37]

To fight the charge that they supported "Negro domination," as they had in 1892, Populists privileged class over race, stressing that domination by pluto-crats and party bosses was a far greater threat to white manhood and woman-hood than supposed "Negro domination." In their assaults on the Democrats, Populists, however, as always, revealed their own ambivalence toward blacks. This ambivalence, as Democrats rightly perceived, made appeals to white supremacy effective for many rank-and-file Populists, and thus it seems polit-ical, economic, and religious restorationism, in the southern United States at the turn of the century, could only go so far. Even though Populists challenged the emerging corporate order and centralized, single-party political rule in the South, only rarely were they ready to question principles of proper race relations, and, even though many Populists resisted the rhetoric, in the end, the power of these racist ideals did them in.[38]

Such ambivalence was nowhere better illustrated than in the "black sec-ond" congressional race, where Democrats pledged to support a Populist congressional candidate in order to remove black Republican George White from office—a candidate opposed by both parties as an "uppity black" and devout goldbug (Populists had, in fact, for a couple of years advocated run-ning another black, Republican Henry P. Cheatham, second-district con-gressman from 1888 to 1892, who was willing to support silver). Over the summer, Populists nominated J. B. Lloyd, a Methodist lay leader, editor of the old Alliance *Farmers' Advocate,* and a long-time Populist, for Congress. Fulfilling their earlier commitment, Democrats did not put forth a nomi-nee. As the white supremacy campaign kicked into full gear, Democrats, however, demanded that Lloyd take a firm stand for white supremacy and denounce black office holding and Republican fusion. The local Democratic paper laid out its position in no uncertain terms: "Now is the time, Mr. Lloyd, when you can show to the public your boasted honesty in politics. Now is the time that you can show them that you believe in a white man's government." The paper then charged: "From now until election day North Carolina's political war will be waged squarely upon the color line. A Populist will either vote the white man's ticket or else declare by his conduct that he prefers the companionship of Negroes. There is no middle ground. . . . You must either renounce your affiliations or not receive enough votes to cover a dollar bill."[39]

Typical of many Populists, Lloyd had maintained cordial relationships with blacks and had advocated black franchise, yet he generally opposed black candidates on Populist or fusion tickets. Yet, despite this ambivalence, Lloyd refused to bow to Democratic pressure and stood firm against the white supremacy campaign, even when, on the eve of the election, William E. Fountain, former Democratic mayor of Tarboro and a Populist since 1896, under pressure from daily threats of death, returned to the Democrats, advocated white supremacy, and challenged Lloyd for Congress. In the end, George White won the race over the divided white ticket, and, following the election, the *Southerner* gloated that Lloyd was "apparently afraid to return home," since he had "developed an abnormal fondness for the Negro candidate," had "stood squarely in the way of the success of a white man," and had helped to elect "the only Negro Congressman in the United States." Lloyd was, in short, "a man who deserted his race."[40]

* * *

The Democratic strategy worked as splendidly as it had in 1876. The resurgent white man's party decimated the Republicans and Populists, and the massacre of innocent blacks in Wilmington at the hands of prominent white citizens punctuated its victory. Democrats stormed the state legislature, electing 94 of their own compared to 23 Republicans and 3 Populists in the state house and 40 Democrats compared to 7 Republicans and 3 Populists in the state senate. Democrats sent 5 congressmen to Washington City along with 3 Republicans and one Populist.[41]

While many black Populists and Republicans stayed away from the polls in the eastern counties, it is difficult to determine just how many white Populists succumbed to the white supremacy rhetoric and either returned to the Democrats or did not vote. Many, it seems, did, and among them were important leaders like Buck Kitchin, who had come to the party late and predominantly over silver. Democratic newspapers printed stories hailing widespread defection, and some precinct returns confirmed that Populists in eastern counties returned to the Democrats either because of white supremacy or because the party of Jefferson now stood for silver and other Populist reforms.

A good many white and black Populists remained true to their party, but 1898 marked the last time most of them would cast a vote for their movement begun only six years earlier with so much passion and promise. Although Populists ran a state ticket early in 1900 and waged a valiant war against the disfranchisement referendum, by the middle of that election year they had, for the most part, merged with the Republican Party, the new home for most Populists who stayed long enough to read the credits. The only traces at ground level, in fact, that the People's Party ever existed are the oddly out-of-place rural Republican strongholds scattered about the eastern part of the state throughout most of the twentieth century.[42]

In 1899 the Democratic legislature wasted little time in reversing the bitter fruits of fusion rule. The legislature made quick work of the election and county government laws, though, in attempting to appease western whites, it worked out county-by-county regulations to ensure centralized Democratic appointments in the east and self-rule in predominantly white counties to the west—especially those that had sizable Democratic constituencies. The legislature also enacted the first North Carolina Jim Crow railroad car laws, abolished the railroad commission (replacing it with a probusiness North Carolina Corporation Commission), and put forth the disfranchisement referendum.[43]

Knowing that many rural whites of all parties opposed the "suffrage amendment," rather than fight the constitutionality of the measure, Governor Russell and Populist leaders sustained a systematic campaign to mobilize voters to defeat the referendum in 1900. But with new election laws in place, and with many blacks for all intents and purposes already disfranchised because of intimidation, the measure easily passed, and North Carolina entered the twentieth century under Governor Charles Brantley Aycock's smiling, progressive, white Democratic supremacy.[44]

EPILOGUE

The End of an Era, the End of a Dream

What do you do when Satan wins? That was the question facing evangelical Populists after 1900. Of course, some had already found refuge back in the party of white supremacy, but others, disgusted with Democratic tactics and disfranchisement, were left with no obvious places to go. Despising the Democrats, yet out of step with much of the Republican agenda, Populists were in many ways victims of their own absolutized eschatology. Their worst nightmares now a reality, all options seemed dismal.

For black Populists, what to do politically was largely not for them to decide; the Democrats had done that for them. While some blacks urged migration to the North to escape the economic and racial chains of the South, most focused on day-to-day survival and found refuge in an evangelicalism that was becoming more ecstatic and ultimately otherworldly. Among middle-class blacks, as historian Glenda Gilmore has pointed out, women, because they did not threaten whites as voters or rapists, gained a new place as "ambassadors" to the white population through participation in education and voluntary societies. Many Populist men, however, probably resonated with second district Congressman George White's contention that "I cannot live in North Carolina and be a man."[1]

Many white Populists shared White's sentiments. One-armed Disciple Brother Burns, the smell of rotten eggs still in his heart, wrote fellow Populist and Disciple J. J. Rawls a few days after the disfranchisement referendum passed: "*Well the big steal is over,* and freedom of speech is gone in N.C. . . . We are at this time completely in the power of a *corrupt* and *godless Crew!*" Sadly recognizing he was no longer the free man his fathers were, Burns wrote, "Were I a young man I would leave N.C. inside of thirty days and go to some place where a man could have some opinion of his own without being cursed and abused and called all evil names because he had independence to call his *soul* his *own.*" Burns died four years later from *la grippe,* one arm left on a Virginia battlefield and the rest of his body planted in eastern North Carolina sand.[2]

Also, like black evangelicals, many white Populists explored the new otherworldly belief systems that were sweeping the state: premillennial dispensationalism and Pentecostalism. In contrast to the optimism of earlier millennialists who believed that they worked hand in hand with God to bring about the millennial kingdom, physically, on the earth and before Christ's return, premillennial dispensationalists taught that God would wipe sin, the devil, and unregenerate human beings from the earth in an apocalyptic Battle of Armageddon and start again with a millennial clean slate (hence the name "premillennial"—the second coming of Jesus, in their chain of events, coming before the millennium). The good news for believers was that they were not going to be around for the carnage. Seven years prior to Armageddon, they were to be whisked away in the "Rapture" to watch the events from the balcony.

As it settled in among many holiness and Pentecostal devotees and among the forerunners of twentieth-century northern and southern fundamentalism (another evangelical variant), this new belief system embraced a more passive stance toward politics than had other variations of nineteenth-century evangelicalism. Why work to save society, its advocates reasoned, when God was allowing Satan to have his way with the world until the end? With the reform of present society pretty much useless, many premillennialists hoped only to save as many souls as possible before the Rapture while they watched nature and Satan's rule follow their downward course. While premillennialists might have been active in alleviating immediate suffering through benevolence, gone was a vision of ushering civilization toward a worldly millennial paradise.

This outlook was inherently comforting in a world of perplexing change or destitution. It helped make sense of a world, or of a southern political system that for all intents and purposes seemed out of whack to people who felt powerless or otherwise disinclined to do anything about it. Such a belief system therefore held an inherent appeal to Populists who saw their movement crushed by the forces of Satan through political tyranny, economic centralization, and "churchianity." Even before it became apparent that Satan, and not God, would rule America's state of affairs, J. F. Click, who in 1892 had portrayed Jesus as a radical agrarian agitator, in 1897 and 1898 began printing premillennial dispensationalist sermons by D. L. Moody and

Canadian holiness preacher A. B. Simpson on the Rapture in his Populist *Hickory Mercury/Times Mercury.* One *Mercury* reporter even visited the pre-millennialist commune of Zion City, Illinois, headed by faith healer John Alexander Dowie; he returned with glowing reports. The image of William Jennings Bryan, the "great commoner"-turned-fundamentalist, prosecuting John T. Scopes for teaching evolution in Dayton, Tennessee, is not as incongruous as it might seem at first glance.[3]

In 1906, in the second and third congressional districts, where the holiness movement had taken hold in the last five years of the nineteenth century, a far more radical version of this movement combining ecstasy, premillennialism, and speaking in tongues burst onto the scene. Pentecostalism, imported by holiness preachers who had visited the fabled Azusa Street Revival in Los Angeles, raced through the fledgling North Carolina Holiness Church as well as numerous Free Will Baptist and other congregations. The boundaries of the movement's epicenter aligned almost perfectly with one of the most ardent hotbeds of Populism in the state: an area comprising northern Sampson, eastern Harnett, western Duplin, western Wayne, northeastern Cumberland, and southern Johnston counties.[4] It is probably impossible to document whether these Pentecostals were former Populists, since, with the Rapture close at hand, Pentecostals had more important things to do than write down the names of their earliest converts, but if they were Populists, by adopting Pentecostalism's sociopolitical outlook, they rejected the idea that God governed society through human means. For them, God now orchestrated human events through the miraculous while the voice of God became the tongues of angels intelligible only to a heaven-bound group of believers separated from the rest of secular society.

Other evangelicals not so inclined to the otherworldly simply longed for a return to normal church life: the revival season, debates over baptismal formulas, and, with newfound vigor, separation of church and state. While Pentecostals and premillennialists adopted de facto separation of church and state for other reasons, mainline and not-so-mainline denominations like the Disciples of Christ and Methodist Protestants, eager to put the tensions of the Populist revolt behind them, determined to adhere strictly to the doctrine of the spirituality of the church. While the spirituality of the church served the purposes of white supremacy and Democratic dominance among mainline evangelical leaders in the white supremacy campaign, its adoption afterward at the local level marked a deep desire to heal hurt relationships among congregants. Disciples of Christ Rev. W. H. Cobb, a loyal Democrat who had the unenviable task of serving Bethany Christian as pastor through its days as the home of Whitakers Alliance and thus as one of the epicenters of the Populist revolt, longed for such a healing to take place in his congregation. In 1904, after outlining his adamant support for the spirituality of the church, Cobb recalled: "We have experienced political moves in the church where brethren have been estranged one from the other." He continued: "Seeing that the political movement of only a few years past broke the Christians' ties that had before blessed the Disciples of North Carolina, let us as Christians devote our time to serving the Lord more diligently, and let politics rest where it properly belongs, with the majority of the voters."[5] By the mid-1950s, the congregants at Bethany had, in fact, followed a path similar to Pentecostals by splitting from an increasingly theologically liberal Disciples denomination to align with the conservative, premillennial dispensationalist Churches of Christ.[6]

The early twentieth century, then, marked a shift in southern evangelical conceptions of church-state relations. Whereas in the 1870s, 1880s, and 1890s, evangelicals of all types had entertained, as they had in the antebellum days, a variety of stances toward politics ranging from the spirituality of the church to patriotic millennialism, those afterward largely avoided political involvement, save agitation for prohibition (which became law in North Carolina in 1908) and such universally acceptable reforms as regulating child labor. Evangelicals, in adopting a more passive attitude toward political involvement either through premillennialism or the spirituality of the church, helped usher North Carolina into a political climate characterized as the "solid south": voter apathy and Democratic rule—in short, a lack of heartfelt passion for anything other than white supremacy.[7]

This return to normalcy in church life Pastor Cobb hoped for could not be had, however, in political life for those Populists who despised the Democrats. For those who did not forsake politics altogether, the Republican Party offered pretty much the only alternative, though a few Populists here and there joined the Prohibition Party.[8] Butler, Thompson, and "Brother Jimmy" all made their ways into the party of Lincoln. Butler attempted to gain leadership there, but the tensions that had surrounded his leadership of the People's Party left him with no real political future. Years later, Butler supported Teddy Roosevelt's brand of progressivism (not that of Democrat Woodrow Wilson), and the former senator died in relative obscurity in 1938, having lived long enough to see most of the reforms for which he had fought put into place by Democrats Wilson and Franklin Roosevelt.[9] Cy Thompson, too, participated actively in the Republican Party, though most of his attention went to his medical practice. Later in life, Thompson became a card-carrying progressive, fighting for professionalization of the medical community as president of the State Board of

Health and through affiliation with a number of other medical associations. When he died in 1930, no one remembered, except his old nemesis Josephus Daniels, his former exploits as one of the best stump speakers the Populists ever produced. His obituaries did not mention his Populism; labeling him a Republican, they focused on his career as a country physician who brought physical healing to rural folk.[10]

While Thompson returned to doctoring, "Brother Jimmy," like other Populists who did not lose their land, went back to farming. In the first decades of the twentieth century, North Carolina farmers experienced the highest prices for their crops that anyone could remember. At least until the 1920s, the immediate angst of their economic situation abated. Nevertheless, for "Brother Jimmy," like so many others, Populism had been about more than just economic grievances, and so even with the return of good times, Mewborne could not rejoin the despotic Democrats who had slandered and disfranchised the Populists. To forever hammer the point home, "Brother Jimmy" used his allegiance to the party of Lincoln to standardize the spelling of his name. Throughout the 1880s and 1890s, in articles, letters, and even on his own letterhead, his name appeared variously as "Mewboorne," "Mewbourne," "Mewborn," and "Mewborne." To distinguish himself from his Democratic kinfolk bearing the first three variants, "Brother Jimmy" settled on "Mewborne," the final "e" marking his and his children's commitment to the Republican Party.[11]

Taking a more ugly turn, however, were those Populists who set their faces like flint against the black brothers and sisters who had helped them achieve what success they had attained. Taking Georgia Populist Tom Watson as an example, C. Vann Woodward in particular pointed out this ugly turn of events. Watson, undoubtedly one of the most radical Populists in advocating biracial union during the 1890s, turned against blacks out of anger and expediency, blaming them for the devastating success of white supremacy campaigns across the South; Watson then returned to the Democrats as a powerful political boss, white supremacist, and nativist.[12]

Thomas Dixon, too, took this route. Although never very gracious in his racial views to begin with, after leaving the ministry in the late 1890s and pursuing a career on the lecture circuit, Dixon finally found the calling that had for so long eluded him. In response to the criticisms of the South he had endured while in Boston and New York, Dixon determined to set Yankees and the rest of the nation straight regarding the horrors of Reconstruction and the devastation carpetbaggers and blacks had supposedly brought upon the South. In *The Leopard's Spots,* and then in the more popular *Clansman,* Dixon painted members of the KKK as noble champions of southern freedom and

dignity in the face of incompetent and hell-bent Republicans. His views
received a wider audience once *The Clansman* evolved into D. W. Griffith's
Birth of a Nation, after which time Dixon was generally credited with revital-
izing the Klan in the 1920s. Dixon, however, lost his fortune in the stock market crash of 1929 and died in poverty and obscurity in a Raleigh hotel a couple
of decades later.[13]

The venerable *The Progressive Farmer,* under the editorship of Clarence
Poe after 1899, also stunningly took this turn. The *Farmer,* in fact, supported
disfranchisement in 1900 (much to Butler's and other Populists' astonish-
ment), and Poe later advocated an apartheid system in North Carolina similar to the one in South Africa.[14]

While the spelling of "Brother Jimmy's" name marked a Populist legacy
of sorts, as did the pockets of Republican resistance scattered across the
rural east and as did the legislative agenda of progressive Democrats, in the
first decades of the twentieth century it seems many Populists, as well as
their detractors, simply wanted to forget the whole episode, though Josephus Daniels briefly resurrected the specter of 1890s fusion-led black rule in
the 1928 presidential campaign to maintain Democratic unity in the state
behind Al Smith. In the 1920s, Butler and Thompson seemed reluctant to
discuss their involvement; when asked, they simply commented that the
Populists had helped to promote public education. Mostly absent was any
discussion of Democratic crisis, tyranny, or millennial prognostication. For
their part, local historians treated the Populists as noble though misguided
farmers, who, after being duped into fusion by black Republicans, returned
nevertheless to the Democrats once they had seen the error of their ways.
Those who cared to notice also mentioned that the Democrats had adopted
many of their noble reforms as the party of Jackson continued, as it had
from the days of Jefferson, to befriend the common folk.[15]

Yet one gets the sense, as the years rolled on, that the Populists stood for
something—a frame of mind, perhaps—that since has disappeared, though
traces of it continue in certain odd places: the stress on God's moral governance in evangelical fundamentalism; the plain-folk critiques of capitalism
in *I'll Take My Stand* or Huey Long's ideas, and in the stress on Christian liberty in the southern civil rights movement. Attempting to fit the language of
the Populists—or of abolitionists, of Civil War soldiers on either side, of the
Woman's Christian Temperance Union, Henry George, Jacob Coxey, the
Knights of Labor, or of antebellum trade unions—into twentieth-century
socialism, progressivism, or most post–World War II liberation movements
creates incongruities not easily resolved. Indeed, Populists, like other
nineteenth-century reformers, spoke a language and clung to a set of ideals

mingling individual freedom with a confidence that God would, if permitted, hold the nation in harmony, that seem oddly out of step with the language of Woodrow Wilson, FDR, or Tom Hayden. The critical link connecting human conscience to God's governance was "the white winged ballot"—the belief in *vox populi, vox dei*—an ideal crushed by disfranchisement and then eschewed in most forms of southern evangelicalism well into the early twentieth century. Among many black and white southerners, then, the demise of Populism also brought with it the loss of a uniquely democratic vision of America.

Notes

Note: Throughout I have standardized spelling, punctuation, and capitalization in quotations to avoid the repetitive use of "*sic.*" I have not, however, added or deleted words unless so designated by brackets or ellipses.

Introduction

1. ECP; see also *PF,* 13 April 1894, 4.

2. Quotations, in order: *FA,* 30 March 1892, 3, 2. See also Polk to J. W. Denmark, 6 April 1892, Polk/Denmark Collection, NCDAH; *FA,* 30 March 1892; 6 April 1892; Turner and Bridgers, 290–311; Anderson, "Populists and Capitalist America."

3. The two most important local leaders, J. B. Lloyd and M. J. Battle, were Methodist lay leaders. Populists at Bethany included W. F. Draughan, Mayo, J. B. Lane, J. S. Dixon, and J. B. Latham. Members at Whitakers Temple were Cutchin, R. H. Cutchin, and, apparently, Bellamy; see *FA,* 8 April 1891, 4; 17 June 1891, 3; 16 December 1891, 3; Ware, *Coastal Plain Christians,* 7–11; idem, *North Carolina Disciples,* 288; *Our Church Record,* 28 April 1898, 5; 23 June 1898, 8. Populist H. H. Raspberry attended Gethsemane Baptist (*Minutes,* Tar River Baptist Association, 1886–1908); "One-legged" Gus Bryant listed in the flier attended Bradford Chapel Methodist Protestant in Halifax County, which was associated with Whitakers Temple (Roanoke Circuit *Minutes,* 55; Whitaker's Chapel Collection, ECU; Populist Party Executive Communication Forms, Nash County, 22 January 1900, MBP). On Cutchin, Hunt, Bellamy, Mayo, the Moyes, Burns, and Mewborne, see *FA,* 30 March 1892, 2–3; 4 May 1892, 3; 20 July 1892, 3; 27 July 1892, 1; *CA,* 20 April 1893, 4; 21 September 1893, 2; 4 November 1894, 3; 22 August 1895, 1; 3 November 1898, 3; *Biographical Sketches,* 6–7, 64; *Proceedings,* North Carolina Christian Missionary Convention, 1900, 17–19; 1905, 1–5; Hebron Christian Church Minutes, 1878–94; Union Records, Second Evangelistic District, NCDOC; correspondence among Mewborne, Burns, E. A. Moye, J. J. Rawls, and J. H. Foy, NCDOC.

4. Historians have in places connected Populism to religion. Robert McMath ("Populist Base Communities"; *Populist Vanguard,* 62–63, 75, 136; *American Populism,* 7–5, 17,

50, 123, 153) and Bruce Palmer (126–37) examined how the organization, rituals, and rhetoric of evangelicalism influenced and legitimated Populism; Palmer argued, however, that millennialism stymied Populists' efforts. I corroborate many of their observations, though I mitigate their emphases on the conservative aspects of evangelicalism. Martin (85–86), Mitchell (89–90), and Williams and Alexander stress similar religious connections. Bode, Argersinger, and Lengel believe Populists denounced evangelicalism for its political and social conservatism. While they correctly show Populists condemned the church, they seem to misread Populist attacks on "churchianity" as attacks on Christianity in general. Goode, King ("Religious Dimensions," 259), Mitchell (86–92), and Miller (4) connect Populism to the northern social gospel. In Kansas, the Midwest, and the Southwest, this connection seems right; see Dunning, 317; *Southern Mercury,* 2 October 1888, 2; 3 January 1889, 2. I agree with Flynt ("Southern Protestantism and Reform," 138) and Harvey (206–23), however, that in the Southeast, rural evangelicals held, rather, to a mixture of antielitism and biblical injunctions to help the poor that did not include the northern social gospel's theological liberalism or criticism of social structures. Finally, Flynt ("Southern Protestantism"), Harrell ("Evolution"), Crews, Ayers (398–408, 546–47), and King ("Disciples of Christ"; "Religious Dimensions," iv, 64–93) have connected Populism to restorationist groups such as the holiness movement, Baptist landmarkers, radical Disciples of Christ, and Pentecostals, concluding that these sects paralleled the Populist response to the hardships faced by farmers. For Texas, King convincingly connects the Disciples of Christ to Populism. Flynt finds deep affinities between some holiness groups and socialists in the Southwest, corroborating the work of Burbank, Green, and Bissett. Crews, working with the Church of God-Cleveland, Tennessee, notes that A. J. Tomlinson, the group's first general overseer, was a Populist prior to his conversion. Wacker ("Early Pentecostals"), however, argues that there were no substantive connections between Populism and the Pentecostal movement. Populism in North Carolina had a complex relationship to such movements; see Chapter 7 and the Epilogue.

5. The Northern Alliance, or National Farmers' Alliance, was founded in 1877 in upstate New York, moved its base to Chicago in 1880, and then spread into Kansas, Iowa, Wisconsin, Illinois, Minnesota, Michigan, Kansas, and the Dakotas; see Hicks, *Populist Revolt.*

6. Kousser; Key.

7. See Hicks, *Populist Revolt;* Woodward, *Tom Watson;* idem, *Origins;* Goodwyn; Nugent, "Some Parameters"; idem, *Tolerant Populists.*

8. Hofstadter, Chapter 1. Nugent (*Tolerant Populists;* "Some Parameters") demonstrated that Kansas Populists were not nativists and that they suffered from low crop prices and high fixed costs. Hackney, who portrays Alabama Populists as capitalists intent on getting their share of New South prosperity, extends Hofstadter's interpretation to that region.

9. I use the term "restorationist" in the same manner as have Shipps, Blumhofer, and Hughes to describe Mormons, Pentecostals, and Disciples/Churches of Christ.

10. I corroborate Pollack's (recent) and Durden's assessments that Populism was in harmony with classical economic liberalism. This is not intended to be the definitive volume on North Carolina Populism. The most extensive published treatments of North Carolina Populism are Durden's *Climax of Populism,* because it focuses on Marion Butler, and James Hunt's *Marion Butler and American Populism.* (Noblin and Lala

Carr Steelman treat only the North Carolina Alliance in their important works.) The most extensive unpublished assessment of North Carolina Populism is Beeby's "Revolt of the Tar Heelers"; I concur with most of his, Durden's, and Hunt's portrayals. Both Goodwyn and Palmer also treat North Carolina Populism extensively, arguing, in contrast to Durden, Hunt, and Beeby, that Populists there were out of step with the more important and radical southwestern Populists.

11. Corroborating this assessment are Flynn, 97–98; Beeby, 13, 23, 149–50; Hunt, 1, 42. There was not a direct causal connection between economic destitution and Populist voting; see Ayers, 280–81; Anderson, "Populists and Capitalist America," 125; McMath, "Agrarian Protest," 47; Flynn, 82.

12. On South Carolina, see Kantrowitz. The following corroborate this assessment of black support: Ayers, 270; Anderson, *Race and Politics*, 178–79, 194–205; Gaither, 87–94, 128; Beeby, 93–94, 135–91; Kousser, 36. Palmer disagrees, arguing from negative evidence that after 1892 North Carolina Populists did not seek black support (52–53, 56, 153). My almost exclusive reliance on white sources in my religion-to-Populism connections is due to a lack of black sources. Based, however, on a few letters and comments by blacks in white Populist papers, and on the ways blacks connected religion to support for the Republican Party, I assume that black Populists drew on their religious ideals in much the same way white Populists did.

13. Because I focus on North Carolina I deal almost solely with evangelicals, since they constituted over 90 percent of the state's churchgoing population. Handfuls of Catholics, Jews, and Universalists were scattered about the state, but research has not revealed their relationship to Populism. As Nugent (*Tolerant Populists*, 67–70; "Some Parameters," 257–58) and King ("Religious Dimensions," 112, 153–57, 163–72) have pointed out, in Kansas, Texas, and elsewhere, Populism also attracted Roman Catholics and United Brethren, along with a few Mennonites, Lutherans (depending on temperance views), Quakers, Unitarians, Universalists, Swedenborgians, Spiritualists, and assorted religious do-it-yourselfers. On problems posed by using the term "evangelical" in southern religion, see Schweiger's comments in Mathews, Hill, Schweiger, and Boles, "Forum: Southern Religion," 162.

14. Howe, 125–30; Isaac; C. Smith, "Correcting"; Hatch. Since the publication of Hatch's *Democratization of American Christianity,* debate has raged over the nature of antebellum evangelicalism that has spilled over into general discussions about the nature of evangelicalism. Hatch and scholars such as Rhys Isaac and Mark Noll have stressed the egalitarian aspects of evangelicalism and its support for countercultural social impulses, economic liberalism, and popular democracy. On the other hand, historians such as Wilenz, Johnson (*Shopkeepers Millennium*; Book Review of *Democratization*), and Wills have stressed evangelicalism's conservative, legitimating side. Somewhere in between have been scholars such as Mathews (*Religion in the Old South*) and Heyrman, who cast *early* evangelicalism as radical but detail its increasing role as guardian of the status quo. I agree with Howe, Noll, and others who argue that evangelicalism has held both impulses in tension.

15. I am broadening certain interpretations of postbellum southern evangelicalism by such historians such as Hill ("Northern and Southern Varieties"; *South and North*), Boles ("Discovery"), Wilson, and Faust (23–40), who, to varying degrees, focus on its

conservative, legitimating aspects while deemphasizing its countercultural or liberal tendencies and political activism. Harvey (4, 17–18), Ayers (398–408), Flynt ("Southern Protestantism"; "One in the Spirit"; *Alabama Baptists*), and Harrell ("Evolution"; "South") corroborate my assessment. Some of my generalizations about evangelicalism in the Southeast might not apply to Tennessee, Kentucky, or the Old Southwest.

16. Woodward, *Origins*; idem, *Strange Career*; Ayers; Kousser; Anderson, *Race and Politics*.

17. See Van Kley; Hilton; Carwardine; C. Smith ("Correcting a Curious Neglect"; *Resisting Reagan*). Larger structural change in society (urbanization) and events (the nomination of William Jennings Bryan) certainly influenced Populism, but I focus on how individuals interpreted these matters and how those interpretations shaped their responses. In doing so, however, I avoid the terms "ideology" or "worldview," since they have become burdened by theoretical baggage.

18. My thoughts on the reciprocal relationships among religion, culture, and society and on the power of religion or the transcendent to motivate action have been shaped by Geertz, Berger, Lindbeck, Niebuhr, Tillich, and Abzug. I especially find helpful Christian Smith's argument that, while established religion typically acts as a conservative force by giving meaning to the pervasive culture, because these meanings are rooted in transcendent realities, such religion has the potential to judge that culture on the basis of its transcendence. Thus, legitimation and a prophetic stance are mutually dependent; religion can produce such intense, devout reform because what it judges is itself so sacralized; see "Correcting a Curious Neglect"; *Resisting Reagan*, 372–85. I also draw on Smith's idea that reform identities are transferable as I argue that many evangelicals transferred their restorationist to their populist identities (*Resisting Reagan*, 382–83).

Section 1. Evangelical Establishment

1. *Hebron Record Book*, NCDOC; Lala Carr Steelman, "James Marion Mewborne," in *Dictionary of North Carolina Biography* (Chapel Hill: University of North Carolina Press, 1979).

2. *WT*, December 1876, 177–78.

3. *Hebron Record Book*, 25 October 1888.

4. *Proceedings*, North Carolina Christian Missionary Convention, 1890, 8.

5. *Hebron Record Book*, 5 October 1890; 11 October 1891.

6. *Hebron Record Book*, 6 March 1892.

7. *WT*, December 1876, 176–77; June 1877, 320–23; August 1877, 363–73.

8. *WT*, October 1877, 411; see also August 1877, 361–63; October, 1877, 409–13; and Circular Letter from Mewborne, F. W. Dixon, and John R. Dixon, 15 May 1880, NCDOC.

9. Quotations, in order: *NCB*, 11 November 1891, 2; 18 March 1891, 2. See also undated clipping, John Alexander Oates Papers, NCBHC; *NCB*, 23 March 1892, 2; 13 July 1892, 1.

Chapter 1. An Established Antiestablishmentarianism

1. Paschal; Harvey; Spain; Wills; C. B. Williams; Wigger; Holifield, 16, 26, 36–44; Calhoon, 152. For general religious developments, see Woodard; G. G. Johnson, 331–463; Paschal.

2. Calhoon, xi, 61, 123; Holifield, 11–20, 36–52, 147–49; Mathews, *Religion in the Old South,* xvii–xviii, 34–35, 81–135, 242–43; Heyrman, 5–27, 254–55; Harvey, 77–106; Loveland, 48–50, 109–10; Snay; Schweiger.

3. Woolverton; Rankin, 27–51 and *passim;* Rumple; T. C. Johnson; Thompson; Bost and Norris. Some rural Episcopal churches resembled other rural churches.

4. Barfield and Harrison, 34 and 36; see also Pelt.

5. See Wacker, "Playing for Keeps," 197–215. On O'Kelly, see Stokes and Scott, 37.

6. *BR,* 6 January 1892, 1; Wills, 98–115; Graham, 6–11; Tull; Hinson; Wigger.

7. Wyatt-Brown, 501–29; Tull, 81–107; Hassell.

8. Quotations from Wigger, 39. See also Ware, *North Carolina Disciples;* Hughes; Wigger, 39–41, 136; Stokes and Scott; Morrill; Drinkhouse; Carroll; Davis; Bassett.

9. Barfield and Harrison, 223; Morrill, 129–35; *Minutes,* North Carolina Conference, Methodist Protestant Church, 1894, 4–5, 19; 1902, 21.

10. *Report on Statistics of Churches, 1890,* 164, 193, 204, 290, 350, 387, 570, 587; *Board of the Census, Special Reports, Religious Bodies, Part I (1906),* 242–45; Creech, Chapter 2.

11. Lincoln and Mamiya, 17. See also Higginbotham; Montgomery; Raboteau; Mathews, *Religion and the Old South,* 136–236; Whitted; Boles, "Slaves in Biracial Churches"; J. T. Campbell; Gilmore; Logan, 164–73; Graves; Walls; Barber.

12. Faust, 58–81; Loveland, 186–265; Calhoon, 9, 163–91; Snay; Mathews, *Religion in the Old South,* 136–236; Carwardine, 133–73; Boles, *Irony,* 75–101; McCurry, 208–38.

13. Stowell, "Why 'Redemption'?"; idem, *Rebuilding Zion;* Wilson; Faust, 22–40; Snay, 2–5, 199–218; Thompson, vol. 2, 36; Farish, 22–162.

14. Harvey, 3–35; Thompson, vol. 2, 198–99; Stowell, *Rebuilding Zion,* 6–8; Gilmore, 3–89; Farish, 209–33; *Baptist Quarterly,* November 1896, 12; Montgomery, 78–79, 91, 142–90; Campbell, 60–62; Whitted, 18–36, 64–74; *NCB,* 15 June 1892, 2; *Church Worker,* August 1900, 1.

15. Stowell, *Rebuilding Zion,* 15–32; Thompson, vol. 2, 89–150; Farish, 28–64; Harvey, 21–31.

16. Harvey, 17–43, 86–106, 137–66; Barnes, 74–81; Farish, 87–91; Thompson, vol. 2, 294–307; Ware, *North Carolina Disciples,* 142–84, 203–14; Grantham, 246–74; Stowell, *Rebuilding Zion,* 110–29; *CA,* 10 October 1889, 1; numerous Baptist association resolutions, such as *Minutes,* Atlantic Baptist Association, 1886, 5; 1889, 14; 1893, 11.

17. Quotations, in order: *Southern Baptist,* 23 January 1896, 4, and Graham, 106–7.

18. Whitted, 112–18; Gilmore; Hall; Yohn; Ware, *North Carolina Disciples,* 150–56; Harvey, 27–29; *Minutes,* North Carolina Conference of the Methodist Protestant Church, 1890, 16, 22–24; 1891, 16–19; *WT,* 1 March 1886, 2.

19. See Masters.

20. *NCB,* 30 September 1891, 2; also see note 19 in Chapter 2.

21. Harvey, 2–4, 45–74, 107–35; Montgomery, 84–86, 118–37; Higginbotham; Gilmore; J. T. Campbell, ix, 28.

22. Farish, 70–76; Harvey, 96; *BR,* 25 January 1893, 2.

23. Jones; Barber; J. E. Campbell; Pelt, 189–93; Goff, FWB; Creech; *WT,* 1 March 1897, 3.

24. Quotation from *NCB,* 22 June 1892, 1. See also 23 December 1891 to 7 November 1894; *BR,* from 16 March 1892 to 4 October 1893; Creech, 191–95; contribution charts in

Minutes, Raleigh, Eastern, South Fork, Atlantic, Kings Mountain, and South River Baptist Associations, 1890–1905.

Chapter 2. Men and Machines

1. Loveland, ix–x, 1–16; Stowell, *Rebuilding Zion,* 8; Snay, 3, 8, 12; Mathews, *Religion in the Old South,* 4; Noll.

2. Holifield, ix, 4, 72–154; Calhoon; Loveland, 108–24, 161–62; and, more generally, the work of George Marsden, James Turner, Mark Noll, Daniel Walker Howe, Bruce Kuklick, and Henry May. Of course, commonsense had other dimensions.

3. Holifield, 152; Loveland, x; T. C. Johnson, 414; McCurry; Edwards.

4. *NCB,* 17 February 1892, 1. See Harvey, 6–7; Loveland, 31–32, 69–71; Wills, 3–6, 33; Mathews, *Religion and the Old South,* 25–46; Isaac; Hatch, especially 9–16, 76–81, 162–89.

5. Quotations, in order: Barfield and Harrison, 13, 32–33, and *BR,* 17 February 1892, 2. See also Hatch; Calhoon, 67–130.

6. *BR,* 17 February 1892, 2. See also Wills, 9, 24, 38–60; Calhoon, 102–40; Mathews, *Religion and the Old South,* 46.

7. Drinkhouse, vol. 1, 419–25.

8. Morrill, 64, 89, 98. See also Drinkhouse, vol. 1, 4, 236–37; vol. 2, 220–22, 279; *Our Church Record,* 28 April 1898, 1; *BR,* 20 June 1888, 2; 17 August 1892, 3; *Corinthian,* October 1900, 4; *CA,* 6 June 1889, 1–2; *HM,* 23 February 1898, 3; Morrill, 15–67, 85–100; C. B. Williams, 33–35, 46–70. Many antebellum southern evangelicals held democratic thinking in contempt and wanted to limit franchise. In postbellum sources, such notions, except in reference to white supremacy, were rare. I use the terms "republican" and "democratic" interchangeably. In this chapter, I often cite sermons appearing in Populist papers; these papers reprinted sermons that usually were not related directly to Populism, so unless otherwise noted, these citations reference general evangelical thinking.

9. *BR,* 26 September 1888, 2; see also 26 September 1888, 2; 24 June 1896, 1–2; 8 February 1899, 1; Loveland, 109–12; C. B. Williams, 45–70; *Minutes,* North Carolina Conference of the Methodist Protestant Church, 1898, 9; *PF,* 8 October 1895, 4; *FA,* 10 June 1981, 1; *Central Protestant,* 18 January 1890, 1; *NCB,* 27 May 1891, 2; 6 July 1892, 2.

10. Quotations, in order: Drinkhouse, vol. 1, 419–21; vol. 2, 605. See also *PF,* 7 January 1896, 4.

11. Quotations, in order: *WT,* 7 June 1901, 4, and *FA,* 21 September 1892, 1. See also Carroll, 11–13, 16–21; Davis, 7–13, 37–49; Drinkhouse, vol. 1, 1–10, 219; Bassett, 22–26; Morrill, 15–67, 85–99; *Church Worker,* March 1899, 1; May 1899, 1; *PF,* 30 April 1895, 4; *Christian Sun,* 23 April 1891, 98; *BR,* 26 September 1888, 2; 11 May 1892, 2; *CA,* 28 November 1889, 1; *WT,* 15 March 1901, 2; T. C. Johnson, 320–25.

12. Bode; Ford, 34–36; Loveland; Startup; *CA,* 8 April 1897, 1.

13. *NCB,* 28 June 1893, 2.

14. Bode, 4–7, 11, 66–67; Barnes, 93; Harvey, 197–206; Walsh; Holifield, 11–13, 36–44, 147–49; Edwards, 184–217.

15. Quotations, in order: *HM,* 5 January 1898, 7, and *Toisnot Transcript,* 4 May 1876, 1. See also *CA,* 6 June 1889, 1–2; 11 August 1892, 1; Thompson, vol. 3, 240–43; *BR,* 18 April 1888, 1; 22 August 1894, 1; 5 September 1894, 1; 2 March 1898, 4; 28 February 1900, 1; *Corinthian,* September 1894, 2; March 1895, 1, 4; November 1898, 2; *HM,* 16 March 1898,

1; *WT,* 15 June 1893, 3; 15 April 1894, 7; Walsh; Flynt, "Southern Protestantism"; Harrell, *Sources,* 91–118; Freeze; Startup; Harper.

16. *NCB,* 14 January 1891, 3; see also N. L. Shropshire, "Nobility of Labor" (1899), No. 2 Exhibit Book, NCDOC; Harvey, 206–26.

17. Harrell, *Sources,* 46–49; Startup, 47–66; *WT,* 1 June 1896, 1; 12 August 1899, 4–5; 25 May 1900, 1; 9 August 1901, 2; *Western North Carolina Baptist,* 8 December 1887, 1; *Central Protestant,* 29 May 1880, 1; Harper Sermon Book, 1885, 33, NCDOC; Thompson, vol. 2, 387.

18. Quotations from *FA,* 27 January 1892, 3, and Dixon, *Living Problems,* 35–36. See also Harvey, 137–52, and *WT,* December 1876, 177–79.

19. *BR,* 17 August 1892, 2. See also 25 May 1888, 1; 13 November 1893, 1, 2; *HM,* 16 March 1898, 1; Harvey, 165; *NCB,* 18 April 1894, 2.

20. See *PF,* 17 July 1888, 1; 9 July 1895, 4; *Corinthian,* June 1894, 1; *BR,* 6 January 1892, 1; *NCB,* 8 April 1891, 4; 25 November 1891, 2; Herring, *Manly Boy,* NCBHC; *Minutes,* Presbyterian Synod of North Carolina, 1895, 360; *FA,* 10 June 1891, 1; *Minutes,* Eastern Baptist Association, 1897, 14–15; *CA,* 26 September 1889, 1; 10 October 1889, 1; 26 March 1891, 4; *Proceedings,* Classis of North Carolina of the Reformed Church, 1886, 23–26; Edwards, 5–106, 161–77, 219; McCurry, 5–91.

21. *HM,* 6 October 1897, 4; *Journal of Proceedings,* North Carolina Annual Conference, United Methodist Church, South, 1890, 31; *Reformed Church Standard,* 1 July 1908; *CA,* 4 March 1897, 1.

22. Davis, 12; *CA,* 3 March 1892, 1, 4; Edwards; McCurry.

23. T. C. Johnson, 379–81; Graham, 143.

24. *WT,* June 1877, 320–23; August 1877, 361–73; 30 November 1900, 1; *NCB,* 11 March 1891, 1; 11 November 1891, 2; 6 July 1892, 2; 24 May 1893, 2; *BR,* 20 June 1888, 1–2; 6 January 1892, 1; 27 April 1892, 3; 4 May 1892, 4; Ware, *North Carolina Disciples,* 125; *PF,* 9 July 1895, 4; Graham, 6–8.

25. Drinkhouse, vol. 1, 418, 419–20; vol. 2, 606. See also *WT,* 27 July 1900, 1; *BR,* 22 February 1888, 1; *Central Protestant,* 18 January 1890, 1; *NCB,* 18 March 1891, 1.

26. *NCB,* 21 June 1893, 2; see also 11 November 1891, 2; 3 February 1892, 2; 24 February 1892, 2; 6 July 1892, 2; 17 August 1892, 1; 21 June 1893, 2; *BR,* 20 January 1892, 1; 30 November 1892, 6; Harvey, 88–91.

27. *WT,* 15 November 1883, 2; 1 September 1897, 3; Graham, 85; *BR,* 29 August 1888, 2; 3 July 1893, 1; *Minutes,* Atlantic Baptist Association, 1892, 13–14; 1893, 11; Bode, 64–66, 197–226. "Taxation" quotation from *HM,* 16 March 1898, 1.

28. *BR,* 23 May 1888, 1; Alexander, xi–xii, 95, 138–41.

29. *Christian Sun,* 12 April 1891, 56; *NCB,* 9 December 1891, 2; 25 May 1892, 2; 19 October 1892, 2; 23 May 1894, 2; *Asheville Baptist,* 24 September 1889, 2; *BR,* 14 February 1894, 1; *Corinthian,* August 1896, 2; *WT,* 13 October 1899, 3; Harper Sermon Book No. 10 (1894), 10; *CA,* 17 October 1895, 2–3.

30. Loveland, 108–25; Carwardine, 8–9, 25–28.

31. Snay, 9–12; Thompson, vol. 2, 403–13; Holifield, 154; Mathews, *Religion in the Old South,* 156–57; Wilson; T. C. Johnson, 424–31; Stowell, *Rebuilding Zion,* 147–48; *Reformed Church Standard,* 1 May 1907, 1. Many northerners also held this view.

32. T. C. Johnson, 424; *TS,* 4 February 1892, 4.

33. *Corinthian*, September 1896, 2; see also March 1896, 2; *NCB*, 23 September 1891, 2; 10 February 1892, 2; 27 July 1892, 2; 23 November 1898, 1; *FA*, 25 November 1891, 1; *WT*, 15 June 1900, 2; 7 June 1901, 4; *BR*, 27 April 1892, 1; 21 September 1898, 4; *Our Church Record*, 24 January 1895, 1; Alexander, 110–11, 138.

34. Grantham; Harvey, 24–25; Grill, 76–77; Thompson, vol. 3, 264; Farish, 325–61; *CA*, 8 April 1897, 1.

35. *Asheville Baptist*, 2 July 1889, 2.

36. *BR*, 11 May 1892, 2. See also *NCB*, 14 October 1891, 1; 9 December 1891, 2; 10 February 1892, 2; *WT*, 9 February 1900, 1; 2 March 1900, 2; *BR*, 16 February 1898, 1; *Little River Record*, September 1907, 2; *CA*, 26 December 1889, 3.

37. Bode, 5–7, 20–38; *Minutes*, Eastern Baptist Association, 1896, 15; 1897, 14–15; *NCB*, 9 May 1894, 2; 16 May 1894, 1; *BR*, from 17 January 1894 through 14 September 1898.

38. *Minutes*, Kings Mountain Baptist Association, 1894, 11; *Christian Sun*, 26 March 1891, 36; *Minutes*, Atlantic Baptist Association, 1894, 7; *Minutes*, North Carolina Conference, Methodist Protestant Church, 1890, 30; *WT*, 1 February 1886, 2; Nash, 32–34, 62–63; Goff, 35–37, FWB; Whitener.

39. *NCB*, 7 September 1892, 1. Previous quotation is from 9 December 1891, 2. See his columns in the *NCB* from December 1891 through April 1894, along with 23 December 1891, 2, and *Christians' Almanac and Annual*, 1892, 28.

Section 2. *The Voice of God in the Alliance Whirlwind*

1. Noblin; *PF*, 1886–92; Polk's letters, LPP and the Polk/Denmark Collection, NCDAH.

2. *NCB*, 14 January 1891, 2. Editor Rev. J. A. Oates, Jr., was an Alliance lecturer (*CA*, 20 August 1891, 4; 24 December 1891, 3); his father, J. A., Sr., was president of the Sampson County Alliance (*CA*, 7 March 1889, 2); Editor Rev. William B. Oliver was also active (*CA*, 14 November 1889, 2), and Editor Rev. E. J. Edwards was Cumberland County Alliance business agent and the first chaplain of the state Alliance (*PF*, 13 October 1887, 1). See also *NCB*, 14 January 1891, 2; 4 February 1891, 4; 1 April 1891, 4; *PF*, 30 July 1889, 6.

3. OCALA, 4–5.

4. *PF*, *CA*, and *Southern Mercury*.

5. Quotations, in order: *FA*, 1 July 1891, 1; Jamestown Alliance Minutebook, DU, 23 May 1891; *PF*, 7 March 1891, 4; 4 November 1890, 2; *CA*, 19 November 1891, 1. See also *CA*, 12 September 1889, 1; 18 December 1890, 1, 2; 25 December 1890, 1; 10 December 1891, 1; 20 July 1893, 3; *PF*, 8 July 1890, 6.

6. Cook, *Thomas Dixon*; idem, *Fire from the Flint*; Crowe; *BR*, 18 July 1888, 1.

7. Dixon, *Living Problems*, 133–34; see also 18, 35, 39, 40–43, 50–69, 163, 189, 244–54; *PF*, 10 February 1891, 7; 2 June 1891, 5; 9 June 1891, 5; *CA*, 16 April 1891, 1; 23 April 1891, 1; 30 July 1891, 1–4; 11 February 1892, 1; 18 February 1892, 1; 17 March 1892, 2; 7 April 1892, 2; 28 April 1892, 1; and other sermons in *PF*, *CA*, and *FA*, from 1891 to 1893.

8. *PF*, 4 November 1890, 2.

9. *PF*, 23 December 1890, 6.

10. *PF*, 4 November 1890, 2.

11. PNCFA, 1888, 3; 1889, 6; 1891, 4.

12. Goodwyn, 656.

13. *PF,* 16 February 1888, 2; *CA,* 7 August 1890, 2. By emphasizing the "Alliance crucible," I stress with McMath the cultural antecedents of evangelicalism, classical political economics, and democratic/republican thinking, yet, with Goodwyn, I see the Alliance as a place where a unique understanding of these issues formed.

Chapter 3. The Alliance *Vorzeit*

1. G. G. Johnson; Escott, *North Carolina Yeoman.*

2. Nugent, *Money and American Society,* 58–59, 160–61, 226–27; Ritter; Unger; Goodwyn, 4–24. The Coinage Act of 1873 dropped the standard 412 grain silver dollar but did not drop trade-use silver dollars or "subsidiary silver" from the list (half-dollars and smaller coins with silver content).

3. Woodward, *Origins,* 183.

4. Goodwyn, 11–15.

5. Nugent, *Money and American Society,* 34–47.

6. Powell, 406–21; Lefler and Newsome, 474–97; Billings, 25–95; Wood, 22–156; Ayers, 14–15, 33–37, 187–213; Noblin, 87–108; Saloutos, 1–68; Fite, 1–47.

7. See Ayers.

8. Dixon, *Life Worth Living,* 41–51.

9. Fite, xii.

10. Chaffin Journal, 1888–94, DU.

11. Graham, 173–74.

12. "Hard Times," Harper Sermon Book, no. 5, 1889, 124–29, NCDOC.

13. Quotations, in order: *NCB,* 2 November 1892, 2; *PF,* 16 February 1887, 2; see also *CA,* 28 March 1889, 1; 21 November 1889, 3; 19 December 1889, 1, 2.

14. *TS,* 4 February 1892, 4.

15. *PF,* 31 July 1888, 6; see also 19 January 1887, 4; 13 March 1888, 2; Noblin, 91–102; McMath, *Populist Vanguard,* 20–21; *BR,* 18 April 1888, 1. The Greenback Party had little impact in North Carolina (Ritter, 113–23).

16. The clubs initially blossomed in the central part of the state and then expanded east and west and existed formally into 1888; see *PF,* 1886–87, especially 31 March 1886, 4; 1 December 1886, 4; 13 October 1887, 1; 19 January 1888, 2–3; Noblin, 149–82, 190–298; L. C. Steelman.

17. *PF,* 9 June 1886, 1. See also 24 February 1886, 3–4; 17 April 1886, 2; 26 May 1886, 5; 20 October 1886, 1; 3 July 1888, 1.

18. *PF,* 2 March 1887, 1. See also 10 November 1887, 2; 27 November 1888, 4; 7 January 1890, 2. Some urban Democrats also supported this view; see T. J. Jarvis to Carr, 25 April 1889; 21 April 1890, ECP; *CA,* 21 March 1889, 1, 4.

19. *PF,* 3 March 1886, 7; 31 March 1886, 3. Not all Association or Alliance farmers were antielitists; see, for example, *CA,* 17 October 1889, 2.

20. *PF,* 21 April 1886, 1, 2; 3 March 1886, 4; 27 October 1886, 4; 3 November 1886, 4; 22 May 1888, 1; 4 November 1890, 2; Ayers, 55–80.

21. *PF,* 31 July 1888, 6. See also 3 March 1886, 1; 20 March 1888, 2; 3 April 1888, 3.

22. *PF,* 31 March 1886, 4; 7 July 1886, 4; 29 September 1886, 1, 4.

23. *PF,* 23 February 1887, 1. See also 21 April 1886, 4; 5 May 1886, 2; 2 June 1886, 2; 19 January 1887, 2; 30 June 1887, 1; 5 March 1889, 1, 4; 7 October 1890, 6; 21 July 1891, 1; *CA,* 12

December 1889, 3. The Association and Alliance in North Carolina from the start saw political action as the primary means for economic reform. I agree with McMath ("Agrarian Protest"), though, that after about 1888, this politicization intensified. Goodwyn (110–53), however, detects a shift from cooperative economic ventures to political action after such enterprises failed, which might well have been the case in Texas.

24. *PF,* 10 April 1888, 1. Goodwyn (47–49, 111–21) identifies enmity between local furnishing merchants and farmers as the chief source of Alliance hostilities. In North Carolina, Alliance targets were primarily local political figures, monopolists, and, initially, Republicans.

Chapter 4. *Religion and the Rise of the Farmers' Alliance*

1. *PF,* 23 June 1887, 2; 14 July 1887, 3. Sealy was assisted by Rev. J. A. Smith, Rev. S. Ivey, and Baptist lay leader Thaddeus Ivey.

2. *CA,* 15 October 1891, 3; D. D. Wells to Thompson, 8 December 1892, CTP; John Dail, *A History of Wilmington Presbytery* (n.p.: n.d.), 26–28, quotation on 26. Thanks to Rev. Neal Carter for the information on Shaw. Rev. W. I. Smith, *North Carolina Baptist* editor W. B. Oliver, and other Baptist ministers helped establish the Alliance in Duplin County (*PF,* 23 February 1888, 6; note 3, below). Presbyterians and German Reformed ministers organized Cabarrus County (*PF,* 17 November 1887, 1; 11 September 1888, 7).

3. In Nash, Wilson, and Edgecombe counties, see activities of Baptist Revs. G. M. Duke and Lunsford Lloyd and of John Ammons in the mountains (*PF,* 17 April 1988, 6; 28 July 1891, 2). Duke was the first president of the Nash County Alliance, Lloyd was a Populist in the 1893 state legislature, and Ammons was a Populist in the 1895 state senate. On Whitakers, see notes 1 and 3 in the Introduction. Other Disciples in the Alliance in Pitt County included A. B. Congleton of Oak Grove Christian Church, whose Carolina Alliance met there (*PF,* 3 September 1889, 4), and F. M. Kilpatrick of Salem Christian Church, whose Experiment Alliance met there (*PF,* 9 December 1890, 4; Salem Church Records, NCDOC). Other Disciples Alliancemen included lecturer Rev. John Respess (Respess Sermon Books, NCDOC); F. M. Dixon and F. D. Koontz of Greene and Onslow (*PF,* 23 July 1889, 2), and Rev. D. H. Petree of Stokes County (*PF,* 4 November 1890, 1). Methodist Protestant Rev. G. E. Hunt was an organizer in Nash and then Davidson counties; see note 3, Introduction; *PF,* 16 April 1889, 1. On W. A. Graham, see Graham; *PF,* 7 May 1889, 2; PNCFA, 1888 to 1892. On the Catawba County area, see information on Col. H. A. Forney (*PF,* 5 November 1889, 2; Clapp, RCA; biographical sketch, H. A. Forney, RCA); Rev. J. L. Murphy, editor of *The Corinthian* (numerous articles in *HM* by Murphy), and Baptists J. F. Click, Rev. G. E. Gower, Rev. C. M. Murcheson, and Rev. R. L. Patton (*HM,* 16 April 1892, 7; 14 September 1892, 4; PNCFA, 1892, 26). Baptist lay leader J. Y. Hamrick was active in the Cleveland County Alliance (*PF,* 21 August 1888, 2). Local Methodist organizers included Dr. R. L. Abernathy, Rev. L. A. Shuford, Rev. M. A. Abernathy, and J. M. "Plateau Kicker" Clampitt (*PF,* 11 September 1888, 1; 12 November 1889, 1; *HM,* 6 April 1892, 5). Other ministers included I. A. Rector of Burke, J. P. Miller and J.T.B. Hoover (Methodist) in Catawba, and L. T. Speight (*PF,* 12 August 1890, 1; 28 July 1891, 2; *HM,* 6 April 1892, 1). In the Cape Fear region, on Oates, Oliver, and Edwards, see note 3, Introduction to Section 2. On Baptist ministers, see also J. M. Byrd (*PF,* 7 August 1888, 6); O. P. Meeks (*CA,* 6 August 1891, 3); William Bland (*CA,* 24 December 1891, 3);

D. W. Tew (*PF,* 3 April 1888, 5); Wiley M. Page (*CA,* 24 December 1891, 3); J. O. Tew (*CA,* 7 March 1889, 3); J. W. Bell (*CA,* 28 July 1892, 4); J. A. Oates, Sr. (*CA,* 7 March 1889, 2); S. B. Page (*PF,* 28 August 1888, 1); J. L. Stewart (*CA,* 16 April 1891, 2). Bland, Oates, Jr., and Page oversaw the South River Alliance Union in Sampson. One leader in the South River Association, Isham Royal, was an Alliance organizer (*CA,* 28 March 1889, 2). On William Byrd, see *PF,* 28 February 1888, 7; 7 August 1888, 2; Goff, 17, FWB. Alliance Methodist Rev. J. B. Jernigan was pastor of Antioch church in Johnston, the first Pentecostal congregation in the North Carolina holiness church (*PF,* 9 April 1889, 8; 17 June 1890, 8; and J. E. Campbell, 227–28). I have located other holiness folk who became Populists (Henry J. Faison and A. B. Crumpler [*CA,* 12 October 1893, 3; 27 August 1896, 3]), but Byrd is the only one I have located in the Alliance. G. F. Taylor, a holiness leader in the Pentecostal Holiness denomination, read *The Caucasian* as a child, writing a letter to the editor published on 10 March 1898, 4. Taylor wrote a paper on Populism when completing his master's degree in history at the University of North Carolina. Along with Methodist J. G. Johnson (*PF,* 19 May 1891, 4) and J. B. Jernigan, other active Methodist ministers in the area were T. H. Sutton (*CA,* 18 August 1892, 4); P. J. Wray (*PF,* 17 April 1888, 7); and Erskin Pope (*PF,* 16 April 1889, 3). Also involved in the Sampson County area were Free Will Baptist Rev. R. A. Johnson (*CA,* 22 August 1889, 1); Quaker Rev. B. E. Perkins (*CA,* 20 July 1893, 3); and ministers of unknown denomination: Z. J. Needham (*PF,* 17 April 1888, 4); T. W. Kendall (*PF,* 22 May 1888, 1); Gray Culbreth (*PF,* 24 July 1888, 4); A. J. Bordeaux (*PF,* 26 June 1888, 7); J. E. Bristowe and J.D.O. Culbreth (*CA,* 18 July 1889, 3); W. R. Johnson (*CA,* 27 July 1893, 3); J. F. Usery (*CA,* 12 October 1893, 3); L. Culbreth and Henry Duncan (*CA,* 1 January 1891, 2). On Francis Joyner, see *PF,* 13 November 1888, 4. On Chatham, see Baptist Rev. O. T. Edwards (*PF,* 22 July 1890, 7); Mt. Elam Christian Church (*PF,* 12 January 1888, 2); Asbury Chapel (Methodist, *PF,* 15 April 1890, 6); Hickory Mountain (Methodist), Sandy Branch, and New Salem churches (*PF,* 15 May 1888, 6); Mays Chapel (*PF,* 19 May 1891, 4); and Reive's Chapel (Baptist, *PF,* 18 June 1889, 1). On Franklin, see Baptist Revs. Baylus Cade and W. A. Barnett, and Methodist lay pastor D. P. Meacham among Popes Chapel Christian Church and Baptist churches Mt. Olive, Perry's, Social Plains, Poplar Springs, and Cypress Chapel(*PF,* 22 September 1887, 1; 26 January 1888, 7; 2 February 1888, 6; 17 April 1888, 4). On O'Kelly Alliance, see *PF,* 2 February 1888, 1. On Moore and Primitive Baptists, see *TS,* 23 July 1891, 3; *FA,* 2 September 1891, 3; 5 October 1892, 3; McMath, "Agrarian Protest," 48. For documentation on ministerial affiliation for listed ministers, see Creech.

4. On editors, see issues of their papers. On Denmark, see letters in LPP and the Polk/Denmark Collection (NCDAH) on the Baptist Student Aid Association and *PF.* See also the correspondence between Ayers and Butler in MBP. On Patillo and Rogers, see L. C. Steelman, 178–79; *PF,* 26 May 1886, 3; 26 August 1890, 2; Whitted, 52, 85–86, 111. On Fife, see *FA,* 27 January 1892, 3; *CA,* 6 August 1891, 3; 24 September 1891, 1–2; 8 October 1891, 3. Ministers were also organizers in Rowan (B. A. York and A. L. Coburn, *PF,* 8 October 1889, 1), Randolph (the centrality of Trinity College to Polk's Association and Dr. D. R. Parker and Rev. B. F. Hayworth, *PF,* 1886 to 1887; 31 July 1888, 7), Vance (*PF,* 16 February 1888, 6), Guilford (Guilford College and Quaker Albert Peele, *PF,* 10 April 1888, 3), Warren (L. C. Perkinson *PF,* 10 April 1888, 3), Alexander (Baptist J. T. Stover, Methodist J.T.B. Hoover, and Baptist churches Pleasant Hill, Little River, and Poplar

Springs, *PF,* 5 February 1889, 3; 19 April 1892, 1), Madison (Baptist S. J. Morgan, *PF,* 16 April 1889, 3), and Clay (J. W. Farmer, J. T. Platt, and J. G. Mashburn, *PF,* 14 May 1889, 8; 11 June 1889, 1). Others leaders in the state Alliance included Methodist lay leaders E. A. Thorne (*FA,* 15 April 1891, 1), Drs. A. B. Nobles and Cyrus Thompson (*FA,* 15 July 1891, 3); M. J. Battle (multiple references, *PF* and *FA*); Methodist Rev. P. H. Massey (*PF,* 4 June 1889, 3); and Quaker W. H. Worth and Methodist W. A. Darden, both of Lenoir County and vital to the State Business Agency (PNCFA, 1888, 18; 1889, 27).

5. Sparta Minutebook, ECP; *PF,* 17 April 1888, 4; Brown, 119–25; Johnson Papers, which include the Centre Minutebook, DU. In Wilson, Freeman was joined by Methodist minister J.T.B. Hoover, and in Onslow, Thompson was joined by Baptist lay leader Hill E. King and Revs. H. Lennon, M. M. Walker, D. E. Green, D. F. Aman, and J. J. Baker (*PF,* 12 January 1888, 3; 27 March 1888, 6; 24 April 1888, 7).

6. Quotations, in order: *PF,* 8 March 1892, 1; Jamestown Minutebook, DU, 28 March 1891. It is unclear if the original Farmers' Clubs included women, but by 1888 many suballiances did. No pattern seems to determine which suballiances allowed women, but there appears to have been countywide agreement. For male/female ratios in suballiances, see Creech, 296–97.

7. *PF,* 22 May 1888, 1.

8. *CA,* 3 September 1891, 1; *PF,* 8 March 1892, 8.

9. Salem Church Records. In Whitakers, Whitakers Temple Methodist Protestant Church, Bethany Christian Church, and Gethsemane Baptist established the Alliance; in Pitt County, Oak Grove and Corinth Christian churches did (note 3, above, and, on Nash, *PF,* 17 April 1888, 6). Penelope's minister, C. M. Murcheson, was an Alliance leader, as were Rev. G. E. Gower and P. K. Morgan of Penelope (note 3, above). On Click, see *HM,* in general; Abernathy and Greenhill, 49–122. For churches as organization bases, see note 2 on Chatham and Franklin, above. See also Falling Creek, Daniels, Salem Methodist, Indians Springs, and Oakland in Wayne (*PF,* 22 March 1892, 5; *CA,* 22 September 1895, 4); numerous churches in Sampson, including Mt. Moriah, Hopewell, and Andrews Chapel Methodist churches (*PF,* 17 April 1888, 4; *CA,* 16 January 1890, 2; 7 January 1892, 3), and Galacia in Cumberland (*PF,* 23 February 1888, 6). On Hebron, see Hebron Church Records, NCDOC; *PF,* 17 March 1888, 7; 10 April 1888, 3; 17 September 1889, 5; Creech, 298. See the exceptional example of Zion Alliance in *PF,* 16 April 1889, 1.

10. *PF,* 23 July 1889, 1. See also 6 March 1888, 3; 24 December 1889, 2; 4 November 1890, 1; 6 October 1891, 2; *CA,* 13 August 1891, 3.

11. Sparta Alliance Minutes, 20 December 1889; *PF,* 3 November 1891, 1; Centre Alliance Minutebook, 19 October 1889 through February 1890; 13 April 1889; Salem Church Records, Alliance section, 1 January 1891.

12. *PF,* 26 August 1890, 2; see also note 4, above; Goodwyn, 276–306; *PF,* 10 July 1888, 2; 31 July 1888, 4; Gaither, 1–25. Rev. Robert Ikard organized the Colored Alliance in the Catawba area (*HM,* 9 March 1892, 7). My discussion of the Colored Alliance and black Populists is based mostly on white accounts, for, except for a few letters and articles in white Alliance newspapers, virtually no accounts from black perspectives exist. This paucity demonstrates how the prevailing white supremacy dictated that the reflections of blacks not be published in white Alliances and Populist newspapers. Goodwyn (276–77) corroborates this.

13. *CA,* 20 June 1889, 4; 26 September 1889, 1; 16 January 1890, 1; 12 May 1892, 3; 23 June 1892, 3; *PF,* 4 August 1887, 1.

14. *PF,* 10 March 1886, 4, 7.

15. *CA,* 27 June 1889, 1; see also *PF,* 29 January 1889, 6.

16. Undated clipping, *Journal of Industry,* LPP. See also *CA,* 30 March 1893, 1.

17. *FA,* 23 September 1891, 1; see also *PF,* 15 September 1891, 2; *TS,* 13 March 1892, 3.

18. Periodically I use citations that range widely in time, but I am careful to do so only with ideas that were consistent over time.

19. *PF,* 2 February 1892, 6; *FA,* 8 April 1891, 2; Rev. D. P. Meacham to Polk, 23 February 1887, LPP; McMath, "Agrarian Protest." For North Carolina, I disagree with Hahn's assessment that Populism was a radical departure from liberalism (3). See also *PF,* 15 September 1886, 4; *CA,* 22 January 1891, 2; 12 February 1891, 2; Palmer, 9–19, 30, 41–46; Pollack, xii–ix. For concise statements on God's moral governance, see *PF,* 19 January 1887, 2; 28 February 1888, 2; 3 April 1888, 2; 23 April 1889, 4; 16 December 1890, 4.

20. *CA,* 1 May 1890, 1; 28 May 1891, 2; 4 February 1892, 3; PNCFA, 1892, 25; *PF,* 26 February 1889, 6; 20 January 1891, 2, 6; 19 May 1891, 1.

21. *CA,* 11 February 1892, 1; see also 21 August 1890, 2; 18 February 1892, 1; *PF,* 14 April 1886, 4; 28 April 1886, 2, 4; 17 July 1888, 2; 12 January 1892, 8; Goodwyn, 51–54.

22. Jamestown Minutebook; Salem Church record book; Centre Minutebook; *PF,* 30 October 1888, 1; 12 February 1889, 1; *CA,* 16 May 1889, 1. Alliance farmers in Texas pooled their cotton; North Carolina Alliance farmers seem only to have pooled tobacco.

23. Correspondence among Carr, W. A. Darden, and W. A. Graham in 1889, ECP; *PF,* summer and fall, 1888; PNCFA, 1888, 1889, and 1892; Centre Minutebook, 25 February 1889; *PF,* 29 January 1889, 3; *PF,* resolutions from the fall of 1888 to the fall of 1889; McMath, *Populist Vanguard,* 54–56.

24. Pollack on "democratic capitalism," ix and xii; OCALA, 22, 33; *PF,* 15 December 1886, 2; 15 December 1887, 1; 21 July 1891, 2; 5 January 1892, 4; *CA,* 9 June 1892, 2. J. M. Mewborne, however, argued that, given how the plutocrats had disrupted the system, "there must of necessity be some paternalism," *PF,* 23 February 1892, 4.

25. PNCFA, 1892, 13–14; Noblin, 208; *PF,* 5 March 1889, 1, 2, 4; 19 March 1889, 2; 7 October 1890, 4; 17 March 1891, 1, 2.

26. Restorationism is explored in Section 3, but see *PF,* 21 July 1891, 8; Dunning.

27. *PF,* 23 April 1889, 4. See also M. H. Rand to Carr, 14 September 1890, ECP.

28. Quotations, in order: Polk, *Protest,* ECP, 1; *PF,* 17 July 1888, 1; see also 2 December 1890, 4.

29. *PF,* 19 February 1889, 1; see also 24 November 1891, 1; *FA,* 13 May 1891, 2; *CA,* 21 August 1890, 2; PNCFA, 1891, 7.

30. Quotations, in order: *PF,* 22 July 1890, 4; *HM,* 6 April 1892, 3. See also *CA,* 2 November 1893, 1; *PF,* 3 April 1888, 1; 4 February 1890, 1; 2 September 1890, 4; 3 February 1891, 7; 11 August 1891, 1; 15 March 1892, 1; 29 March 1892, 6; Rev. James Pitchford to Carr, 1 January 1891, ECP. Alliancefolk did, however, celebrate Confederate mythology.

31. Quotations, in order: *PF,* 16 December 1890, 4; 12 November 1889, 1; 8 December 1891, 2. See also 18 November 1890, 1; 4 August 1891, 4; 16 February 1892, 1.

32. *PF,* 30 July 1889, 6. See also *CA,* 14 April 1892, 2.

33. Quotations, in order: *PF,* 29 March 1892, 1; 2 February 1892, 6. See also 9 February 1892, 1 ("Brimstone"); *CA,* 2 June 1892, 1, 2.

34. *PF,* 29 July 1890, 4; see also 25 August 1887, 1; 23 March 1889, 2; 28 May 1889, 1; *Windsor Public Ledger,* 19 October 1887, 1; *FA,* 2 December 1890, 4; 25 November 1891, 1.

35. *CA,* 20 April 1893, 4.

36. *CA,* 9 September 1897, 4; see also 17 October 1889, 6.

37. *PF,* 21 July 1887, 1; 25 June 1889, 1; 24 September 1889, 6; 22 December 1891, 1; *CA,* 5 September 1889, 1; 18 December 1890, 2; 28 January 1892, 4; PNCFA, 1892, 32–33; Edwards, 145–52; McCurry, 72–85.

38. *PF,* 18 June 1889, 2; 7 October 1890, 7; 3 March 1891, 3; 23 June 1891, 1; PNCFA, 1889, 8, 23; *CA,* 7 August 1890, 3; notes 42 and 43, below.

39. This language intensified in 1891 and 1892, but it was there from 1886; see *PF,* 10 February 1886, 4; 18 June 1889, 1, 2; 5 August 1890, 4; 17 March 1891, 2; 24 November 1891, 1; *CA,* 12 May 1892, 1; Hunt, 38–43.

40. Quotations, in order: *PF,* 21 April 1891, 4; Polk, *Protest,* 1–2, Elias Carr Papers. See also *PF,* 7 May 1889, 2; 7 June 1892, 4; E. A. Thorne, undated letter to *Dispatch,* Thorne Papers, DU; Dunning, 1–10.

41. *PF,* 14 April 1887, 3; 23 June 1891, 4; 14 July 1891, 2; 9 August 1892, 4; D. H. Rittenhouse to E. A. Thorne, 21 May 1890, Thorne Papers.

42. OCALA, 4. See also *TS,* 30 March 1891, 1; *CA,* 12 December 1889, 3; 12 February 1891, 2; PNCFA, 1891, 4–8.

43. *PF,* 17 November 1891, 1; see also 23 September 1890, 4; 7 April 1891, 4; 2 February 1892, 2; 8 March 1892, 3; 22 March 1892, 4; *HM,* 2 December 1891, 5.

44. *PF,* 10 February 1891, 6; see also 28 February 1888, 2; 12 March 1891, 5; 7 April 1891, 4; 26 January 1892, 1; 9 February 1892, 1; 29 March 1892, 1, 6; *FA,* 24 June 1891, 2.

45. *PF,* 2 September 1890, 4; 26 September 1893, 1. On Kansas, see Nugent, *Tolerant Populists.*

46. *CA,* 18 December 1890, 2. "Moral plague" and "great moral revolution" come from PNCFA, 1891, 7; *PF,* 6 May 1890, 1. See also W. K. Carr to Carr, 18 December 1891, ECP; *CA,* 24 October 1889, 2; 18 December 1890, 1, 2; 25 December 1890, 1; 3 December 1891, 4; *PF,* 20 November 1888, 6; *FA,* 1 July 1891, 2; 2 December 1891, 1; 2 March 1892, 1; Pollack, ix–x, xii.

47. *HM,* 15 June 1892, 2.

48. *PF,* 22 September 1891, 1.

49. Mewborne to Carr, 25 May 1890, ECP.

50. *PF,* 1 December 1891, 8. The "vine and fig tree" refers to the millennium in Zechariah 3:10 and Micah 4:4 and to peace and prosperity in I Kings 4:25.

Section 3. Vox Populi, Vox Dei

1. *CA,* 12 January 1893, 4. See also Anderson, "Populists and Capitalist America," 109–12; Battle and Yelverton, 595, 602–3; *TS,* 21 April 1892, 2.

2. *FA,* 2 December 1891, 3.

3. Quotations, in order: *FA,* 23 September 1891, 3; 30 March 1892, 2.

4. *FA,* 23 March 1892, 3.

5. *FA,* 30 March 1892, 3.

6. *FA,* 20 April 1892, 2.

7. *TS,* 3 November 1892, 2; see also 15 September 1892, 2.

8. *FA,* 20 April 1892, 2. See also 6 April 1892, 3; 13 April 1892, 2; *TS,* 8 September 1892, 1.

9. Populist Redmond Winstead started People's Chapel in Elm City, near Whitakers, in 1893; see Populist Party Executive Communication Forms, Nash, 22 January 1900, MBP; People's Chapel FWBC Cemetery Records, NCDAH; Barfield and Harrison, 335.

10. Carwardine, 126–27; *Zion's Landmark,* 15 October 1892, 549–52; 15 December 1892, 57–59; *Gospel Messenger,* June 1892, 222–26.

11. *TS,* 20 October 1892, 2.

12. *FA,* 26 October 1892, 3.

13. *FA,* 30 March 1892, 2.

14. *FA,* 29 April 1891, 1.

15. *PF,* 12 April 1892, 1.

16. Quotations, in order: *CA,* 31 March 1892, 4; *FA,* 12 October 1892, 2; *PF,* 26 April 1892, 1; *CA,* 5 December 1895, 1.

17. *PF,* 8 November 1892, 1.

Chapter 5. *"Pure Democracy and White Supremacy"*

1. The historical narrative in this section is highly compressed. For more detail, see Creech; Noblin; Beeby, 17–55; Crow and Durden; Edmonds; J. F. Steelman, 1–56; L. C. Steelman; Escott, "White Republicans"; *PF,* 1886–92; *CA,* 1889–92.

2. Harvey, 21–43.

3. Anderson, *Race and Politics;* Edmonds, 9.

4. Ritter, 210–26; Noblin, 135–36.

5. Bode, 95–121; Noblin, 147–49.

6. In J. F. Steelman, 18; see also *CA,* 20 June 1889, 4.

7. Centre Minutebook, 14 July 1888; 22 December 1888, DU.

8. *PF,* 14 July 1886, 1; 3 November 1886, 4; Noblin, 163–82.

9. *PF,* 10 March 1886, 3; 26 January 1887, 4; 20 March 1888, 1; 15 January 1889, 2; 5 February 1889, 2; 19 March 1889, 2; 3 March 1891, 2; *CA,* 19 March 1891, 1. Alliancefolk waffled on the Australian ballot (*CA,* 24 October 1889, 1), often opposed state aid to the university (*PF,* 26 January 1887, 4), and a few opposed prohibition (*PF,* 24 March 1891, 1).

10. *PF,* 30 April 1889, 4. See the resolutions of suballiances in the *Farmer* and *The Caucasian* after 1889 and especially *PNCFA,* 1889, 17; 1891, 5.

11. *FA,* 6 January 1892, 1; *CA,* 22 May 1890, 2; 5 June 1890, 2, 4.

12. *PF,* 21 July 1891, 2. See also 14 January 1890, 1; 6 January 1891, 1; *CA,* 3 July 1890, 1; Goodwyn, 149–76.

13. McMath, *Populist Vanguard,* 59–61, 90–150; Noblin, 83–84; F. E. Smith, 56–74.

14. *CA,* 3 July 1890, 1. See also Josephus Daniels to Carr, 20 August 1889, ECP; *PF,* 29 September 1887, 2; 3 February 1891, 1; *TS,* 15 January 1891, 2; 18 June 1891, 2; *CA,* 18 April 1889, 1; 7 August 1890, 3.

15. Carr to S. J. Westall, 27 September 1890, ECP. See also *TS,* 10 December 1891, 1; L C. Steelman, 32–33.

16. See note 28, below.

17. Goodwyn, 651–52.

18. *PF*, 5 May 1886, 3; 19 January 1887, 2; 16 February 1887, 4.

19. L. C. Steelman, 30–42; *PF*, 23 February 1888, 2; 27 March 1888, 2, 7; 3 April 1888, 2; 17 April 1888, 2.

20. *PF*, 16 February 1888, 2.

21. L. C. Steelman, 36–37.

22. *PF*, 12 February 1889, 4. See also 13 November 1888, 2; 5 February 1889, 2; 5 March 1889, 4; 19 March 1889, 2; *CA*, 7 March 1889, 1; Crowe and Durden, 49.

23. L. C. Steelman, 59–123; Noblin, 229–53; Bromberg.

24. *PF*, 30 April 1889, 4; 10 September 1889, 2; 11 March 1890, 1; 29 April 1890, 1; 23 September 1890, 1, 4; 30 September 1890, 6; 7 October 1890, 4; *PNCFA*, 1889, 6, 12; J. A. Fink to Carr, 15 February 1890, ECP; *CA*, 22 May 1890, 1, 2; 29 May 1890, 1.

25. Quoted in Noblin, 233–34.

26. Anderson, *Race and Politics*, 173–85; B. F. Scarborough to Carr, 19 May 1890, ECP; *PF*, 12 August 1890, 2; 20 January 1891, 1.

27. See *HM*, 14 September 1892, 3.

28. E. Chambers Smith to R. W. Winston, 1 September 1890, Winston Papers, SHC. See also Spier Whitaker to Carr, 11 July 1890; Josephus Daniels to Carr, 20 August 1889, ECP; J. F. Steelman, 21.

29. J. M Mewborne to Carr, 5 August 1890; E. C. Beddingfield to Carr, 18 July 1890; Zebulon Vance to Carr, 29 June 1890; W. H. Rand to Carr, 14 September 1890, ECP; *CA*, 17 July 1890, 4; 31 July 1890, 1; 13 November 1890, 1; *PF*, 8 July 1890, 2; 15 July 1890, 2; 23 December 1890, 1.

30. Contrast T. J. Jarvis to Carr, 21 [November] 1890, to L. L. Polk to Carr, 9 September 1890, ECP, cited in Creech, 501. See also Polk to R. W. Winston, 11 September 1890, Winston Papers; Josephus Daniels to Carr, 31 July 1890 and 23 August 1890, ECP.

31. C. C. King to Carr, 21 June 1890; R. F. [Gary] to Carr, 12 July 1890; S. J. Westall to Carr, 8 September 1890, ECP; *PF*, 4 February 1890, 1.

32. Mewborne to Carr, 4 May 1890, ECP. See also *PF*, 14 October 1890, 1.

33. Mewborne to Carr, 15 July 1890, ECP. See also Mewborne to Carr, 29 October 1890, ECP.

34. *PF*, 17 June 1890, 8.

35. Polk to Carr, 26 December 1890, ECP; weekly coverage in *CA*, January to March 1891; L. C. Steelman, 125–65.

36. *PF*, 3 February 1891, 7.

Chapter 6. Crossing the Rubicon

1. *HM*, 6 April 1892, 7. On 1891–92 generally, see Anderson, *Race and Politics*, 186–205; J. F. Steelman, 27–37; L. C. Steelman, 171–268; Noblin, 268–98; Beeby, 17–129; *PF*, 23 January 1894, 1.

2. J. D. Thorne to Polk, 11 April 1892, LPP.

3. *PF*, 7 April 1891, 4. See also 15 September 1891, 4; McMath, *Populist Vanguard*, 116–17.

4. John Graham to E. A. Thorne, 23 May 1891, Thorne Papers, DU. See also *FA*, 22 April 1891, 2; *PF*, 31 March 1891, 1; *TS*, 18 June 1891, 2; 18 November 1891, 2; L. C. Steelman, 33–34.

5. *PF*, 7 April 1891, 4.

6. Compare *PF,* 3 June 1888, 3, to 23 June 1891, 2. Calls for free silver were ubiquitous from the summer of 1891 forward. A few Alliancefolk continued to attack the tariff (*CA,* 16 June 1892, 1).

7. D. H. Rittenhouse to J. M. Mewborne, 4 August 1890, ECP; *TS,* 14 August 1891, 3; L. C. Steelman, 105–6, 178–79.

8. *PF,* 16 June 1891, 5. See also S. B. Alexander to Carr, 23 May 1891; 1 September 1891; Polk to Carr, 24 November 1891, ECP.

9. E. J. Brooks to Carr, 13 May 1891; Carr to E. J. Brooks, 22 May 1891, ECP; *PF,* 28 April 1891, 1; 16 June 1891, 2, 5; *CA,* 21 May 1891, 4; 28 May 1891, 1; *FA,* 27 May 1891, 1, 2.

10. *HM,* 2 December 1891, 5. See also Polk to J. W. Denmark, 21 August 1891, LPP; *TS,* 21 May 1891, 2; *PF,* 7 July 1891, 4; 6 October 1891, 1; 20 October 1891, 4; 29 September 1891, 1, 4; 1 December 1891, 6, 7; *FA,* 16 September 1891, 1; 23 September 1891, 1, 3; 14 October 1891, 1; 21 October 1891, 1, 2; 11 November 1891, 2, 3; 9 December 1891, 1, 3; *CA,* 30 April 1891, 3; 23 July 1891, 1, 2; Hunt, 38–43.

11. *Second Declaration of American Independence.* For the state platform, see *PF,* 23 August 1892, 2.

12. Dixon to Polk, 26 April 1892, LPP. See also Polk to J. W. Denmark, 8 February 1892; 26 March 1892; A. L. Swinson to Polk, 10 April 1892; Rev. J. H. Gilbreath to Polk, 6 April 1892, LPP; letters to the *Farmer* such as on 22 March 1892, 3. In addition, see *PF,* 2 February 1892, 2; 9 February 1892, 1; 8 March 1892, 3; 22 March 1892, 1, 2, 3; 10 May 1892, 1,2; *FA,* 6 April 1892, 2; 13 April 1892, 3.

13. J. E. Robinson to J. B. Grimes, 14 May 1892, Grimes Papers, SHC; *TS,* 15 January 1891, 2.

14. *PF,* 3 May 1892, 1. See also 5 January 1892, 2; 29 March 1892, 1, 6; 10 May 1892, 1, 2; 28 June 1892, 1, 12 July 1892, 4; *CA,* 1 September 1892, 1; 15 September 1892, 1, 2; *HM,* 6 April 1892, 1, 3; 14 September 1892, 3.

15. Quotations, in order: *CA,* 22 June 1893, 1; *PF,* 4 October 1892, 4. "Heathens" from *PF,* 28 June 1892, 4. See also *PF,* 1 March 1892, 2; 22 March 1892, 4; 24 May 1892, 1; 1 November 1892, 1.

16. Quotations, in order: *CA,* 27 October 1892, 1; *PF,* 29 March 1892, 1. See also *PF,* 4 August 1891, 2; 17 November 1891, 1; 4 October 1892, 2, 4; 25 October 1892, 1; *CA,* 25 February 1892, 1; 31 March 1892, 4; 12 May 1892, 1; 15 September 1892, 1.

17. For example, *TS,* 8 January 1892, 3.

18. *PF,* 5 January 1892, 1; 29 March 1892, 1; 4 October 1892, 4.

19. Carr to Polk, 8 April 1892, LPP.

20. *HM,* 29 June 1892, 6; D. F. Talfaia to J. B. Grimes, 25 April 1892, Grimes Papers; W. F. Korngay to Polk, 11 April 1892, LPP; *PF,* 8 March 1892, 3; 19 July 1892, 1; *CA,* 14 July 1892, 1.

21. Carr to J. Reid, 13 January 1896, and Thaddeus Ivey to Carr, 25 October 1892, ECP; Delap, 51; Carr to Polk, 25 April 1892, LPP; S. B. Alexander to J. B. Grimes, 2 October 1892, Grimes Papers; *PF,* 25 October 1892, 6; 20 June 1893, 7; F. E. Smith, 96.

22. W. A. Graham to Carr, 27 June 1892, ECP; W. A. Graham to A. W. Graham, 20 September 1898 and 7 November 1898, A. W. Graham Papers, SHC; *FA,* 17 February 1892, 1; W. H. Kitchin to J. B. Grimes, 19 January 1892 and 1 February 1892, Grimes Papers.

23. J. D. Thorne to Polk, 18 April 1892, LPP ("exterminate"); *PF,* 10 May 1892, 3; 28 June 1892, 4; *TS,* 25 February 1892, 2.

24. J. E. Robinson to J. B. Grimes, 16 March 1892, Grimes Papers; *CA,* 26 May 1892, 1; 16 June 1892, 1, 3; *PF,* 24 May 1892, 7; 23 August 1892, 2. The state Democratic platform, like the Populists', demanded free silver and the abolition of national banks. Unlike the Populists, the Democrats denounced the tariff and the "Force Bill." The Populists, like the Democrats, wanted "the strictest economy in the administration of the State Government" but also the 6 percent cap on interest rates. The most important differences—Populist support of the subtreasury plan and government ownership of railroads, telephones, and telegraph services—had been absent from the Democratic platform supported by most Alliancefolk in 1890.

25. Polk to Carr, 11 April 1892, ECP; *PF* 24 May 1892, 2; 5 July 1892, 2.

26. Polk to S. B. Alexander, 31 May 1892, and Alexander to Polk, 2 June 1892, LPP; *PF,* 7 June 1892, 2.

27. *FA,* 20 July 1892, 3; *PF,* 9 August 1892, 3.

28. *CA,* 21 July 1892, 1–4; 28 July 1892, 1, 2; 11 August 1892, 1; 15 September 1892, 3.

29. *PF,* 15 March 1892, 1.

30. *TS,* 11 August 1892, 2. See also 30 June 1892, 2; 21 July 1892, 2; 4 August 1892, 2; *HM,* 14 September 1892, 5, 6; *CA,* 1 September 1892, 1.

31. *PF,* 29 March 1892, 6; 13 June 1893, 2; *CA,* 25 August 1892, 1, 2; 17 November 1892, 2; 7 March 1895, 3; *HM,* 21 September 1892, 1.

32. Gaither, 69, 75; Cyrus Murphey Endorsement, Folder 720, MBP; marginalia, list of Robeson County Democrats and Populists, folder 727, MBP; W. B. Fleming to Butler, 11 February 1897, MBP; *CA,* 11 May 1893, 3.

33. *CA,* 30 March 1893, 1. See also 3 November 1892, 2; 30 March 1893, 1; *HM,* 31 August 1892, 6; *PF,* 4 October 1892, 6.

34. Quotations, in order: *HM,* 9 March 1892, 5; *PF,* 3 October 1893, 2. See also *CA,* 25 August 1892, 2; Pollack, 59–80; Gaither, xii; Beeby, 15; Palmer, 63, 145.

35. Undated newspaper clipping from 1898, "Race Relations" file, J. A. Campbell Papers, Campbell College Archives; *PF,* 1 November 1892, 1.

36. *PF,* 25 October 1892, 6.

37. Anderson, *Race and Politics,* 199; *CA,* 18 June 1896, 1; *FA,* 13 April 1892, 3; Suggs, ECU; Beeby, 114–43; *TS,* 8 September 1892, 1; 29 September 1892, 3.

38. See Gavins, 211.

39. Gavins, 211; Abrahamowitz, 143–205.

40. *TS,* 13 August 1891, 3; L. C. Steelman, 178–79; *CA,* 30 April 1896, 1; 5 March 1896, 1.

41. A. J. Moye to Butler, 30 April 1896; 7 September 1896, MBP; *CA,* 5 March 1896, 1; 19 March 1896, 1; 2 April 1896, 1; 14 May 1896, 2; 11 June 1896, 1.

42. *CA,* 25 August 1892, 2; 7 November 1895, 2; Edmonds, 218.

43. In Wilson County, this is clear in Saratoga, Stantonburg, and Taylor townships, and probable in Cross Roads, Gardner, and Toisnot. In Edgecombe, this seems clear in township 13 and is probable in townships 9 and 10. In Johnston, this is clear in Wilder's and O'Neal's (*PF,* 12 May 1896, 7), and probable in Bentonville, Beulah, and Meadow townships. In Nash, this is clear in Castalia, Griffins, Jackson, Mannings, Nashville, and North Whitakers townships and probable in South Whitakers. This pattern is apparent in Falling Creek, Mosely Hall, Neuse, and Vance townships in Lenoir, Jamesville and Robersonville townships in Martin, and Dismal Township in Sampson. See also *PF,* 28

April 1896, 6; *Windsor Public Ledger,* 15 August 1894, 2. For a full account of these and other voting records, see Creech, Appendix.

44. See returns for Oakland, Albright, Baldwin, Cape Fear, Center, Gulf, Hadley, Hickory Mountain, New Hope, and Williams townships. See also L. C. Steelman, 253–55; Abrahamowitz, 281–89; Beeby, 119–23, 366–67; Gaither, 42, 87–94, 128; Kousser, 183–95. Palmer disagrees with this assessment (52–53, 145).

45. L. C. Steelman, 232.

46. *CA,* 4 August 1892, 3; 3 November 1892, 2; *HM,* 31 August 1892, 4, 5; *PF,* 4 October 1892, 2–4; 25 October 1892, 1; Daniels, *Tar Heel Editor,* 497–503; L. C. Steelman, 249; *FA,* 5 October 1892, 2.

47. *North Carolina Manual,* 989–90, 1005–6. Populists won a true majority only in Chatham County; they were strong in Wilson, Wake, Sampson, Nash, Franklin, Cumberland, Pitt, and in seaboard counties such as Hyde, Brunswick, and Tyrrell. Often in counties such as Johnston and Edgecombe that had low Populist percentages overall (14 percent and 19 percent respectively), Populists won township majorities (Bentonville in Johnston and Numbers 2 and 13 in Edgecombe).

48. Election records for Wilson County, reprinted in Creech. See also returns for Townships 1 and 12 in Edgecombe; Kinston Township in Lenoir; Rocky Mount Township in Nash; and Goldsboro Township in Wayne. See also *PF,* 8 November 1892, 1; Goodwyn, 651–52; Hahn, 1–11.

49. Returns for Catawba and Iredell do not display this pattern; neither did highly rural counties such as Chatham, Sampson, and Duplin. Wilson County returns indicate that a closer proximity to urban areas might have increased Populist excitement.

50. For Populists, see Townships 2, 4, 5, 9, 13, and 14 in Edgecombe; Falling Creek, Mosely Hall, Vance, and Woodington townships in Lenoir; and Beargrass, Jamesville, and Robersonville Townships in Martin. For the Democrats, see Cline Township in Catawba; Kenansville and Smith in Duplin; New Hope and Shiloh in Iredell; Ocracoke in Hyde; and Great Swamp in Wayne.

51. *FA,* 9 November 1892, 3. See also *CA,* 16 February 1893, 4.

Chapter 7. Religion and the Populist Revolt

1. *HM,* 6 April 1892, 3; *PF,* 8 January 1895, 1. See also *PF,* 11 September 1894, 1; *TS,* 15 September 1892, 2. This chapter cites materials from 1892 to 1898 but always with close attention to context and contingency.

2. *HM,* 6 April 1898, 2.

3. Quotations, in order: *NCB,* 26 October 1892, 1 (rpt., *Raleigh Christian Advocate*); *WT,* 15 September 1892, 4. See also *BR,* 1 June 1892, 1; 19 October 1892, 2; *NCB,* 12 October 1892, 2; 16 November 1892, 3.

4. *NCB,* 27 July 1892, 2. Editors J. A. Oates, Jr., associated with the Prohibition Party (John Alexander Oates papers, NCBHC), and E. J. Edwards became a Populist (*PF,* 7 June 1892, 7).

5. Quotations, in order: *PF,* 10 May 1892, 4; 17 October 1893, 8; 4 October 1892, 4; and *HM,* 6 April 1892, 8. See also *PF,* 28 June 1892, 4; 26 February 1895, 8; 9 June 1896, 8; 22 September 1896, 4; *CA,* 2 April 1896, 1, 4; 30 July 1896, 1; 18 February 1897, 2; 2 August 1894, 1; 22 August 1895, 1–4.

6. Quotation in Freeze, 210. See also the Introduction to Section 3; *BR*, 21 March 1894, 1.

7. *FA*, 24 August 1892, 2. See also *PF*, 12 July 1892, 4; 21 August 1894, 4; *CA*, 13 July 1893, 1; 4 June 1895, 3. Alliance lay leaders and ministers mentioned in Chapter 4 who became Populists included J. F. Click (*HM*); H. A. Forney (*PF*, 21 June 1892, 2); A. C. Shuford (*CA*, 28 March 1895, 1); Baptist Rev. R. L. Patton (*PF*, 7 August 1894, 2); W. M. Byrd (*PF*, 7 June 1892, 7); J. M. Byrd (*CA*, 19 May 1898, 2); J.T.B. Hoover (*PF*, 21 June 1892, 1); and Lunsford Lloyd (Tomlinson, 95). Populist ministers and lay leaders in the 1895 legislature included John Ammons; J.T.B. Hoover; H. W. Norris; J. M. Mewborne; J. C. Bellamy; Council S. Wootin; William R. Dixon; I. W. Taylor; L. L. Smith; J. T. Phillips; J. P. Smith; and A. J. Moye (*Biographical Sketches*, 1895). Rev. C. H. Martin was elected to Congress from the sixth district in 1895 (*PF*, 8 January 1895, 4).

8. *PF*, 11 September 1894, 1; 29 September 1896, 2; *CA*, 4 January 1894, 2; 28 November 1895, 3; 27 August 1896, 3; 21 April 1898, 3; Dixon to Butler, 14 April 1898; 19 April 1898, MBP.

9. *NCB*, 21 September 1892, 2; 28 September 1892, 2; *CA*, 18 August 1892, 1; 30 March 1893, 1; 20 April 1893, 4; 21 September 1893, 2; 21 February 1895, 1; Freeze, 209. (I assume that Dixon was a Democrat.)

10. My association of holiness folk with Populism is speculative and based on observations of a few leaders. In North Carolina, most holiness folk eventually embraced Pentecostalism, which was apolitical. No doubt some holiness folk were apolitical earlier as well.

11. Holsey, 257–65; and Stowell, *Rebuilding Zion*, 184–85.

12. *PF*, 26 September 1893, 1; see also 18 July 1893, 1; 17 October 1893, 8; 13 March 1894, 4; 3 July 1894, 4; 17 July 1894, 1; 21 August 1894, 4; 30 April 1895, 4; *CA*, 26 January 1893, 4; 8 June 1893, 3; 20 June 1895, 4; 21 November 1895, 3; 30 July 1896, 1.

13. Populist Rev. R. L. Patton was a Gospel Missioner (note 7); see also Chapter 2.

14. *Zion's Landmark*, 15 December 1892, 57–59.

15. *WT*, 1 May 1894, 1; *Corinthian*, September 1894, 2; *FA*, 9 March 1892, 2; *CA*, 28 June 1894, 1; 8 April 1897, 1; 28 October 1897, 1; 7 July 1898, 3; 29 September 1898, 2; *BR*, 19 October 1892, 2; 21 March 1894, 1; 21 November 1894, 1; 27 February 1895, 1; 23 September 1896, 1; Josiah Bailey to Butler, 22 July 1897, MBP; *PF*, 23 April 1895, 1. Bailey was attached to the reform wing, Kilgo the conservative wing.

16. Florence Kent to Thompson, 16 November 1877, CTP; Brown, 119–25; Bode, 41; Daniels, *Editor in Politics*, 298.

17. *News and Observer*, 22 September 1895, 3; 18 September 1895, 4.

18. *CA*, 12 December 1895, 1.

19. *News and Observer*, 17 September 1895, 2. See also *CA*, 19 September 1895, 2; 12 December 1895, 1; 19 December 1895, 1; 2 January 1896, 1, 4; 9 January 1896, 1; 16 January 1896, 4; 6 February 1896, 4, along with: 8 June 1893, 1; 23 January 1896, 1, 2; 9 July 1896, 1; *PF*, 18 July 1893, 1.

20. *CA*, 19 December 1895, 1. Although Populists regularly denounced Catholicism, only rarely were they anti-Semitic, sometimes invoking the "Shylock" stereotype (*CA*, 9 June 1898, 2).

21. *CA*, 16 January 1896, 1; 6 February 1896, 4.

22. *News and Observer*, 17 September 1895, 2; *CA*, 19 December 1895, 4.

23. *CA*, 6 February 1896, 4.

24. *CA*, 21 November 1895, 2; see also *PF*, 17 July 1894, 1.

25. *CA*, 2 January 1896, 4.

26. *CA*, 6 February 1896, 4.

27. *News and Observer*, 18 September 1895, 4.

28. *CA*, 7 November 1895, 1; see also 10 October 1895, 1.

29. *News and Observer*, 22 September 1895, 3; *CA*, 10 October 1895, 1; 12 December 1895, 1.

30. *News and Observer*, 22 September 1895, 3.

31. *CA*, 20 September 1894, 2. See also 8 March 1894, 1; 19 September 1895, 1, 2, 4; 27 February 1896, 1; 2 July 1896, 1; 9 July 1896, 1; *PF*, 9 August 1892, 4; 8 January 1895, 1; 30 April 1895, 4; 8 October 1895, 4; *HM*, 14 September 1892, 3; 19 January 1898, 2; 9 February 1898, 8; *FA*, 2 March 1892, 1.

32. *CA*, 6 February 1896, 4; see also 10 October 1895, 1; 17 October 1895, 2, 3.

33. Quotations, in order: *CA*, 6 February 1896, 4; F. S. Blain to Thompson, 20 September 1895, CTP; see also *PF*, 11 September 1894, 1; *HM*, 22 June 1898, 2.

34. *CA*, 6 February 1896, 4.

Chapter 8. *Victory, Defeat, and Disfranchisement, 1893–98*

1. *CA*, 30 March 1893, 1. See also 16 February 1893, 4; 13 April 1893, 1; *PF*, 15 November 1892, 4; 13 December 1892, 7; 20 December 1892, 6. On 1893 to 1895 generally, see *TS*, 19 July 1894, 2; Trelease; Daniels, *Editor in Politics*, 120–35; J. F. Steelman, 119–23; Beeby, 135–91; Edmonds, 34–47; Hunt, 64–76; *PF*, 7 February 1893, 1.

2. *CA*, 15 March 1894, 1. See also 9 March 1993, 2; 4 May 1893, 1; 11 January 1894, 3; 8 March 1894, 1; 13 September 1894, 1; 21 March 1895, 2; *PF*, 8 January 1895, 1, 2. Changing the county government law represented a shift in Alliance thinking (*PF*, 26 July 1892, 2), though some Alliances had supported the measure (*PF*, 6 January 1891, 1; 24 March 1891, 1).

3. *PF*, 13 June 1893, 1. Similar denunciations filled *The Farmer* and *The Caucasian* from February to May 1893(see *PF*, 14 March 1893, 4).

4. *PF*, 12 September 1893, 1, 4; 23 January 1894, 1, 4; 15 May 1894, 2; *CA*, 18 May 1893, 3; 2 August 1894, 2.

5. *PF*, 4 September 1894, 2.

6. Quotations, in order: *CA*, 15 April 1894, 1; 3 May 1894, 1; see also 22 March 1894, 2; 16 August 1894, 1; 6 September 1894, 1; 11 October 1894, 1; *PF*, 7 August 1894, 2, 4, 6, 7; [L.N. Perkins?] to Butler, 2 September 1893, MBP.

7. *CA*, 15 November 1894, 1; see also 22 November 1894, 1, 2.

8. *PF*, 20 November 1894, 2; 17 January 1895, 5, 6; *CA*, 8 November 1894, 3. For blacks voting Populist, see Townships 9 and 10 in Edgecombe, and Old Fields, Saratoga, Springhill, Stantonsburg, and Taylor (and possibly Cross Roads and Black Creek) townships in Wilson. For Democratic declines, see 1894 returns for Catawba, Chatham, Duplin, Hyde, Iredell, Martin, Wilson, and especially Hall, Honeycutt, Mingo, North Clinton, and Piney Grove townships in Sampson.

9. Daniels, *Editor in Politics*, 124; Martin quotation from Ayers, 293.

10. *CA*, 21 March 1895, 2; see also Edmonds, 41–45, 67–81; *CA*, weekly, from 10 January 1895 to 21 March 1895.

11. On the 1896 election, see Durden, who argues Butler's fusion agreement was consistent with Populist thinking and marked the high point of Populist influence; Hunt agrees (92–123). In contrast, Goodwyn believes fusion made the People's Party a "shadow movement" of the Alliance; see also endorsement notes, folder 720, MBP; Crow and Durden, 50–74; Beeby, 281–355.

12. *CA,* 6 February 1896, 1; 13 February 1896, 1, 2; 16 April 1896, 1; 11 June 1896, 1; 13 August 1896, 1; 15 October 1896, 2; *PF,* 4 February 1896, 2; 7 April 1896, 2. The focus on Butler reflects his centrality in these fusion arrangements; it also offers a shorthand approach to covering the main issues. Butler's correspondence demonstrates his close touch on the movement in North Carolina.

13. *PF,* 13 October 1896, 4.

14. *PF,* 18 February 1896, 6; 3 March 1896, 4; 17 March 1896, 4, 6; 7 April 1896, 3, 4; 28 April 1896, 2, 8; 5 May 1896, 3; 16 June 1896, 6; 15 September 1896, 6, 7; J. W. Dixon to Butler, 22 April 1896; and H. W. Butler to Butler, 1 May 1896, MBP; *CA,* 13 February 1896, 2; 20 February 1896; 1, 2; 16 April 1896, 1; 23 April 1896, 1, 2; 7 May 1896, 2.

15. *PF,* 21 July 1896, 2; 15 September 1896, 3; 22 September 1896, 2, 3; 29 September 1896, 4, 7; 27 October 1896, "Extra"; 3 November 1896, 2, 6; *CA,* 16 July 1896, 1, 2; 30 July 1896, 2, 3; 20 August 1896, 1, 3; 27 August 1896, 1; 24 September 1896, 1, 2; 15 October 1896, 2; 3 December 1896, 1; J. Z. Green to Butler, 6 October 1896; J. D. Mears to Butler, 17 September 1896, and W. O. Stratford to Butler, 30 April 1896, MBP, and J. M. Mewborne to Thompson, 11 November 1896, CTP.

16. *PF,* 9 June 1896, 8. See also *CA,* 26 March 1896, 1; 16 April 1896, 1.

17. Quotations, in order: *PF,* 7 April 1896, 4; *CA,* 23 July 1896, 1. See also Durden, 14–15; *CA,* 12 March 1896, 1; *PF,* 28 April 1896, 6; 5 May 1896, 3; Charles Martin to Butler, 11 December 1896; E. D. Thompson to Butler, 8 October 1896; and J. W. Lassiter to Butler, 9 May 1898, MBP.

18. Crow and Durden, 68–73; Edmonds, 56.

19. *CA,* 30 April 1896, 1; see also 7 November 1895, 2; *PF,* 28 February 1893, 2; 5 September 1893, 4; 28 April 1896, 6; *Hayseeder,* 22 October 1896, 1, 2; A. J. Moye to Butler, 30 April 1896, and 7 September 1896, MBP.

20. *CA,* 20 August 1896, 1; note 36, below.

21. *CA,* 9 July 1896, 1; Crow and Durden, 64–69.

22. *CA,* 5 March 1896, 1; 19 March 1896, 1, 2; 18 June 1896, 1; Y. C. Morton to Butler, 30 April 1896, MBP.

23. *North Carolina Manual,* 1004, 1006; *PF,* 10 November 1896, 2. The returns from Duplin, Hyde (Fairfield and Lake Landing townships), Martin (Jamesville Township), Chatham (Cape Fear, Center, Hickory Mt., New Hope, and Oakland townships), and Wilson (Saratoga, Stantonsburg, and Taylor townships) indicate loss of black Populist votes to the GOP.

24. *CA,* 15 April 1897, 1, 2; 1 July 1897, 1; 16 September 1897, 4; 20 January 1898, 1; *PF,* 12 January 1897, 1, 2; *Hayseeder,* 1897 through 1898; J. I. Lewis to Butler, 16 January 1897; G. E. Hunt to Butler, 2 December 1896; R. J. Peele to Butler, 21 December 1896; Walter Henry to Butler, 7 January 1897; and A. D. McGill to Butler, 19 February 1897, MBP. On 1897 to 1898 generally, see Crow and Durden, 75–159; Beeby, 298–99, 356–485; Hunt, 124–55; Wat-

son; J. F. Steelman, 124–55; Edmonds, 136–54. About three in four North Carolina Populists seem to have supported Butler.

25. *HM*, 20 October 1897, 2; 27 April 1898, 1; *CA*, 17 March 1898, 1; *TS*, 5 May 1898, 2; J. R. Jones to Butler, 10 June 1898, C. E. [Latern] to Butler, 20 July 1898, and E. F. Patterson to Butler, 26 July 1898, MBP.

26. *CA*, 10 March 1898, 1, 2; 24 March 1898, 1–4; 28 April 1898, 1, 2, 4; 5 May 1898, 1, 2; 19 May 1898, 2; 26 May 1898, 1–2; *HM*, 2 March 1898, 3; W. W. Barber to Butler, 20 May 1898, and J. A. Sherrill to Butler, 25 March 1898, MBP.

27. *CA*, 2 June 1898, 1, 2; 9 June 1898, 1.

28. Ayers, 300. See also Crow and Durden, 134; Anderson, *Race and Politics*, 268–69.

29. *TS*, 14 July 1898, 2; 28 July 1898, 2; 22 September 1898, 2; 20 October 1898, 3; *CA*, 29 September 1898, 1; 6 October 1898, 2; 27 October 1898, 2, 3; T J. Jarvis to Thompson, 22 August 1898, CTP; Gilmore, 61–146; Woodward, *Strange Career*, 83.

30. Bode, 122–40; *CA*, 15 December 1898, 2; *BR*, 28 September 1898, 1; 26 October 1898, 1; 16 November 1898, 1; 8 August 1900, 1; Luftman.

31. In Bode, 125.

32. *WT*, 1 September 1897, 4; *NCB*, 26 October 1898, 1; *Our Church Record*, 6 October 1898, 1; 17 November 1898, 1; *Corinthian*, February 1900, 4.

33. *CA*, 3 November 1898, 3. Would that space provided the opportunity for a more thorough examination of race and evangelicalism in these decades, especially pertaining to disfranchisement, lynching, and segregation. For a careful exploration of these issues, see Gilmore; Mathews, "Southern Rite."

34. *CA*, 20 October 1898, 1; see also 14 April 1898, 2; 6 October 1898, 1; 3 November 1898, 3; *HM*, 17 November 1897, 2; 6 April 1898, 2, 6; 14 September 1898, 2; *Hayseeder*, 20 January 1898, 3.

35. *CA*, 2 June 1898, 1; see also 23 September 1897, 2. I agree here with Ayers's (132–59, 489) and Anderson's (*Race and Politics*) assessments. On gender, see Gilmore.

36. Quotations, in order: W. B. Fleming to Butler, 11 February 1897, MBP; *CA*, 23 December 1897, 1. See also *CA*, 12 May 1898, 2; T. L. James to Butler, 19 May 1896, MBP; Anderson, *Race and Politics*, 256; Beeby, 494–95; Hunt, 172–73; Crow and Durden, 148–49; notes 32 and 41 in Chapter 6.

37. A. W. Jordan to Butler, 9 July 1898; W. W. Teague to Butler, 17 October 1898; A. C. Shuford to Butler, 14 November 1898; A. E. Smith to Butler, 12 July 1898; A. J. Moye to Butler, 5 October 1898, MBP.

38. *CA*, 11 November 1897, 1; 2 June 1898, 1; 14 July 1898, 2; 1 September 1898, 1, 2, 4; 8 September 1898, 2, 3; 22 September 1898, 1, 2; 29 September 1898, 1; 20 October 1898, 1, 2, and "Extra"; 27 October 1898, 3; *HM*, 14 September 1898, 2; *Hayseeder*, 20 January 1898, 2; I. H. Bright to Butler, 15 October 1898, MBP; W. A. Graham to A. W. Graham, 7 November 1898, A. W. Graham Papers.

39. *TS*, 8 September 1898, 2; see also 15 September 1898, 2; Anderson, *Race and Politics*, 267–75; Edmonds, 145; D. S. Moss to Butler, 20 June 1896, MBP.

40. *TS*, 9 February 1899, 2.

41. *CA*, 10 November 1898, 1, 2; 17 November 1898, 1; Edmonds, 158–78.

42. Suggs, Suggs Papers, ECU, 48; W. A. Graham to A. W. Graham, 20 September 1898, A. W. Graham Papers; Anderson, *Race and Politics*, 277; and the 1898 and 1900 election

returns for Cross Roads, Gardners, Old Fields, Taylor, and Toisnot townships in Wilson; Chatham County; Piney Grove, South Clinton, and Westbrooks townships in Sampson; Currituck and Lake Landing townships in Hyde; Davidson and Shiloh townships in Iredell.

43. Edmonds, 178–93.

44. Folders 721–38, MBP; *TS,* 30 March 1899, 2; 8 February 1900, 4; 24 May 1900, 2; 14 June 1900, 3; E. P. Deal to Butler, 2 April 1900, and E. M. Wellborn to Butler, April 2, 1900, MBP; Edmonds, 198–214; Anderson, *Race and Politics,* 296–312; Hunt, 156–85; Beeby, 486–542; Crow and Durden, 138–59.

Epilogue

1. In Anderson, *Race and Politics,* 296; see also Gilmore, 119–75.

2. Burns to J. J. Rawls, 18 August 1900, NCDOC; Burns obituary, Bethany Church Records, Pamlico County, NCDOC.

3. *HM,* 24 November 1897, 8; 26 January 1898, 2; 20 July 1898, 2, 6; 31 August 1898, 6.

4. See precinct returns from these areas, NCDAH. On Pentecostalism, see Chapters 1, 2, 4, and 7.

5. *WT,* 8 April 1904, 3; see also 2 March 1900, 2; 7 June 1901; *CA,* 23 December 1898, 1.

6. Bethany Church disappeared from the Disciples' records in the mid-1950s (NCDOC) and is currently affiliated with the Churches of Christ.

7. Grantham, 14–25, 160–245.

8. Wade, Horton, and Strowd, 115; Pelser, 250–51; F. E. Smith, 177–78.

9. F. E. Smith, 177–78; Hunt, 247–57.

10. Presidential address before the Seaboard Medical Association of Virginia and North Carolina, December 1920, by Cyrus Thompson; obituary in *Elizabeth City Advance,* 21 November 1930, and eulogy, 1 May 1931, CTP.

11. Martha Marble, electronic correspondence with author, 9 February 1999 and 10 February 1999; Hunt, 186–253.

12. Woodward, *Strange Career,* 89–90; idem, *Tom Watson;* Hunt, 172–73.

13. Dixon citations throughout, along with Crowe.

14. *TS,* 8 February 1900, 4; 2 August 1900, 4; Crow; Hunt, 160–61.

15. Florence Smith, 177–184; Hunt, 247–257; Wade, Horton, and Strowd; Turner and Bridgers; Brown, 123; Lefler and Newsome.

Bibliography

Primary Sources: Manuscripts

Buies Creek, N.C.: Campbell College Archives, Campbell College
  J. A. Campbell Papers
Chapel Hill, N.C.: Southern Historical Collection, UNC-Chapel Hill
  Marion Butler Papers
  A. W. Graham Papers
  J. Bryan Grimes Papers
  Stuart Noblin Papers
  William Joseph Peele Papers
  L. L. Polk Papers
  Cyrus W. Thompson Papers
  William Henry Wills Papers
  Robert W. Winston Papers
Durham, N.C.: Manuscript Division, Duke University Library
  Butler, Jesse Armon. "Methodism in North Carolina, 1800–1837." Graduate Thesis
    Trinity College, n.d.
  W. S. Chaffin Journal
  Charles Carroll Dodson Papers
  Jamestown Alliance Minute Book
  Hugh W. Johnson Papers, including Centre Alliance Minutebook
  E. A. Thorne Papers
Greenville, N.C.: East Carolina Manuscript Collection, J. Y. Joyner Library, East Carolina
  University
  Elias Carr Papers, including Sparta Alliance A#218 Minutebook and L. L. Polk, *The
    Protest of the Farmer: Address of President L.L. Polk to Citizens Alliance No. 4 of
    Washington, D.C., at Concordia Hall, April 14, 1891*
  Harold G. Sugg Papers, Unpublished Manuscript, "1898 In Pitt County, N.C.: The
    Fusion Movement in North Carolina Seen Through the Focus of a Critical Locality"
  Whitaker's Chapel Collection

Mount Olive, N.C.: Free Will Baptist Historical Collection, Moye Library, Mt. Olive College
  Goff, Florence. *Tests and Triumphs.* N.p., 1924
Raleigh, N.C.: North Carolina Division of Archives and History
  County Election Books
  People's Chapel Free Will Baptist Church Cemetery Records
  Polk/Denmark Collection
Salisbury, N.C.: Reformed Church of America Archives, Catawba College
  Biographical Sketch, Col. Hiram Asbury Forney
  Clapp, Rev. Carl H. *Historical Sketch of Grace Reformed Church, Newton, NC.* N.p.: 1937
Wilson, N.C.: North Carolina Discipliana Collection, Barton College
  Church Records for:
    Gordon Street Christian Church, Lenoir County
    Hebron Church, Lenoir County
    Salem Church, Pitt County
  North Carolina Christian Missionary Convention. *Proceedings* (1885–1908)
  Sermon Books of J. J. Harper and John Bunyan Respess
  Shropshire, N. L. "The Nobility of Labor." Speech dated 1899
  Union Records for Second Evangelistic District and Old Ford and Roanoke Union Meetings, 1887–1996
Winston-Salem, N.C.: Smith Reynolds Library at Wake Forest University
The North Carolina Baptist Historical Collection:
  Atlantic Baptist Association. *Minutes*
  Cedar Creek Baptist Association. *Minutes*
  Eastern Baptist Association. *Minutes*
  W. A. Graham Papers
  D. W. Herring Papers, including Herring, D. W. *A Manly Boy.* N.p.: n.d.
  Little River Baptist Association. *Minutes*
  Kings Mountain Baptist Association. *Minutes*
  John Alexander Oates Papers
  Raleigh Baptist Association. *Minutes*
  South Fork Baptist Association. *Minutes*
  South River Baptist Association. *Minutes*
  Tar River Baptist Association. *Minutes*

Primary Sources: Published Minutes and Proceedings Available Outside Manuscript Collections

Christian Church (O'Kellyite) South. *The Christians' Almanac and Annual* (1886–1906)
Classis of North Carolina of the Reformed Church in the United States. *Proceedings* (1886–1906)
National Farmers' Alliance and Industrial Union. *Proceedings* (1890)
North Carolina Annual Conference of the Methodist Episcopal Church, South. *Journal* (1886–1908)

North Carolina Conference of the Methodist Protestant Church. *Minutes* (1886–1908)
North Carolina Farmers' State Alliance. *Proceedings* (1888, 1889, 1891, 1892)

Primary Sources: Populist Periodicals

Hayseeder (Raleigh, N.C.)
Hickory Mercury/Mercury Times (Hickory, N.C.)
Southern Mercury (Dallas, Tex.)
The Caucasian (Clinton, Goldsboro, Raleigh, N.C.)
The Farmers' Advocate (Tarboro, N.C.)
The Progressive Farmer (Winston, Raleigh, N.C.)

Primary Sources: Religious Periodicals

Asheville Baptist (Asheville, N.C.)
Baptist Quarterly (Black Baptists, Raleigh, N.C.)
Biblical Recorder (Baptist, Raleigh, N.C.)
Central Protestant (Methodist Protestant Church, High Point, N.C.)
Christian Advocate (Methodist Episcopal, South, Raleigh, N.C.)
Christian Sun (Christian Connection, Elon College, N.C.)
Church Worker (Baptist, Lexington, N.C.)
Corinthian (Reformed Church of America, Hickory, N.C.)
Free Will Baptist (Ormondsville, Ayden, N.C.)
Little River Record (Baptist, Buies Creek, N.C.)
North Carolina Baptist (Fayetteville, N.C.)
North Carolina Christian Advocate (Methodist Episcopal South, Greensboro, N.C.)
Our Church Record (Methodist Protestant Church, High Point, N.C.)
Reformed Church Standard (Reformed Church of America, Salisbury, N.C.)
Southern Baptist (Asheville, N.C.)
The Gospel Messenger (Primitive Baptist, Butler, Ga.)
Toisnot Transcript (Free Will Baptist, Toisnot, N.C.)
Watch Tower (Disciples of Christ, Wilson, N.C.)
Western North Carolina Baptist (Asheville, N.C.)
Zion's Landmark (Primitive Baptist, Wilson, N.C)

Primary Sources: Democratic Periodicals

News and Observer (Raleigh, N.C.)
Tarboro Southerner (Tarboro, N.C.)
Windsor Public Ledger (Windsor, N.C.)

Primary Sources: Statistical Data

Census Reports, Vol. I: Twelfth Census of the United States Taken in the Year 1900: Population, Part I. Washington, D.C.: U.S. Census Office, 1901.
The North Carolina Manual. Raleigh, N.C.: The Historical Commission, 1913.

Report on Population of the United States at the Eleventh Census: 1890, Part I, Vol. I. Washington, D.C.: Government Printing Office, 1895.

Report on Statistics of Churches in the United States at the Eleventh Census: 1890. Washington, D.C.: Government Printing Office, 1894.

Special Reports, Religious Bodies: 1906. Part I: Summary and General Tables. Washington, D.C.: Government Printing Office, 1910.

Special Reports, Religious Bodies: 1906. Part II: Separate Denominations: History, Description, and Statistics. Washington, D.C.: Government Printing Office, 1910.

Books and Articles

Abernathy, Raye, and Loree Greenhill. *Penelope: Her First One Hundred Years, 1888–1988.* Hickory: Clay Printing Co., 1988.

Abrahamowitz, F. Jack. "The Negro in the Populist Movement." *Journal of Negro History* 38 (1953): 257–89.

Abzug, Robert H. *Cosmos Crumbling.* New York: Oxford University Press, 1994.

Alexander, Gross. *A History of the Methodist Church, South.* New York: The Christian Literature Co., 1894.

Anderson, Eric. "The Populists and Capitalist America." In *Race, Class, and Politics in Southern History.* Ed. Jeffrey Crow, Paul Escott, and Charles Flynn, Jr. Baton Rouge: Louisiana State University Press, 1989, 106–25.

———. *Race and Politics in North Carolina, 1872–1901.* Baton Rouge: Louisiana State University Press, 1981.

Argersinger, Peter H. "Pentecostal Politics in Kansas." *Kansas Quarterly* 1 (1969): 24–35.

Ayers, Edward L. *The Promise of the New South.* New York: Oxford University Press, 1992.

Barber, William Joseph. *The Disciple Assemblies of Eastern North Carolina.* St. Louis: The Bethany Press, 1966.

Barfield, J. M., and Thad Harrison. *History of the Free Will Baptists of North Carolina.* Ayden: Free Will Baptist Press, n.d.

Barnes, William Wright. *The Southern Baptists Convention, 1845–1953.* Nashville: Broadman Press, 1954.

Bassett, Ancel H. *Concise History of the Methodist Protestant Church . . .* Pittsburgh: Wm. McCracken, 1887.

Battle, Herbert Bemerton, and Lois Yelverton. *The Battle Book.* Montgomery, Ala.: The Paragon Press, 1930.

Beeby, James M. "Revolt of the Tar Heelers." Ph.D. diss., Bowling Green State University, 1999.

Berger, Peter. *Sacred Canopy.* Garden City: Doubleday, 1967.

Billings, Dwight B. *Planters and the Making of the "New South."* Chapel Hill: University of North Carolina Press, 1979.

Biographical Sketches of the Members of the General Assembly of North Carolina, 1895. Raleigh: Edwards and Broughton, 1895.

Bissett, Jim. *Agrarian Socialism in America.* Norman: University of Oklahoma Press, 1999.

Bode, Frederick A. *Protestantism and the New South.* Charlottesville: University of Virginia Press, 1975.

Boles, John B. *The Irony of Southern Religion.* New York: Peter Lang, 1994.

———. "Slaves in Biracial Churches." In *Varieties of Southern Religious Experience.* Ed. Samuel S. Hill. Baton Rouge: Louisiana State University Press, 1988, 95–113.

———. "The Discovery of Southern Religious History." In *Interpreting Southern History.* Ed. John B. Boles and Evelyn Nolen. Baton Rouge: Louisiana State University Press, 1987, 510–48.

Bost, Raymond M., and Jeff L. Norris. *All One Body: The Story of the North Carolina Lutheran Synod 1803–1993.* North Carolina Synod, Evangelical Lutheran Church, 1994.

Bradley, David Henry. *A History of the African Methodist Episcopal Zion Church.* Nashville: Parthenon Press, 1956.

Brasher, J. Lawrence. *The Sanctified South: John Lakin Brasher and the Holiness Movement.* Urbana: University of Illinois Press, 1994.

Bromberg, Alan B. "The Worst Muddle Ever Seen in N.C. Politics." *North Carolina Historical Review* 56 (1979): 19–40.

Brown, Joseph Parsons. *The Commonwealth of Onslow.* New Bern, N.C.: The Owen G. Dunn Co., 1960.

Burbank, Garin. *When Farmers Voted Red.* Westport, Conn.: Greenwood, 1976.

Calhoon, Robert M. *Evangelicals and Conservatives in the Early South, 1740–1861.* Columbia: University of South Carolina Press, 1988.

Campbell, James T. *Songs of Zion: The African Methodist Episcopal Church in the United States and South Africa.* New York: Oxford University Press, 1995.

Campbell, Joseph E. *The Pentecostal Holiness Church, 1898–1948.* Franklin Springs: Publishing House of the Pentecostal Holiness Church, 1951.

Carroll, J. Elwood. *History of the North Carolina Annual Conference of the Methodist Protestant Church.* Greensboro: McCulloch & Swain, 1939.

Carwardine, Richard J. *Evangelicals and Politics in Antebellum America.* New Haven: Yale University Press, 1993.

Cook, Raymond A. *Fire from the Flint: The Amazing Careers of Thomas Dixon.* Winston-Salem: John F. Blair, 1968.

———. *Thomas Dixon.* New York: Twayne Publishers, 1974.

Creech, Joseph. "Righteous Indignation: Religion and Populism in North Carolina, 1886–1906." Ph.D. diss., University of Notre Dame, 2000.

Crews, Mickey. "Populistic Religion: The Social Origins of the Church of God." *Cultural Perspectives on the American South* 5 (1991): 1–16.

Crow, Jeffrey J. "An Apartheid for the South." In *Race, Class, and Politics in Southern History.* Ed. Jeffrey Crow, Paul Escott, and Charles Flynn, Jr. Baton Rouge: Louisiana State University Press, 1989, 216–59.

Crow, Jeffrey, and Robert Durden. *Maverick Republican in the Old North State: A Political Biography of Daniel L. Russell.* Baton Rouge: Louisiana State University Press, 1977.

Crowe, M. Karen. "Southern Horizons: The Autobiography of Thomas Dixon. A Critical Edition." Ph.D. diss., New York University, 1982.

Daniels, Josephus. *Editor in Politics.* Chapel Hill: University of North Carolina Press, 1941.

———. *Tar Heel Editor.* Chapel Hill: University of North Carolina Press, 1939.

Davis, Lyman Edwyn. *Democratic Methodism in America.* New York: Fleming H. Revell Co., 1921.

Delap, Simeon Alexander. "The Populist Party in North Carolina." *Trinity College Historical Society Papers,* no. 14. Durham: Seeman Printery, 1922, 40–74.

Dixon, Thomas, Jr. *Living Problems in Religion and Social Science.* New York: Charles T. Dillingham, 1889.

———. *The Life Worth Living.* New York: Doubleday, Page, & Co., 1905.

Drinkhouse, Edward J. *History of Methodist Reform* . . . 2 vols. Baltimore: Board of Publication of the Methodist Protestant Church, 1899.

Dunning, Nelson A. *The Farmers' Alliance History and Agrarian Digest.* Washington, D.C.: Alliance Publishing Co., 1891.

Durden, Robert F. *The Climax of Populism.* Lexington: University of Kentucky Press, 1965.

Edmonds, Helen G. *The Negro and Fusion Politics in North Carolina, 1894–1901.* Chapel Hill: University of North Carolina Press, 1951.

Edwards, Laura F. *Gendered Strife and Confusion.* Urbana: University of Illinois Press, 1997.

Escott, Paul. "White Republicans and Ku Klux Klan Terror." In *Race, Class, and Politics in Southern History.* Ed. Jeffrey Crow, Paul Escott, and Charles Flynn, Jr. Baton Rouge: Louisiana State University Press, 1989, 230–51.

———. *Many Excellent People.* Chapel Hill: University of North Carolina Press, 1985.

———, ed. *North Carolina Yeoman: The Diary of Basil Armstrong Thomason, 1853–1862.* Athens: University of Georgia Press, 1996.

Farish, Hunter Dickinson. *The Circuit Rider Dismounts.* Richmond: Dietz Press, 1938.

Faust, Drew Gilpin. *The Creation of Confederate Nationalism.* Baton Rouge: Louisiana State University Press, 1988.

Fite, Gilbert. *Cotton Fields No More.* Lexington: University of Kentucky Press, 1984.

Flynn, Charles L., Jr. "Procrustean Bedfellows and Populists." In *Race, Class, and Politics in Southern History.* Ed. Jeffrey Crow, Paul Escott, and Charles Flynn, Jr. Baton Rouge: Louisiana State University Press, 1989, 81–105.

Flynt, Wayne. *Alabama Baptists.* Tuscaloosa: University of Alabama Press, 1998.

———. "Dissent in Zion." *Journal of Southern History* 35 (1969): 523–43.

———. "One in the Spirit, Many in the Flesh." In *Varieties of Southern Evangelicalism.* Ed. David Edwin Harrell, Jr. Macon, Ga.: Mercer University Press, 1981, 23–44.

———. "Southern Protestantism and Reform, 1890–1900." In *Varieties of Southern Religious Experience.* Ed. Samuel S. Hill. Baton Rouge: Louisiana State University Press, 1988, 135–57.

Ford, Lacy K., Jr. *Origins of Southern Radicalism.* New York: Oxford University Press, 1988.

Freeze, Richard Gary. "Model Mill Men of the New South." Ph.D. diss., University of North Carolina at Chapel Hill, 1987.

Gaither, Gerald Henderson. *Blacks and the Populist Revolt.* University: University of Alabama Press, 1977.

Gavins, Raymond. "The Meaning of Freedom." In *Race, Class, and Politics in Southern*

History. Ed. Jeffrey Crow, Paul Escott, and Charles Flynn, Jr. Baton Rouge: Louisiana State University Press, 1989, 175–215.

Geertz, Clifford. *Interpretation of Cultures.* New York: Basic Books, 1973.

Gilmore, Glenda. *Gender and Jim Crow.* Chapel Hill: University of North Carolina Press, 1996.

Goode, Richard C. "The Godly Insurrection in Limestone County." *Religion and American Culture* 3 (1993): 155–69.

Goodwyn, Lawrence. *Democratic Promise.* New York: Oxford University Press, 1976.

Graham, W. A. *The History of the South Fork Baptist Association . . .* Lincolnton, N.C.: Journal Printing Co., 1901.

Grantham, Dewey W. *Southern Progressivism.* Knoxville: University of Tennessee Press, 1983.

Graves, C. F. *The Story of the Negro Baptists of North Carolina From 1620–1955.* N.p., n.d.

Green, James R. *Grass-Roots Socialism.* Baton Rouge: Louisiana State University Press, 1978.

Grill, C. Franklin. *Methodism in the Upper Cape Fear Valley.* Nashville: Parthenon Press, 1966.

Grissom, William L. *History of Methodism in North Carolina from 1772 to the Present Time.* Vol. 1. Nashville: Publishing House of the M.E. Church, South, 1905.

Hackney, Sheldon. *Populism to Progressivism in Alabama.* Princeton: Princeton University Press, 1969.

Hahn, Stephen. *The Roots of Southern Populism.* New York: Oxford University Press, 1983.

Hall, Prathia. "Woman's Space, Women's Place." Paper presented at the Women and Twentieth-Century Protestantism Conference, Chicago, 23–25 April 1998.

Harper, Keith. *The Quality of Mercy: Southern Baptists and Social Christianity, 1890–1920.* Tuscaloosa: University of Alabama Press, 1996.

Harrell, David Edwin, Jr. "The Evolution of Plain Folk Religion in the South." In *Varieties of Southern Religious Experience.* Ed. Samuel S. Hill. Baton Rouge: Louisiana State University Press, 1988, 24–51.

———. *The Sources of Division in the Disciples of Christ, 1865–1900.* Atlanta: Publishing Systems, Inc., 1973.

———. "The South: Seedbed of Sectarianism." In *Varieties of Southern Evangelicalism.* Ed. David Edwin Harrell, Jr. Macon, Ga.: Mercer University Press, 1981, 45–58.

Harvey, Paul. *Redeeming the South.* Chapel Hill: University of North Carolina Press, 1997.

Hassell, Cushing Biggs. *History of the Church of God . . .* Orange City: Gilbert Beebe's Sons, 1886.

Hatch, Nathan O. *The Democratization of American Christianity.* New Haven: Yale University Press, 1989.

Heyrman, Christine Leigh. *Southern Cross.* New York: Alfred A. Knopf, 1997.

Hicks, John D. "The Farmers' Alliance in North Carolina." *The North Carolina Historical Review* 2 (1925): 162–87.

———. *The Populist Revolt.* Minneapolis: University of Minnesota Press, 1931.

Higginbotham, Evelyn Brooks. *Righteous Discontent in the Black Baptist Church, 1880–1920.* Cambridge, Mass.: Harvard University Press, 1993.

Hill, Samuel S. *Southern Churches in Crisis.* New York: Holt, Rinehart and Winston, 1967.

———. *The South and North in American Religion.* Athens: University of Georgia Press, 1980.

———. "Northern and Southern Varieties of American Evangelicalism." In *Evangelicalism.* Ed. Mark Noll, David Bebbington, and George Rawlyk. New York: Oxford University Press, 1994, 275–87.

Hilton, Boyd. *The Age of Atonement.* Oxford: Oxford University Press, 1988.

Hinson, E. Glenn. *A History of Baptists in Arkansas 1818–1978.* Little Rock: Arkansas Baptists State Convention, 1979.

Hofstadter, Richard. *The Age of Reform.* New York: Alfred A. Knopf, 1956.

Holder, Naomi Dail. *History of Wheat Swamp Christian Church Including the Conditions in Europe and the Colonies.* Private, 1977.

Holifield, E. Brooks. *The Gentleman Theologians.* Durham: Duke University Press, 1978.

Holsey, L. H. *Autobiography, Sermons, Addresses, and Essays.* Atlanta: The Franklin Printing and Publishing Company, 1898.

Howe, Daniel Walker. "Religion and Politics in the Antebellum North." In *Religion and American Politics.* Ed. Mark Noll. New York: Oxford University Press, 1990, 121–46.

Huggins, Maloy A. *A History of North Carolina Baptists.* Raleigh: The General Board, Baptist State Convention of North Carolina, 1967.

Hughes, Richard T. *Reviving the Ancient Faith: The Story of the Churches of Christ in America.* Grand Rapids, Mich.: Wm. B. Eerdmans Pub. Co., 1996.

Hunt, James L. *Marion Butler and American Populism.* Chapel Hill: University of North Carolina Press, 2003.

Isaac, Rhys. *The Transformation of Virginia, 1740–1790.* Chapel Hill: University of North Carolina Press, 1982.

Johnson, Guion Griffis. *Ante-Bellum North Carolina: A Social History.* Chapel Hill: University of North Carolina Press, 1937.

Johnson, Paul. Book Review of *Democratization of American Christianity. Journal of Social History* 24 (1991): 843–50.

———. *Shopkeepers Millennium.* New York: Hill and Wang, 1978.

Johnson, T. C. *A History of the Presbyterian Church, South.* New York: The Christian Literature Co., 1894.

Jones, Charles Edwin. *A Guide to the Study of the Holiness Movement.* Metuchen, N.J.: The Scarecrow Press, Inc., 1974.

Kantrowitz, Stephen. *Ben Tillman and the Reconstruction of White Supremacy.* Chapel Hill: University of North Carolina Press, 2000.

Key, V. O., Jr. *Southern Politics in State and Nation.* New York: Alfred A. Knopf, 1949.

King, Keith L. "Disciples of Christ and the Agrarian Protest in Texas, 1870–1906." *Restoration Quarterly* 35 (1993): 81–91.

———. "Religious Dimensions of the Agrarian Protest in Texas, 1870–1908." Ph.D. diss., University of Illinois, Champaign-Urbana, 1985.

Kousser, J. Morgan. *The Shaping of Southern Politics.* New Haven: Yale University Press, 1974.

Lefler, Hugh, and Albert Newsome. *North Carolina.* Chapel Hill: University of North Carolina Press, 1954.

Lengel, Leland. "Radical Crusaders and a Conservative Church." *American Studies* 18 (1972): 49–59.

Lincoln, C. Eric, and Lawrence Mamiya. *The Black Church in the African American Experience.* Durham: Duke University Press, 1990.

Lindbeck, George. *Nature of Doctrine.* Philadelphia: Westminster, 1984.

Logan, Frenise A. *The Negro in North Carolina, 1876–1894.* Chapel Hill: University of North Carolina Press, 1964.

Loveland, Anne C. *Southern Evangelicalism and the Social Order.* Baton Rouge: Louisiana State University Press, 1980.

Luftman, Austin J. "Negro Disfranchisement in North Carolina: A Baptist Editor's Campaign." Master's thesis, Wake Forest University, 1977.

Martin, Roscoe C. *The People's Party in Texas.* Austin: University of Texas Press, [1933] 1970.

Masters, Victor I. *Country Church in the South.* Atlanta: Southern Baptist Convention, 1916.

Mathews, Donald G. "'Christianizing the South'—Sketching a Synthesis." In *New Directions in American Religious History.* Ed. Harry Stout and D. G. Hart. New York: Oxford University Press, 1998, 84–115.

———. *Religion in the Old South.* Chicago: University of Chicago Press, 1977.

———. "The Southern Rite of Human Sacrifice." *Journal of Southern Religion* 3 (2000), at http://jsr.fsu.edu.

———. "'We have left undone those things which we ought to have done.'" *Church History* 67 (1998): 305–25.

Mathews, Donald G., Samuel S. Hill, Beth Schweiger, and John B. Boles. "Forum: Southern Religion." *Religion and American Culture* 8 (1998): 147–78.

McCurry, Stephanie. *Masters of Small Worlds.* New York: Oxford University Press, 1995.

McDowell, John P. *The Social Gospel in the South.* Baton Rouge: Louisiana State University Press, 1982.

McMath, Robert C., Jr. "Agrarian Protest at the Forks of the Creek." *North Carolina Historical Review* 51 (1974): 41–63.

———. "Populist Base Communities." *Locus* 1 (1988): 53–63.

———. *American Populism.* New York: Hill and Wang, 1993.

———. *Populist Vanguard.* New York: W. W. Norton & Co., Inc., 1977.

Miller, Timothy A. "Religion and Populism: A Reassessment." *Religion* 8 (1971): 1–6.

Mitchell, Theodore R. *Political Education in the Southern Farmers' Alliance, 1887–1900.* Madison: University of Wisconsin Press, 1987.

Montgomery, William E. *Under Their Own Vine and Fig Tree: The African-American Church in the South, 1865–1900.* Baton Rouge: Louisiana State University Press, 1993.

Morrill, Milo True. *A History of the Christian Denomination in America: 1794–1911.* Dayton, Ohio: The Christian Publishing Association, 1912.

Muller, Philip Roy. "New South Populism: North Carolina, 1884–1900." Ph.D. diss., University of North Carolina at Chapel Hill, 1969.

Nash, L. L. *Recollections and Observations.* Raleigh: Mutual Publishing Co., 1916.

Niebuhr, H. Richard. *Meaning of Revelation.* New York: Macmillan, 1941.

Noblin, Stuart. *Leonidas Lafayette Polk: Agrarian Crusader.* Chapel Hill: University of North Carolina Press, 1949.

Noll, Mark. *America's God.* New York: Oxford University Press, 2002.

Nugent, Walter. "Some Parameters of Populism." *Agricultural History* 40 (1966): 255–70.

———. *Money and American Society, 1865–1880.* New York: The Free Press, 1968.

———. *The Tolerant Populists.* Chicago: University of Chicago Press, 1963.

Ormond, Jesse Marvin. *The Country Church in North Carolina.* Durham: Duke University Press, 1931.

Owenby, Ted. *Subduing Satan.* Chapel Hill: University of North Carolina Press, 1990.

Palmer, Bruce. *"Man Over Money": The Southern Populist Critique of American Capitalism.* Chapel Hill: University of North Carolina Press, 1980.

Paschal, George Washington. *History of North Carolina Baptists.* Raleigh: The General Board, North Carolina Baptist State Convention, 1930.

Pelser, Charles J., Jr. *A History of Catawba County.* N.p., 1954.

Pelt, Michael R. *A History of Original Free Will Baptists.* Mount Olive, N.C.: Mount Olive College Press, 1996.

Polk, Leonidas L. *Agricultural Depression, Its Causes—The Remedy.* Raleigh: Edwards and Broughton, 1890.

Pollack, Norman. *The Humane Economy.* New Brunswick: Rutgers University Press, 1990.

Powell, William S. *North Carolina Through Four Centuries.* Chapel Hill: University of North Carolina Press, 1989.

Raboteau, Albert J. *Slave Religion.* Oxford: Oxford University Press, 1978.

Rankin, Richard. *Ambivalent Churchmen and Evangelical Churchwomen.* Columbia: University of South Carolina Press, 1993.

Ritter, Gretchen. *Goldbugs and Greenbacks.* Cambridge: Cambridge University Press, 1997.

Rumple, Jethro. *The History of Presbyterianism in North Carolina.* Richmond: Library of Union Theological Seminary, 1966.

Saloutos, Theodore. *Farmer Movements in the South, 1865–1933.* Berkeley: University of California Press, 1960.

Schweiger, Beth. *The Gospel Working Up.* New York: Oxford University Press, 2000.

Second Declaration of American Independence. Platform Adopted by the Confederated Industrial Organization at St. Louis, Mo., 22–24 February 1892.

Smith, Christian. "Correcting a Curious Neglect, or Bringing Religion Back In." In *Disruptive Religion.* Ed. Christian Smith. New York: Routledge, 1996, 1–25.

———. *Resisting Reagan.* Chicago: University of Chicago Press, 1996.

Smith, Florence Emeline. "The Populist Movement and Its Influence in North Carolina." Ph.D. diss., University of Chicago, 1929.

Snay, Mitchell. *Gospel of Disunion.* Cambridge: Cambridge University Press, 1993.

Spain, Rufus. *At Ease in Zion.* Nashville: Vanderbilt University Press, 1967.

Startup, Kenneth Moore. *The Root of All Evil: The Protestant Clergy and the Economic Mind of the Old South.* Athens: University of Georgia Press, 1997.

Steelman, Joseph F. "The Progressive Era in North Carolina, 1884–1917." Ph.D. diss., University of North Carolina, 1955.

Steelman, Lala Carr. *The North Carolina Farmers' Alliance: A Political History, 1887–1893.* Greenville: East Carolina University Publications, 1985.

Stokes, Durwood T., and William T. Scott. *A History of the Christian Church in the South.* Burlington: Southern Conference of the United Church of Christ, 1975.

Stowell, Daniel W. "Why 'Redemption?' Religion and the End of Reconstruction." Paper presented at the sixty-fourth annual meeting of the Southern Historical Association, Birmingham, Ala., 11–14 November 1998.

———. *Rebuilding Zion.* New York: Oxford University Press, 1998.

Thompson, Ernest Trice. *Presbyterians in the South.* 3 vols. Richmond: John Knox Press, 1973.

Tillich, Paul. *Dynamics of Faith.* New York: Harper, 1957.

Tomlinson, W. A. *Biography of the State Offices and Members of the General Assembly of North Carolina, 1893.* Raleigh: Edwards and Broughton, 1893.

Trelease, Allen M. "The Fusion Legislatures of 1895 and 1897." *North Carolina Historical Review* 57 (1980): 280–309.

Tull, James E. *A History of Southern Baptist Landmarkism in the Light of Historical Baptist Ecclesiology.* New York: n.p., 1980.

Tullos, Allen. *Habits of Industry.* Chapel Hill: University of North Carolina Press, 1989.

Turley, Briane Keith. "A Wheel within a Wheel: Southern Methodism and the Georgia Holiness Association." Ph.D. diss., University of Virginia, 1994.

———. "A Wheel within a Wheel: Southern Methodism and the Georgia Holiness Association." *Georgia Historical Quarterly* 75 (1991): 295–320.

Turner, J. Kelly, and John L. Bridgers, Jr. *History of Edgecombe County, North Carolina.* Raleigh: Edwards and Broughton, 1920.

Turner, James. "Understanding the Populists." *Journal of American History* 67 (1980): 354–73.

Unger, Irwin. *The Greenback Era.* Princeton: Princeton University Press, 1964.

Van Kley, Dale. *The Religious Origins of the French Revolution.* New Haven: Yale University Press, 1996.

Wacker, Grant. "Early Pentecostals and the Almost Chosen People." *Pneuma* 19 (1997): 141–66.

———. "Playing for Keeps." In *The American Quest for the Primitive Church.* Ed. Richard T. Hughes. Urbana: University of Illinois Press, 1988, 197–215.

Wade, Hampton Hadley, Doris Goerch Horton, and Nell Craig Strowd. *Chatham County, 1771–1971.* Durham: Moore Publishing Co., 1976.

Walls, William Jacob. *The African Methodist Episcopal Zion Church.* Charlotte: A.M.E. Zion Publishing House, 1974.

Walsh Julia. "Strike and Be Saved: Religion and the 1886 Strike in Augusta, Georgia." Unpublished paper presented at the sixty-fourth annual meeting of the Southern Historical Association, Birmingham, Ala., 11–14 November 1998.

Ware, Charles Crossfield. *Coastal Plain Christians.* Wilson: Private Printing, 1964.

———. *North Carolina Disciples of Christ.* St. Louis: Christian Board of Publication, 1927.

Watson, Richard L. "Furnifold M. Simmons and the Politics of White Supremacy." In *Race, Class, and Politics in Southern History.* Ed. Jeffrey Crow, Paul Escott, and Charles Flynn, Jr. Baton Rouge: Louisiana State University Press, 1989, 126–72.

Weathers, Lee B. *The Living Past of Cleveland County.* Reprint: Spartanburg: The Reprint Company Publishers, 1980.

Weisenfeld, Judith. "On Jordan's Stormy Banks." In *New Directions in American Religious History.* Ed. Harry Stout and D. G. Hart. New York: Oxford University Press, 1998, 417–44.

Whitener, Daniel Jay. *Prohibition in North Carolina, 1715–1945.* Chapel Hill: University of North Carolina Press, 1945.

Whitted, J. A. *A History of the Negro Baptists of North Carolina.* Raleigh: Edwards and Broughton, 1908.

Wigger, John H. *Taking Heaven by Storm.* New York: Oxford University Press, 1998.

Wilenz, Sean. *Kingdom of Matthias.* New York: Oxford University Press, 1994.

Williams, Charles B. *A History of Baptists in North Carolina.* Raleigh: n.p., 1901.

Williams, Rhys H., and Susan M. Alexander. "Religious Rhetoric in American Populism." *Journal for the Scientific Study of Religion* 33 (1994): 1–15.

Williamson, Joel. *The Crucible of Race.* New York: Oxford University Press, 1984.

Wills, Gregory A. *Democratic Religion.* New York: Oxford University Press, 1997.

Wilson, Charles Reagan. *Baptized in Blood.* Athens: University of Georgia Press, 1980.

Wood, Philip J. *Southern Capitalism: The Political Economy of North Carolina, 1880–1980.* Durham: Duke University Press, 1986.

Woodard, John R. "North Carolina." In *Religion in the Southern States: A Historical Study.* Ed. Samuel S. Hill, 213–37. Macon, Ga.: Mercer University Press, 1983.

Woodward, C. Vann. *Origins of the New South.* Baton Rouge: Louisiana State University Press, 1951.

———. *The Strange Career of Jim Crow.* New York: Oxford University Press, 1974.

———. *Tom Watson: Agrarian Rebel.* New York: Rinehart & Co., Inc., 1938.

Woolverton, John F. *Colonial Anglicanism in North America.* Detroit: Wayne State University Press, 1984.

Wyatt-Brown, Bertram. "The Antimission Movement in the Jacksonian South." *Journal of Southern History* 36 (1970): 501–29.

Yohn, Susan M. "Let Christian Women Set the Example in Their Own Gifts." Paper presented at the Women and Twentieth-Century Protestantism Conference, Chicago, 23–25 April 1998.

Index

on, 26, 28–31, 36, 76–80, 111, 120, 129, 186, n. 10, 197 n. 19, 197 n. 24

Landmarkism, 12, 18–19, 146–146; Populism, relationship to, 145–146, 185–186, n. 4. *See also* Baptists; Gospel Mission Movement; Primitive Baptists; Protestant evangelicalism

Lease, Mary, 137, 155

Liberty, *see* political ideals

Lindsey, W. R., 127–128, 132–133, 139

Lloyd, J. B., xvi, 75, 94–96, 173–174, 185 n. 2

Lutherans, 9–10, 20, 22

Lynching, xxvii, 74, 172

Macune, C. W., xx, 99

Manhood, Manliness, *see* gender roles

Mathews, Donald, xxvii

McMath, Robert, 185–186, n. 4, 193 n. 13, 194 n. 23

McKinley, William, 57, 162, 164, 166

Merchants, Rural, 61–62, 194 n. 24

Methodist Episcopal Church, South, 7–14, 15–16, 18, 20, 22, 28, 29, 35, 37,41, 62, 142, 147–156; relationship to Populism, 70–71, 75, 142, 144, 147–156, 173–174, 185 n. 2, 195–196 n. 4

Methodist Protestant Church, 10, 13, 20, 27, 33, 44, 144, 147, 179; relationship to Populism, xvi–xviii, 71, 73, 144, 147, 179, 185 n. 2, 194–195 n. 3

Mewborne, James Marion (J. M.), xviii, 1–4, 6, 8, 19, 31, 33, 72–73, 89, 91, 99, 111, 117, 119–120, 125, 132, 140, 144, 148, 165, 180–182, 185 n. 2, 197 n. 24

Mid-Road/Mid-Roaders, *see* People's Party in North Carolina

Millennialism, *see* apocalypticism, patriotic millennialism, Protestant evangelicalism

Monetary Policy: banking and currency regulations, 51–57, 64–67, 76–82, 86–89, 94, 106–111, 114, 115–117, 119, 123–124,158–167 ; antebellum,53; banking and currency regulations, during Civil War, 53–54; banking and currency regulations, 1865–1900, 52–57, 61–62, 64–67, 76–82, 86–89, 94, 106–111, 114, 115–117, 119, 123–124, 157–167, 202 n. 24; commodity prices, 54–56, 61–62, 64–67, 78–79, 86, 89, 94; currency volume or scarcity, 52–57, 61–62, 64–67, 78–79, 86, 89, 94, 107, 124; specie backing, 53–55; fiat money or greenbacks, 52–57, 78–79, 114;

interest rates, 52–57, 61–62, 78–79, 86, 89, 109–110, 114; "free silver," "silverites," or bimetallic, xxi–xxii, 52–57, 78–79, 107, 111, 114, 116, 119, 123–124, 157–169, 174, 193 n. 2, 202 n. 24; gold standard or monometallic, 52–57, 119, 123, 157–167; national banking system, 53–57, 61, 64–67, 78–82, 86, 88, 89, 94, 107–111, 115, 202 n. 24. *See also* political thought, National Farmers' Alliance, North Carolina State Farmers' Alliance, People's Party, People's Party in North Carolina

Money Problem or Question, *see* monetary policy

Moody, D. L., 178

Movement Culture, xxiii

National Banking Act, 1863, 53–54

National Banking System, *see* monetary policy, National Banking Act, 1863

National Farmers' Alliance and Industrial Union, xx–xxi, 48, 69, 115; 1890 Ocala Convention and Statement, 43–44, 87, 115; economic cooperation, xxi, 44, 79, 194 n. 23; histories/historiography, xxii–xxiv, 185–186, n. 4, 186–187, n. 10, 187, n. 11, 187, n. 12; jute boycott, 79, 109; political activity, xxi, 43–44, 108–110, 115; political ideals, xxi, 43–44, 69, 115; platforms and agendas, xxi, 95, 109–110, 115, 123; religion, influence on, 44–49; Third Party Activity, xxi, 119–120. *See also* subtreasury plan; political ideals, commonsense thinking, North Carolina State Farmers' Alliance, People's Party, People's Party in North Carolina

National Greenback Party, xxi, 47, 52–56, 98, 106, 137, 163, 193 n. 15

Nativism, 89

New South, 52, 59–60, 65–67, 129, 172. *See also*, Protestant evangelicalism, in the South.

Nineteenth Century South: postbellum agricultural developments, 51–52, 55–67, 93–94, 98, 180–181; postbellum history, social, and economic developments, 51–64, 93–94, 98; postbellum political developments, 98, 103–108, 157–175, 177–181; postbellum religious developments, 7–39, 98, 177–180; Reconstruction, 52, 58, 104–106. *See also* Protestant evangelicalism, South.

Union; North Carolina State Farmers'
Alliance; People's Party (National/
General); patriotic millennialism;
People's Party in North Carolina; political
parties; Protestant evangelicalism;
tyranny

Political Parties: attacks on partisan politics
by populists, 81–82, 86, 88, 100, 108, 114,
133; attacks on partisan politics by
evangelicals, 34–39; bossism, 34–39, 67,
86, 88, 95, 132, 173; denominations,
Protestant, comparisons to, 34–39, 81–82,
86–90, 152

Political Theory, *see* political ideals

Polk, Leonidas Lafayette (L. L.), xxii, 41–45,
48, 51, 64–66, 69, 71, 74, 78, 81, 87, 94–95,
98, 107, 113, 116–117, 124–125, 127, 130–132

Poll Tax, 74

Populist Party, *see* People's Party

Premillennial Dispensationalism, 144–145,
178–180. *See also* patriotic millennialism

Presbyterians/Presbyterian, *see* southern
Presbyterians

Primitive Baptists, 7, 10, 12–14, 20, 22, 37,
63–64, 144, 146–147; relationship to
Populism, 63–64, 70, 96–97, 143, 144,
146–147, 154

Pritchard, Jeter, 161, 167

Private Property, Evangelical or Populist
Views on, 28, 77

Producerism, 28–31, 48, 60, 61, 100

Progressive Farmer, xxii, 42, 44, 51, 64–66, 71,
74, 77, 81, 84, 113, 118, 131–132, 168, 182

Progressive Farming, *see* North Carolina
Farmers' Association; North Carolina
State Farmers Alliance

Progressive/Progressivism, xxiii–xxv, 36, 129,
173–174, 180

Prohibition Party, 106, 142

Prohibition: nationally, 37–38; in North
Carolina, 20, 37–38, 109, 111, 142, 199 n. 9,
203 n. 4

Protective Tariff, 52–53, 61–62, 66, 106, 111,
124, 202 n. 24

Protestant Episcopal Church, *see*
Episcopalians, Protestant evangelicalism

Protestant Evangelicalism, xxv–xxvii;
American democracy or liberty,
influences on, 25–28, 36–37, 145–147,
149–156, 190 n. 8; antebellum history,
7–15, 35; anti-elitism, xxvi, 8, 13, 16, 18–19,

29–31, 33, 45–46, 185–186, n. 4; baptism, 7,
8, 11, 14; benevolence, 28–31; Bible, 24–26,
150; centralization in denominations,
xvii–xix, 2–6, 12–13, 26–38, 140, 144–14-
153; Christian maturity, 31–32; church and
state views, xxviii, 23–28, 34–38, 142–156,
178–180; cities, antipathy towards, 30–33,
62–63, 150; class dynamics, 28–31, 62–64,
144–148, 150–155; conversion experience,
centrality of, xxvi, 22, 25; creeds/anti-
creedalism, 11, 13; democratic and
republican ideals, xvii–xix, 6, 27–28, 34–38,
44–46, 62–64, 97, 140, 144–156, 177–178, 190
n. 8; denominationalism, 2–5, 12–14, 32–38,
146–148, 150–153; discipline, 25;
ecclesiastical tensions, 2–5, 12–14, 26–38,
62–64, 140, 144–148, 150–153; ecclesiology,
xxvi, 12, 27–28, 32–34, 149–151; economic
thought, 26, 28–31, 36, 146–147, 152–153;
education, 26, 32; egalitarianism, 1–5, 22–28,
63–64, 148–159; eighteenth-century history,
7–14, 22; elitism, 29, 62–64; families, 31–33;
fashion, opposition to, 18, 30–31; foreign
missions, 3, 18–19; fundraising, 2–3, 17, 34;
history/historiography, 187, n. 14; holy
communion, 8; individualism, xxvi, 25, 44,
140, 146–147; law of love, 27, 30, 78–79, 83,
97; lay leadership, 1, 33; liberal and
conservative tendencies, xix–xx,
xxvi–xxviii, 5–6, 7–10, 16, 22–31, 34–39, 44,
45–46, 49, 62–64, 96–98, 139–156, 171–172,
177–180, 187, n. 14; millennialism, xxvi, xxix,
5–6, 13,23, 26–28, 34–38, 44–45, 46, 48–49,
139–141, 145–147, 149–156, 178–179;
ministers/ministry, 8, 10, 16–17, 30, 44, 143;
politics, 25–32, 44–45, 139–144, 148–156,
178–179; preaching, 30; religious and
political liberty, xviii–xix; 23–29, 32–38,
44–46, 140, 144–156, 190 n. 8; revivalism,
9–10, 13, 22; slavery, 9, 14–15, 35, 148, 149,
154–155; social conservatism, xix–xx,
xxvi–xxviii, 7–10, 28–31, 35–38, 62–64,
146–148, 149, 151–155, 170–172; theology,
18–38, 45, 151–153; tyranny, religious,
political, or economic, accusations of,
xvii–xix, 2–6, 12–13, 26–38, 140, 144–156;
voluntarism, xxvi, 11–12, 33; women, 12, 17,
22–24, 31–32, 35–37, 45, 154–155; worldliness,
8–9, 13. *See also* apocalypticism; black
church; commonsense thinking;
denominations by name; ecclesiology;

The University of Illinois Press
is a founding member of the
Association of American University Presses.

University of Illinois Press
1325 South Oak Street
Champaign, IL 61820-6903
www.press.uillinois.edu